THE **boat** MAINTENANCE BIBLE

REFIT, IMPROVE AND
REPAIR WITH THE EXPERTS

THE boat
MAINTENANCE BIBLE

Pat Manley • Rupert Holmes

Adlard Coles Nautical
London

Published by Adlard Coles Nautical
an imprint of A & C Black Publishers Ltd
36 Soho Square, London W1D 3QY
www.adlardcoles.com

Copyright © Adlard Coles Nautical 2011
First edition 2011

ISBN 978-1-4081-2479-6

This book is produced using paper that is made from
wood grown in managed, sustainable forests. It is
natural, renewable and recyclable. The logging and
manufacturing processes conform to the
environmental regulations of the country of origin.

Produced for Adlard Coles Nautical
by Ivy Contract

Project editors: Nic Compton and Sarah Doughty
Project designer: Lisa McCormick
Designer: Alistair Plumb

Typeset in Veljovic Book and Bliss
Printed in China by RR Donnelley South China Printing Co

Contents

Welcome to boat maintenance

It is said that owning a boat is like standing under a shower and tearing up money. Well, no more. This book shows you how to perform all those essential jobs on your boat – whether it be a sailboat, powerboat or dinghy – without having to call in expensive expert help. From cleaning off rust stains to servicing your engine and refurbishing the woodwork, it's all explained in clearly illustrated, easy-to-follow stages.

Above: **A hull with an osmosis problem. Use a small mechanical grinder to remove osmosis blisters from the hull and then repair by filling with gel coat.**

Essential tools

What tools do you need to get the job done, without buying a whole tool shop? Here's a guide to what you really need, with separate lists for different departments.

General boat care

Everything you need to know about keeping your boat spic and span, from washing the hull to cleaning the bilges and maintaining the upholstery.

Hull and deck repairs

If your boat is looking a bit the worse for wear, here are some simple steps that you can take to spruce it up and make it look like new. If the damage is more serious, there's general advice on working with fibreglass and wood, as well as detailed instructions on specific jobs, such as how to reseal a leaking deck, how to re-bed deck fittings and how to repair crazed gel coat.

Painting and varnishing

How to prepare fibreglass, wood and steel to achieve a perfect finish, plus invaluable advice about applying paint by brush, roller or spray. And how to varnish like a professional.

Below: **Lowering a yacht onto a trailer at the end of the season. The hull is cleaned off ready for polishing and repainting.**

General mechanics

This section of the book describes how the principal systems work – including water, gas and toilets – and explains how to repair some common faults. It also shows how you can pre-empt problems by servicing vital bits of equipment, such as the anchor winch and sea cocks, before they break.

Electrics

Electrics need not be the dark art they're made out to be. This section describes typical wiring installations and considers some common tasks – from changing fuses to re-soldering loose connections, replacing navigation lights and fitting solar panels and wind turbines.

Engine maintenance

Whether you're a sailboat or a powerboat enthusiast, engines will probably play a part in your boating experience. This section includes a description of a typical motor installation, with details of how to deal with common problems, such as bleeding the fuel system, adjusting the belt drive and replacing an impeller. Plus there's a servicing schedule, a list of spare parts and that all-important troubleshooting guide.

Powerboat maintenance

For those who like to put their trust in more predictable sources of power than the fickle wind, this section is devoted entirely to the mighty powerboat, including trim tabs, stern drives and jet drives.

Sailboat maintenance

Yachts have many maintenance issues peculiar to themselves – masts, rigging and sails, for a start. This section provides advice on

checking wood and aluminium spars, servicing roller reefing and winches, and the fine art of sail repair (easy when you know how).

Dinghy maintenance

Just because they're smaller doesn't mean they don't need looking after. Damaged centreboards, loose fittings and seized-up trailers are just a few of the topics covered. And there's advice on that perennial bugbear: how to patch an inflatable dinghy.

Outboard engines

Here are step-by-step instructions on how to get a stubborn outboard started, changing a spark plug and

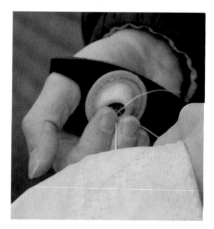

Above: **Apply antifouling with a roller to save time. For best results, do this just before the boat goes back in the water.**

replacing a sheer pin. Plus there's general advice on looking after your outboard, including daily and annual servicing schedules, and a handy troubleshooting guide.

Safety gear

This section includes advice on testing lifejackets, updating the first aid kit and checking flares, liferaft, and EPIRBs. Don't leave harbour without reading this chapter.

Laying up for winter

Lastly, how to make sure your boat is safely tucked up at the end of the season and stays in the best possible shape for the beginning of the next.

Comprehensive, authoritative and accessible, we hope this book will put the pleasure back into boat maintenance. Happy boating!

Left: **Carrying out a small sail repair using a sailmaker's palm (similar to a dressmaker's thimble).**

Essential
tools

Safety first

If you're doing any maintenance on your boat, you'll need a variety of tools and products, many of which need to be used with care to avoid injury. It is essential to familiarise yourself with the use of your tools and the various techniques required – and think SAFETY all the time.

General safety
- ✪ Ensure that the material is held firmly, ideally in a vice or clamped to something that won't move.

Hand saws
- ✪ When cross-cutting, use a saw hook or clamp to hold the material.

Hand tools with sharp blades
- ✪ Keep both hands behind the blade at all times.
- ✪ Keep the blade sharp – a sharp blade is safer than a blunt one.
- ✪ Work away from your body, not towards it.
- ✪ Always ensure that a sharp tool is put away safely so that you don't cut yourself while searching for it. Retract the blade if possible as soon as you have finished with it.

Hand tools with blunt blades
- ✪ Blunt blades, such as screw drivers, can be just as dangerous as a saw, because you can stab yourself.
- ✪ Keep your hands behind the 'blade' or tip.
- ✪ Use the tool only for the purpose for which it was designed.

Electric hand tools
- ✪ All electric tools are a potential danger because of their inherent power.
- ✪ Read the manual supplied with the tool and observe all the safety instructions.
- ✪ If the trigger can be locked ON, think carefully before you do so. In the event of an accident it will keep running, possibly with dire results.
- ✪ If the tool has a safety guard, always use it, even if it seems inconvenient. If you can't do the job with the guard in place, then the tool is inappropriate – find another tool.

Above **When going aloft, tie the halyard to your harness as well as using the shackle. Use a secondary halyard as back-up.**

- ✪ Take care with mains-powered tools to ensure you don't cut or entangle the power lead (cord).
- ✪ Ensure the mains supply has an ELCB or RCCB so that the current will be cut off immediately should any fault occur.
- ✪ Always disconnect the power from the tool before you insert or remove a tool from the chuck – your fingers may slip and operate the trigger.
- ✪ When you release the trigger, let the tool stop rotating before you lay it down. High speed rotation can cause a strong gyroscopic effect of the tool as you move it and you may drop the rotating tool.

Below **Sitting comfortably when working at height is much safer than reaching across, and much easier as well.**

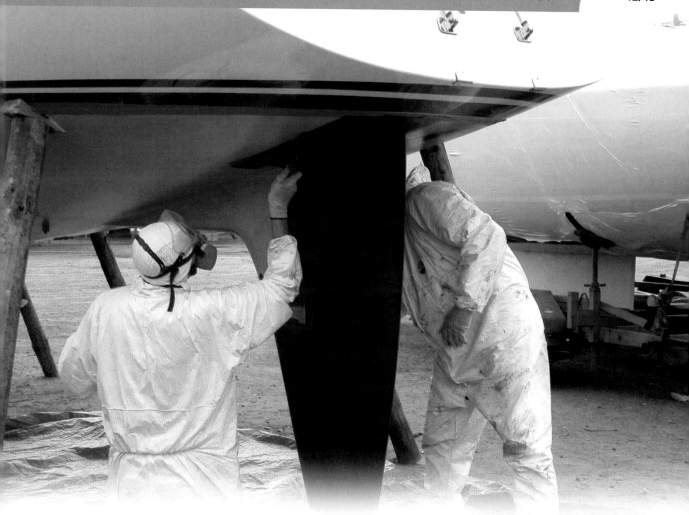

Glues, paint and chemicals

✪ Always read and observe the instructions and warnings supplied with the product.

Working at height

Use common sense to ensure your safety when working at height.

✪ When using electric saws, make sure that the power cable is well away from the tool and that any guard is properly fitted to provide adequate protection.

✪ If paint is likely to spatter, wear eye protection. When using antifouling paint, wear skin protection as well.

Above **Antifouling paint is toxic, so always wear protective clothing when rubbing down and repainting.**

Right **Wear eye and ear protection when using power tools, and ensure the guard is properly fitted.**

✪ Use a suitable knot and not a shackle to secure the bosun's chair to the halyard. Always use a secondary safety halyard as well. If possible, choose a halyard that passes through the masthead.

✪ Keep your hand behind the blade and clamp the material if it can move.

General maintenance tools

You will always need to carry some tools onboard your boat, even if you don't do that much maintenance yourself. The problem is, just what tools do you need to carry? To a great extent this will depend on how much of the work you carry out yourself.

The quality of the tools

Unless you are a professional who uses the tools every day, there's no need to aim for professional quality tools to keep on board – they cost too much. For the relatively little use they will get, budget tools will be fine as long as you avoid really cheap tools that will break or deform with use. There's an exception – rigging cutters on a sailing boat. Cheap wire cutters won't cut stainless steel rigging wire.

Tool hire

For both boat and household use, buying expensive specialist tools that you would use only once makes little sense. Hire them instead and you will get professional quality and good advice as well.

'Boat tools'

Even though you may have many tools at home, it's worth having some frequently used 'duplicates' on the boat as well.

Below **Attachments to masts and booms are often made using tubular rivets, for which a heavy duty riveter is needed.**

Above **If you don't have a large hole saw, you can hire one for special jobs.**

Care of 'boat tools'

Tools on a boat are subject to a damp environment and may be thrown around in rough seas. Keep the tools in plastic boxes and it's a good idea to spray them occasionally with water displacing fluid. If you have sharp woodworking tools on board, keep the blades sharp and protected and spray them with water displacing fluid, even though you will have to wipe the blades before use.

Hand tools versus power tools

✪ **Hand tools:** Manual tools such as drills may be old fashioned, but they don't need electricity to run them and this may be important if you are out on the water.

Above **It's essential to keep your chisels sharp, so ensure you have a good sharpening stone and use it frequently.**

✪ **Rechargeable tools:** Probably the most useful power tools on the boat are powered by battery packs. The tools come in plastic protective cases and you can get a set of various tools all powered by the same detachable, rechargeable battery. You must have at least two batteries.

✪ **Mains powered tools:** These are typically more powerful than battery tools and don't need to be charged, but you need access to mains voltage electricity. They are often a better bet for doing heavy duty work.

Above **A mains-powered drill is usually more powerful than a battery drill.**

Above **A battery electric screwdriver is very useful if you have a lot of screws to undo.**

Mechanical tools

A boat owner must have an assortment of tools on board to carry out mechanical repairs, replacements or adjustments, even though you would ordinarily never dream of wielding a spanner at home.

Spanners (wrenches)

- **Open-ended spanners:** These can be slipped onto the nut from the side and grip just two sides.
- **Ring spanners:** These grip the nut all round, but must be fitted from on top and there isn't always room for that.
- **Combination spanners:** These have a ring on one end and an open ended spanner on the other. Seen as a space or money saver, they have the disadvantage that if

you need two spanners of the same size to undo a lock nut, you still need another spanner.

- **Adjustable spanners:** Useful if you don't have the correct size spanner, but may not grip the nut as well.
- **Socket spanners:** These are deep ring spanners with a separate ratchet handle. You can exert a lot of force with these and the ratchet allows their use where there's not much room to turn the handle.

Above **A ratchet socket spanner is a quick means of tightening or untightening nuts and bolts.**

Below **Tools such as these often come in sets in purpose-made tool cases of varying quality and price.**

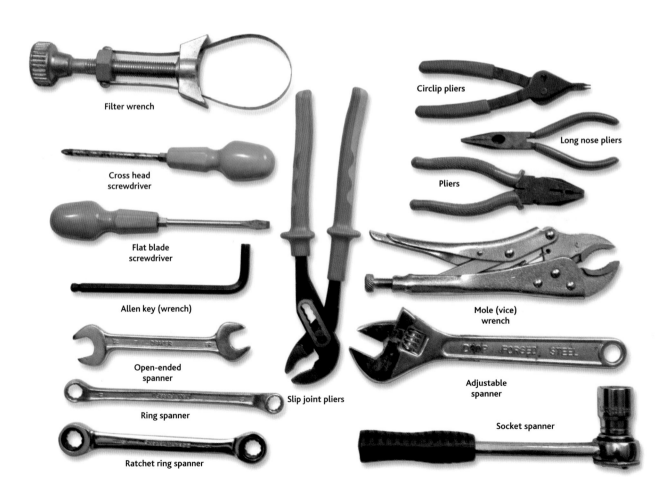

Filter wrench

Cross head screwdriver

Flat blade screwdriver

Allen key (wrench)

Open-ended spanner

Ring spanner

Ratchet ring spanner

Slip joint pliers

Circlip pliers

Long nose pliers

Pliers

Mole (vice) wrench

Adjustable spanner

Socket spanner

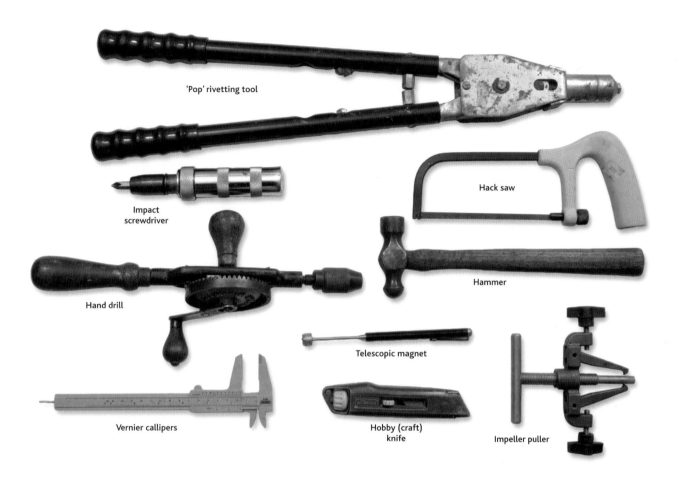

'Pop' rivetting tool

Impact screwdriver

Hack saw

Hand drill

Hammer

Telescopic magnet

Vernier callipers

Hobby (craft) knife

Impeller puller

Screwdrivers

✪ **Cross head screwdrivers:** There are several designs of cross head 'slots' and the correct type and size must be used to avoid damaging the slot beyond use.

✪ **Flat blade screwdrivers:** These are used for screws with slotted heads. Use the correct sized blade for the size of the slot to avoid damage to the screw.

Hexagonal wrenches (Allen keys)

Some bolts have a hexagonal recess in their head and a matching wrench must be used. There are many sizes of key, both metric and imperial, and it's essential that the correct size is used to prevent damage to the head of the bolt.

Pliers and grippers

These are used to grip a metal object which has no 'flats' for a spanner to grip. A vice grip locks onto the object so you are not relying on the grip of your hand. Although useful, they have one drawback: they can damage whatever you are gripping so can't be used on precision-made parts if they are to be reused.

Drill bits

There are a variety of drill bits available for special tasks but a set of twist drills should be all that you need. Better quality bits won't need to be sharpened very often and are essential if you are going to drill stainless steel.

Above Individual tools, such as those shown here, are best kept in a plastic tool box, away from the reach of water.

Additional tools

In addition you may find that a hammer, small hack saw, hobby knife, a general purpose metal file and a centre punch are all useful.

Multi-purpose tool

The ubiquitous 'multi-purpose' tool has a place on any boat, as you can keep it safely on your belt and you can do many jobs just with this.

Electrical tools

Unless you are planning to call in a professional every time you have a small electrical problem, you should have a basic set of electrical tools on board so that you can troubleshoot and make simple repairs.

Multimeter

This is the most important tool for electrical troubleshooting and you don't have to pay a lot for one. A manual selection meter is the most accurate type, but you do have to have a rough idea of the value volts, current or resistance to preset the meter before you use it. An automatic ranging meter is probably the most useful type for amateurs, as all you need to do is set it to measure volts, current or resistance and the meter does the rest.

Wire cutters

A pair of side cutters will cut any size of wire you are likely to need.

Cable stripper

If you are going to do much wiring, a good pair of cable strippers is worth having, as it makes stripping the insulation from a cable very easy.

Crimping tool

A crimping tool is used to fit cable connectors to electrical wire. It's worth paying a little more to buy a ratchet type which makes a more secure connection. Make sure the tool matches the crimps. Some American tools don't work properly on European crimps and vice-versa.

Below **If you are going to carry out maintenance to the electrical systems, you will need some or all the tools shown here.**

TIP

Crimp cable terminals come in three colours, red, blue and yellow, corresponding to the wire size they are to be used with. Use too big a terminal and it won't grip the wire properly.

Long nose pliers

These are very useful for holding things in awkward places where ordinary pliers are too big.

Electrical screwdrivers

Many electrical jobs require small screwdrivers which would not necessarily appear in your normal, basic toolkit.

Gas soldering iron

12 volt electric soldering iron

Crimp terminals

De-soldering tool

Heavy duty fuse

Multi-core solder   Tubular fuse   Blade fuse

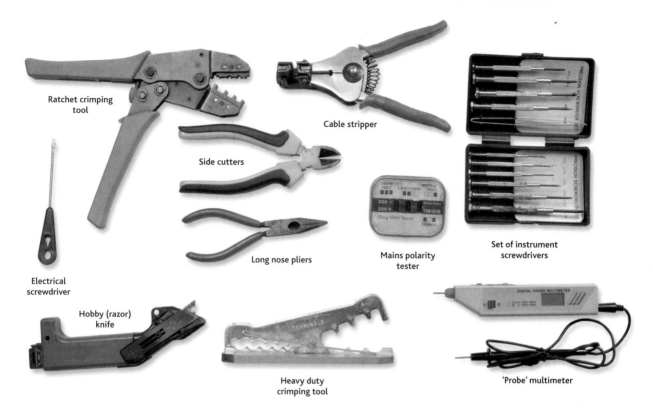

Ratchet crimping tool

Cable stripper

Side cutters

Long nose pliers

Electrical screwdriver

Mains polarity tester

Set of instrument screwdrivers

Hobby (razor) knife

Heavy duty crimping tool

'Probe' multimeter

Small spanners

Some electrical tasks demand small spanners and it's best not to try to make do with a pair of pliers instead.

Soldering irons

Soldering irons come in different wattages and may be mains powered, or powered from your 12 volt system. The power in

watts defines what size of components can be soldered. For soldering small electrical wires, a 25 watt iron will be fine. Small irons heated by butane gas are also available. Very useful on a boat, they can be used to cut rope as well. However, you may find that the cheaper gas irons quickly burn out their catalytic heater.

Above **Some electrical tools might only be used occasionally but are invaluable in an emergency.**

Consumables

In your electrical tool kit you will also need insulating tape, crimp terminals of various types and sizes, a tube of silicone waterproofing grease and a jar of petroleum jelly. If you are doing much rewiring, heat shrink tubing is very useful and much neater than insulating tape.

Left **Crimp terminals can be used to make permanent connections as well as connections which can be disconnected at a later date.**

Woodworking tools

Many boat owners will keep few, if any, woodworking tools on their boat, relying on bringing any necessary tools from home if required. However, a few basic tools kept on board may be useful to make small repairs.

Stowage of woodworking tools

Woodworking tools and a damp environment don't go together because the sharp blades will become rusty and blunt. The blades of woodworking tools kept on board should be kept lightly oiled, but cleaned before use. Because of their sharp blades, they should be kept in a box to protect both them and hands searching the tool stowage.

Saws

❂ **Rip saws:** These have longer flexible blades and coarse teeth for making long, fast cuts.
❂ **Tenon saws:** For more accurate cutting, they have a rigid spine and finer teeth.

Chisels

There are a number of different types of chisel specially designed for particular jobs. For most boat owners a set of bevel edged chisels will be quite adequate. They must be kept properly sharpened.

Sharpening stone

A sharpening stone is used to keep a keen cutting edge on chisel and plane blades. A double sided one is best as it has a different grade of stone on each side.

Planes

Planes make smooth faces on sawn timber. Short planes are used on small areas, but for a long piece of timber you need a long 'jack' plane to ensure the finish is fair along the full length.

Spokeshaves

Spokeshaves are useful for rounding off edges on a piece of timber, although a plane can be used on longer pieces of wood.

Mallet

To prevent damage to the handle, chisels should never be hit with a hammer. A mallet with a wooden head should be used with chisels and for lightly tapping woodwork.

Below **Working with wood requires a selection of basic tools for cutting, smoothing and shaping.**

Above **It's worth acquiring a spokeshave to facilitate rounding off work. Once you've got the hang of it, it's a fun tool to use.**

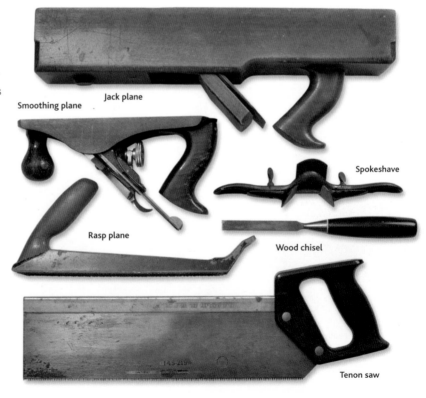

Smoothing plane

Jack plane

Rasp plane

Spokeshave

Wood chisel

Tenon saw

Right **If you're working regularly with wood, you will need a selection of more specialist tools.**

Hammers

In woodworking, a hammer is used for nailing and two types are useful: a pin or tack hammer is best for small nails, as its small head allows precision use. A claw hammer is used for heavier nailing and for pulling out nails and is more of a carpenter's tool.

Set square

This tool ensures that you can draw a line at right angles to a finished edge and make an accurate cut.

Bevel

A bevel is a little like a set square but one edge can be set to any angle. This allows an angle to be reproduced and transferred to the wood that you are shaping to ensure that it fits.

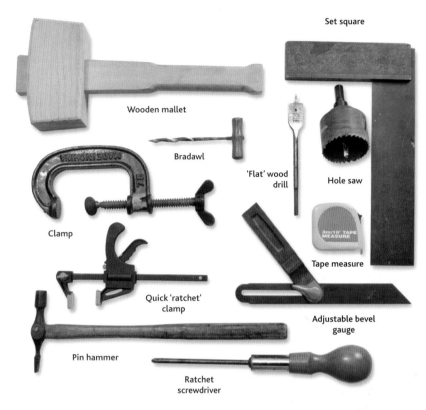

Set square

Wooden mallet

Bradawl

'Flat' wood drill

Hole saw

Clamp

Tape measure

Quick 'ratchet' clamp

Adjustable bevel gauge

Pin hammer

Ratchet screwdriver

Clamps

A clamp or cramp is used to hold two or more pieces of wood together. Metal screw clamps can exert a lot of pressure. Modern plastic friction clamps are quick and easy to use. Several of each type will be useful.

Portable workbench or vice

For safe and accurate work the timber must be held securely. A vice, or better still a portable work-bench, is a necessity for all but the most basic woodwork.

Above **Planing wood is best done at a workbench with a bench stop to prevent the wood moving. Or you can use a piece of wood clamped in place as a stop.**

Above **If you are able, use a workbench when there's chiselling to be done. In any case, ensure the work can't move while you're working on it.**

Essential spares

Some spare parts for general maintenance should always be carried on board. The basic guidelines are: will the lack of this spare stop the boat or affect safety, and what is the chance of it being required?

Engine spares

The engine spares required are listed on pages 212 to 213 and these will be common to any type of boat, whether it be power or sail.

Hull and deck spares

⊕ **Bulbs:** All boats should carry spare bulbs for the navigation and deck lights. Not all navigation light bulbs are necessarily the same, so make a note of which bulb is required in the various lights.

⊕ **Nuts, bolts and split pins:** Make a note of the various pieces of hardware, such as davits, guard rails or wires, blocks and shackles, with items that could work loose and be lost overboard. Have some spares for these items.

⊕ **Steering:** If the steering is hydraulic, carry some spare steering fluid – check the manual for the specification. Spare nuts, bolts and split pins would be a sensible precaution.

Above **Even though an oil change may not be due, a sudden oil leak will require spare engine oil.**

Below **According to the type of boat, there are certain essential spares that should be carried on any journey.**

Drive belt

Fuel filter element

Hose clip

Insulating tape

PTFE tape

Electrical cable

Water pump impeller

Self amalgamating tape

Spare navigation light bulb
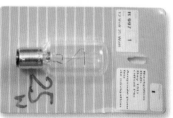

Wire connector

Fuses

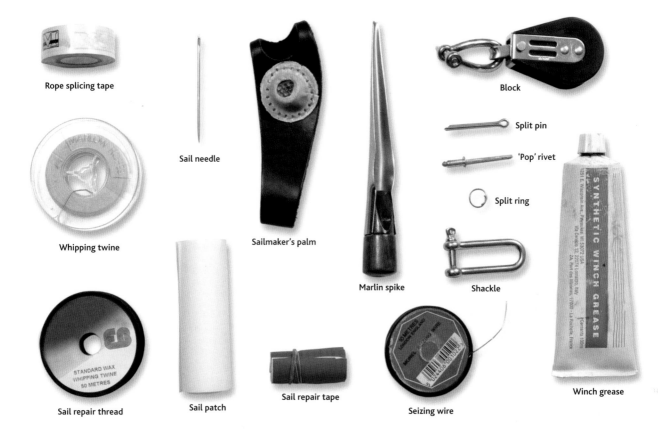

Rope splicing tape

Sail needle

Whipping twine

Sailmaker's palm

Block

Split pin

'Pop' rivet

Split ring

Marlin spike

Shackle

Sail repair thread

Sail patch

Sail repair tape

Seizing wire

Winch grease

Above **If you have a sailing boat, you will need a special selection of spares.**

Interior spares

- ☼ **Bulbs:** Have a look at the various bulbs in the cabins and cockpit lockers and carry spares for these.
- ☼ **Fuses:** It's essential that spare fuses are carried for all the equipment on board. Some fuses are hidden away behind panels (this is bad practice) so you may have to poke around to find them.
- ☼ **Distilled or de-ionised water:** This will be required for topping up domestic and engine start batteries.
- ☼ **Electrical:** Spare wire and connectors will make it possible to replace broken connections.

Safety spares

- ☼ **Lifejackets:** Rearming packs for your lifejackets. These are type specific, so it makes sense to have all your lifejackets of the same make and model, so that all the spares are the same.
- ☼ **Torches/flashlights:** Batteries and bulbs for all torches.

Rigging spares

Any boat with rigging needs to have a stock of rigging spares on board, because things work loose due to vibration, or even break. The spares should include:

- ☼ Shackles, split pins, split rings, pulley blocks, all of various sizes.
- ☼ Seizing wire for locking shackles.
- ☼ Rigging tape to prevent chafe.

Sail and rope repairs

Frayed rope ends and damaged sails can quickly develop into something more serious, so first aid spares should be carried on board. These should include:

- ☼ Sailmaker's palm and needles.
- ☼ Whipping twine of various sizes and colours.
- ☼ Sail repair tape and patches.

Long distance cruising

The long distance cruiser will require a much more comprehensive list of spares to ensure self sufficiency. Chafe, vibration and ultraviolet light on a sailing boat rig will cause damage that must be repaired as soon as it is noticed.

General
boat care

Cleaning hull & deck

Maintaining the appearance of a boat in top condition requires more than a regular scrub with a brush and soapy water. Here are some expert tips for dealing with typical problem areas.

Stubborn marks

Difficult stains, such as the unsightly grey marks that leach from the toe rail of many yachts, normally need to be removed by scrubbing by hand. Where possible, abrasive cleaners should be avoided because they scratch the surface, which will trap more dirt in the future. If you apply a finishing glaze or silicone-free wax after polishing the hull, this will repel dirt, reducing the frequency of cleaning needed in these areas (see page 44).

Another common problem is soot around the exhaust outlet of diesel engines. Again, applying glaze or wax will help prevent it sticking to the hull. But if large amounts of soot are forming, the cause of this should be investigated. It's often a sign that the injectors need cleaning (see page 188).

Weed growth near the waterline is both unsightly and has a detrimental effect on performance. It can be scrubbed away with a stiff brush, working from a pontoon or dinghy. However, if this is a persistent problem the antifouling line should be moved higher.

Above: **A regular scrub will deal with weed that grows on the waterline. If this is a recurring problem, the antifouling should be raised slightly.**

Below **Topsides frequently need little more than periodically rinsing with fresh water, but stubborn stains may need to be removed with detergent and a sponge.**

TIP

Fenders are all that sits between the hull and a potential multitude of ugly marks and scars. Make sure you have plenty of them, including a variety of shapes – big round ones can be very useful – and that they're a good size for your boat. Fender boards give extra protection when moored against a rough quay.

Fender socks and blankets

Socks can be fitted to reduce rubbing between fenders and the boat's topsides. However, if these trap grit, they may actually exacerbate abrasion. A better alternative is a fender blanket – a piece of acrylic canvas hanging between boat and fenders. These are particularly important for boats with vinyl graphics, or those with painted hulls, which are not as resistant to abrasion as those with a gel coat finish.

Cleaning decks

When cleaning decks, start at the top of the coachroof, working down towards to the lowest point in the cockpit. Fibreglass and painted decks can be cleaned with a stiff-bristled deck brush, or with a pressure washer if badly soiled. However, neither of these methods is suitable for teak, which has very soft areas between the grains. Gently brushing across the grain using a soft-bristled brush will avoid removing the soft material. The exact cleaning process and subsequent

Above **A stiff-bristled brush is ideal for cleaning decks, but make sure you're prepared for getting wet feet. And try not to fall over!**

treatment of teak varies, depending on whether it is to be left with a natural silver finish, oiled or varnished (see page 110).

To avoid scratching the surface, varnished wooden trim, hatches and windows should be washed by hand using a soft sponge and soapy water. After rinsing with clean water, they benefit from being buffed with a soft cloth.

Above **Use a biodegradable, non-abrasive cleaner with a soft sponge to clean cabin windows and hatches.**

Canvas care

Immaculate canvaswork is a prerequisite for a boat to look its best, but it is susceptible to the effects of sun and wind, and small areas of damage expand rapidly if appropriate action is not taken quickly.

Fabric types

The most common fabrics used in marine canvaswork are acrylic and PVC/polyester. With care both types can be long-lasting, although marine grade acrylics tend to have better ultraviolet and fade resistance, and also benefit from being breathable.

As with many aspects of boat maintenance, prevention is the key to keeping canvas in good shape. Top quality canvaswork has reinforcement around areas prone to chafe and in high-load areas close to attachment points, and similar features are easy to retrofit to extend the life of existing canvas items. Most domestic sewing machines will sew through two or three layers of acrylic fabric, although some hand finishing may be necessary.

Regular checks should focus on stitching, chafe, studs and other fastenings. In addition, ensure all canvas is firmly secured before leaving the boat. In a gale, even small unsecured areas can flog with enough power to age the material rapidly and loosen fastenings.

Repairing damage

Temporary repairs can be carried out by hand on small areas of damaged stitching, and even with more major damage a few well-placed stitches can prevent a seam continuing to

Above **Regularly examine canvaswork for signs of chafe, and make repairs at the earliest opportunity.**

Below **Any boat can have great-looking canvaswork. The material is long-lasting but requires regular cleaning and reproofing.**

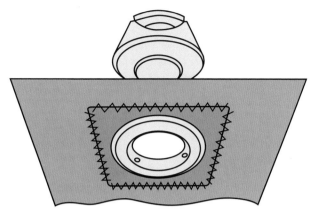

Left **If studs tear away from the material, first sew a patch under the damaged area, then replace the stud with a new one. Studs come in two parts and are a press fit.**

unravel. However, the fact that one area of stitching has failed indicates the likelihood that all the seams will be weak, so it makes sense to re-stitch the entire item.

Rips and tears should have their frayed edges cut away with sharp scissors, and a neat hem sewn around the damage. A slightly larger reinforcing patch can then be stitched around the damage.

The studs commonly used to hold the outer corners of spray hoods to the coachroof can cause problems if they start to tear away from the fabric. Most have two elements that are pressed together through the material. If the two parts cannot be separated, the stud will need to be carefully cut away. A patch can then be sewn over the damaged area, before a new stud is fitted.

Preventing and removing mould

Mould and green algae grow on fabrics that remain damp for extended periods, or where dirt is allowed to accumulate. Regularly washing salt and dirt away with fresh water will help the fabric dry quickly after rain or dew. It will lose its weatherproof properties over time and should be reproofed every few years with the application of a spray-on reproofing liquid. If mould forms it can be treated with a proprietary mould cleaner, scrubbing gently with a soft brush if necessary. Afterwards rinse the fabric thoroughly, then re-treat for water and stain resistance.

Stitching canvas

Tools and materials for canvas repairs: sailmaker's needles, webbing, palm, heavy-duty scissors, twine and a knife.

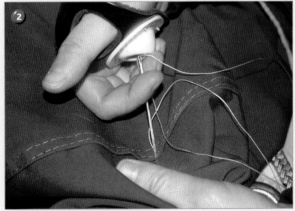

Using a palm to reinforce a seam. Acting promptly to repair loose stitching can save hours of work later.

Rope care

Modern synthetic ropes are available in a wide variety of materials to suit different purposes and budgets. Most are very long-lasting, and with care will give decades of reliable use, but chafe can destroy a line in minutes.

Material choice

Sheets and halyards should 'give' as little as possible, so cruisers usually choose pre-stretched polyester, while race boats go for ultra-expensive high-modulus polyethylenes such as Dyneema and Spectra. By contrast, mooring warps and anchor rodes benefit from being able to stretch, because elasticity reduces peak loads in rough weather, and this makes nylon an excellent choice.

One common synthetic that is not durable is polypropylene, which is rapidly weakened by exposure to sunlight. For this reason it's rarely used afloat, with the exception of man overboard heaving lines, which require a buoyant material. These are stored in a bag, which is designed to protect them from UV degradation as well as to facilitate throwing the line.

TYPES OF ROPE

Three main construction techniques are used in rope manufacture. Braided lines have an outer braid surrounding and protecting a central core of fibres, which may be braided or plaited. Historically three-strand twisted construction (also known as 'laid' rope) was the most popular, but having greater stretch, it is now used primarily for mooring and anchor lines. Multiplait is a newer development for this purpose. It is more comfortable to handle than laid rope, but more expensive.

Chafe protection

Chafe can rapidly weaken a rope, so it is important to ensure that lines are led clear of anything that may cause damage. With running rigging, chafe is usually a gradual process, but strong winds and waves create snatching loads in mooring warps that can make fairleads, or the edge of a quay, cut through a line in hours. The best prevention is to slide a piece of hose pipe (or other stout plastic tube) over the line at the chafe point.

Left **Rinsing lines regularly with fresh water prevents them becoming stiff. Allow them to dry before stowing them away.**

Sailmaker's whipping

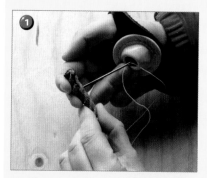

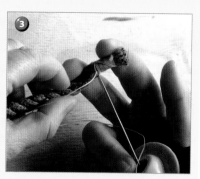

Start by securing the end of the whipping twine by pulling it through the rope with a needle a few times.

Wind the twine tightly round the rope, moving towards the end of the line, making sure the rope strands lie flat.

Finally, pass the twine around the whipping and through the rope three times to hold it securely in place.

Small amounts of chafe won't seriously weaken a line, provided the affected area isn't exposed to further damage. The lifespan of halyards and reefing lines can be extended by 'end for ending' them – reeving them the opposite way round, so that further chafe occurs on undamaged parts (see page 240).

Rope ends need protection against fraying. Most new lines have ends sealed with a hot knife, but a sailmaker's whipping, stitched securely through the rope, is the best permanent solution.

Cleaning rope

Prolonged exposure to seawater makes ropes stiff and awkward to handle. Regular rinsing with fresh water will minimise this problem, although a periodical deeper clean is beneficial. A bath of warm, soapy water is ideal, although badly soiled lines can benefit from being cleaned in a domestic washing machine.

Bending ropes through tight angles reduces their strength, and even knots weaken them. Bowlines and overhand knots reduce a rope's breaking strain by around 50 per cent, whereas a splice or round turn and two half hitches will cause only ten per cent of the strength to be lost. The effect is especially pronounced with hi-tech lines that have minimal stretch.

Below **Short lengths of hose pipe are ideal for protecting mooring lines against chafe and are cheaper to replace than rope.**

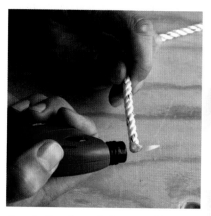

Above **Sealing the end of a rope with a gas-fuelled hot knife prevents it from fraying, but keep fingers well away.**

Cleaning saloon & cabins

Cleaning the interior of a boat can be time-consuming, and often the same problems recur with annoying frequency. Knowing how to deal with these effectively makes this aspect of boat maintenance more efficient and rewarding.

Above **If mains electricity is available, dehumidifiers are effective at banishing damp from the interior of a boat.**

Avoiding damp

This is the most important part of looking after the interior of any boat. Even boats kept in ostensibly dry regions, such as the Mediterranean, can be exposed to significant winter rainfall. Damp conditions promote the growth of mould on interior surfaces and soft furnishings, and give the vessel a musty, unloved smell. Salt crystals readily absorb moisture, so every effort should be made to keep seawater away from the interior, and rinse any fabrics, clothing and surfaces with fresh water after exposure to salt.

Vessels with access to mains electricity can use a dehumidifier to banish damp. These are wonderfully effective, and will also dry foul weather gear and sails, provided the boat is well-sealed to prevent moist air replacing the dry air on board. The alternative is to maximise ventilation, promoting a constant movement of air through the boat (see page 56). This is the only viable option for traditionally built wooden boats, because prolonged use of a dehumidifier will dry out the timber too much.

Interior woodwork

Most older boats have a relatively soft single-pack varnish or oiled finish, which should be fully re-coated every couple of years. Touch up scratches immediately, though, to prevent moisture ingress causing further damage. Newer boats normally use a two-pack varnish system that's very hard-wearing and requires no routine maintenance other than an occasional wash.

Soft furnishings

Modern marine upholstery fabrics have a mould inhibitor, but this cannot prevent mould growing on dirt embedded in the fabric. Remove loose dirt by vacuuming or brushing before it has a chance to be rubbed into the fabric. Covers should be washed periodically. If you don't want to do this by hand, a washing machine set on 'cool wash' is fine, but covers must not be tumble dried, as the polyester base panels will not withstand the heat. Use a carpet-cleaning machine with an upholstery attachment for cushions that can't be removed. Covers should be re-treated with a water- and stain-proofing product after cleaning.

Spilt liquids and stains should be dealt with immediately; the longer they soak into the material the more difficult they are to remove. Salt is an effective first defence against red wine stains, while acetone may work well for chewing gum and greasy marks, and a mix of detergent and vinegar solution is ideal for many food stains. Try a hidden test area first to check the fabric isn't damaged by the mix, especially if using solvents that may affect dyes.

Left **With care, a boat's interior can retain an as-new appearance for decades, as this 20-year-old Contessa 32 shows.**

Banishing mould

Hydrogen peroxide is both a more effective and a less damaging mould cleaner than chlorine bleaches. Use a pre-diluted solution, and apply generously with a damp cloth. Leave it to soak for a while, before washing off with soapy water, gently using a soft-bristled brush if necessary. Wipe surfaces afterwards with white vinegar to kill any remaining fungus.

Above **Most sleeping cabins have poor ventilation, so cushions will benefit from being taken on deck to air in fine weather.**

Right **Attention to detail is crucial. Start by cleaning the debris out of corners, before dealing with more open areas.**

Cleaning heads & galley

There are significant differences between on-board domestic equipment and household equivalents, so specialist knowledge is needed to keep these items operating efficiently and looking their best. Stowage of food also needs careful consideration, especially on smaller boats or when voyaging away from regular sources of provisions.

Marine toilets

A build-up of limescale in pipework, pump seals and valves is one of the biggest causes of problems in marine sanitary systems, so a regular flush with descaler is beneficial. Vinegar solution is very effective, as well as being environmentally friendly and a mild disinfectant. Chlorine bleaches should be avoided – as well as being environmentally destructive, they can damage the rubber components in the pump. Drips or leaks from toilets usually come from the clean water side.

Nevertheless, this is a clear sign that the seals are worn and that the pump needs to be overhauled (see pages 134 to 137).

Unpleasant odours come from two main sources. Firstly, if sanitation grade hose is not used, then the hoses absorb odours and transmit these to their surroundings. This is a particularly important consideration on vessels fitted with holding tanks. Secondly, the seawater inlet hose can harbour microscopic organisms, which gradually die and produce a strong,

Above **Blocked drains are often responsible for ugly smells from top-loading fridges and coolboxes. Keep them clean.**

Below **Avoid using aggressively abrasive cleaners on the plastic basins fitted to many yachts.**

STOWING FOOD

Stowage of provisions is an important consideration, both to maximise the life of fresh produce and to make best use of the space available. Fruit keeps best in nets, which can be hung from the deckhead, but many vegetables prefer a dark, well-ventilated space. Dried goods are especially vulnerable to moisture, and should therefore be stowed in sealed plastic containers.

sulphurous odour. As well as being transmitted through the hose walls, this will be brought out in the open when the toilet is flushed for the first time after being left for a while.

To combat this, flush the toilet with freshwater before leaving the boat, or fit a cleaning system to the inlet hose. The latter course of action will also have the benefit of automatically adding a cleansing agent every time the system is flushed.

Fridges and cookers

Top-loading fridges are popular because the cold air is retained when the lid is opened, and they can also be squeezed into otherwise inaccessible areas. Most have a drain to allow condensation and spilt

liquids to leave the compartment. Check where this drain terminates. It should be led to a skin fitting, enabling liquids to leave the boat, rather than draining into the bilge. Unexplained and unpleasant smells emanating from the fridge can often be traced to blockages or partial obstructions in this drain.

Biodegradable household cleaning agents work well on marine cookers, although the polished stainless steel surface of many models is very easily scratched, so aggressive scourers should be avoided.

Above **The sides of gimballed cookers can quickly collect dirt. Use a long-handled brush to reach inaccessible areas.**

Professional delivery crews, who must present a yacht in pristine condition, even after a 4,000-mile passage, lay aluminium foil in the trays around the burners of the gas hob, making cleaning much easier. While cleaning, check for any damage to the flexible part of the gas pipe leading to the cooker.

Maintaining headlinings

Headlinings provide a neat cosmetic finish below fibreglass decks and insulate against cold and condensation. Both fibreglass inner mouldings and foam-backed vinyl materials were used extensively in the 1970s and 1980s. Since the late 1990s manufacturers have started to produce monocoque deck mouldings with a fair cosmetic finish on both sides and insulation built in.

Problems with vinyl linings

Older fibreglass linings are long-lasting and require no maintenance other than routine cleaning, although condensation readily forms, making good ventilation essential if you are to avoid mould in the off season. Vinyl headlining panels can also be fairly durable, provided they are mounted on small plywood panels. However, the foam backing breaks down over time, and larger areas fall away from the deckhead after a decade or two.

Where it has been glued to plywood panels, vinyl can be given an extra lease of life by using stainless steel staples to reattach the edges of the material to the blind face of the plywood. Slightly stretching the material helps to minimise the amount of droop below the centre of each panel.

If foam-backed vinyl has been glued directly to the deckhead, there's less that can be done to rescue it once the foam fails. It may be possible to make strategic use of decorative wooden strips, screwed through the vinyl and into the deck, to give added support. Screws used for this purpose must not penetrate more than half the deck's thickness.

Below **Foam-backed vinyl headlinings were fitted to many new boats in the 1970s and 80s, but the material has a finite lifespan.**

Permanent solutions

The best long-term solution is to cut panels from 4mm exterior grade plywood, with the edges rounded, onto which the largest expanses of material can be glued. These are then screwed to wooden battens, which are in turn glued to the deckhead using epoxy resin thickened with microfibres. The headlining will remain largely supported, even after the foam has started to fail. Any small gaps between panels can have vinyl glued directly to the deckhead.

To achieve a neat finish, buttons covered in matching material can be used to hide screw heads. These are made in exactly the same fashion as upholstery buttons (see page 38), but are a snap fit into raised washers around each screw.

When foam-backed vinyl is removed, it leaves behind lumps of foam and adhesive that must be stripped before new material can be glued in place. The most efficient way of doing this is using a Face-Off disc (an abrasive-impregnated plastic mesh, which looks a bit like wire wool), or similar product in an electric drill or small angle grinder.

SAFETY

Working with solvent-based adhesives in the tight confines of a boat's interior is fraught with potential hazards. The area must be well ventilated and free of naked flames (including pilot lights), and an organic vapour mask should be worn. Gluing vinyl to plywood panels is best done outside, in a separate well-ventilated area. The dust created by broken-down foam is hazardous, so an effective dust mask should be used at all times.

Applying foam-backed vinyl

Having cut the plywood board to the right size, apply the adhesive with a notched spreader. Getting an even spread is more important than applying a large quantity.

Place the board, with the adhesive facing downwards, onto the headlining. Trim the edges of the material to give an overlap of about 2in (50mm).

Cutting a tongue at the corners helps to create a neat overall finish. It's worth practising this part with scrap material before you start.

Hold the edges of the material in place for a few seconds to allow the adhesive to bond firmly. Note how cutting the tongue prevents bunching at the corner.

Upholstery care

Soft furnishings are one of the most expensive elements of a boat's interior, but also the most easily damaged. A degree of wear and tear is inevitable, but much can be done to keep fabrics in good order and maximise their lifespan.

Ideal fabrics

Modern marine upholstery fabrics are water- and stain-resistant, with good anti-fungal properties. In addition, most suppliers avoid material with a high cotton content, as this readily absorbs moisture. Older upholstery used a vinyl base fabric to protect the underside of the cushions from water ingress, but more modern fit-outs are likely to use an ultra-breathable polyester mesh.

Polyester wadding is often placed between the foam and the cover to provide a soft, slightly domed finish and reduce movement of the fabric relative to the foam. Provided the edges of the foam have not collapsed and it is of a fire-retardant specification, re-covering existing cushions is a cost-effective way of transforming

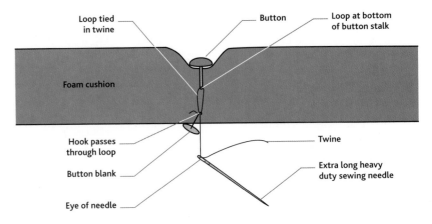

the appearance of a boat's interior.

To remove covers, unzip or pull the hook-and-loop fastenings apart, then manoeuvre the end of the foam out of the cover. This is easier for long, thin cushions than for large square ones. Zips that are seized with salt crystals can generally be

Above **Connecting a button to its blank partner on the underside of the cushion. Pull a loop of twine into the cushion using a long needle, then pass the hook on the stem of the blank button through the loop.**

Below **Taking care of upholstery pays dividends in terms of reducing long-term costs and keeping the boat looking its best.**

WEAR AND TEAR

Tips to minimise wear and tear:

- ✪ On long passages, cover saloon cushions with waterproof material to prevent water absorption.

- ✪ When leaving the boat for long periods, ensure it is well ventilated and stand cushions on edge.

- ✪ Take soft furnishings home over the winter and store in a dry place.

- ✪ Deal with problems, whether stains, damaged stitching or rips, immediately.

Above **When making new cushions, a bread knife makes an effective tool for cutting the foam to size.**

freed by brushing loose salt away, then carefully pouring a small amount of hot water into the zip to dissolve the remainder.

Removing and replacing buttons

Before removing covers, cut the thread that secures buttons. To replace them, use a long needle to connect the button to its blank on the underside of the cushion, and tie the two together. New buttons are created in a press from two components, so it's normally more economical to buy them ready-made from an upholstery supplier than make them yourself.

Repairing stitching and patching holes

Curved needles can be used for stitching small patches and tears in situ, and needles that curve through 180 degrees can be used to repair stitching on internal seams without removing the foam. However, larger repairs are often easiest carried out using a sewing machine after the cover has been removed.

If matching material is available, a tidy job can be done with the cover removed. Use sharp scissors to cut a neat rectangle around the damaged area, and a patch slightly larger than the hole, ensuring that the pattern exactly matches. The patch can then be stitched in place, with a flat seam, allowing it to sit level with the surrounding fabric.

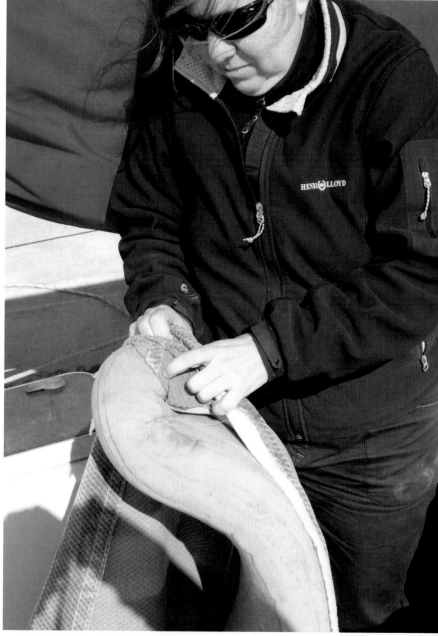

Above **Cushions should be a very snug fit in their covers. Care and patience are needed to remove and replace them without causing damage.**

Lockers & bilges

Don't be tempted to ignore these unseen areas. They demand just as much attention as the rest of the vessel. The reward for complacency in this department is all too often a smelly, slimy gunge that contaminates an ever-larger area.

Avoiding contamination

Every possible effort should be made to prevent engine oil and diesel reaching the main bilge. If it mixes with water here it can slosh around a large area, contaminating other surfaces including lockers. Another problem is that contaminated water must not be pumped out of the bilge into the sea, so disposing of it is an additional hassle. A common misconception is that, because proprietary bilge cleaners are generally labelled as biodegradable, they convert oil and other contaminants in a mucky bilge into biodegradable substances. The fact is, they don't.

Fitting a drip tray under the engine is the best way to prevent oil and diesel reaching the bilge. On some boats, a simple barrier glued across the front of the engine bearers will suffice, although others will need a custom-made aluminium or fibreglass container. On sailing yachts, the tray must be deep enough to retain its contents when the boat is heeled.

Cleaning the bilge

If significant amounts of engine oil or diesel reach the bilge, oil-absorbent pads can be used to remove most of the contamination, but the bilge will still need a thorough clean. Start by washing the bilge with a mix of bilge cleaner and water, using a long-handled brush to reach inaccessible areas. The liquid can then be removed for safe disposal ashore, and the surface of the bilge dried with disposable rags.

Above **An aluminium sheet glued across the front of the engine bearers creates an improvised 'drip tray'.**

Below **Oil absorbent pads help to keep oily residues out of the bilge water. Dispose of them properly ashore.**

Repeat the process if a significant amount of oil residue remains.

Even if water is the only liquid that ever reaches the bilge, it must still be washed out periodically to remove accumulations of dirt and grit brought into the boat from outside, plus dust and dead skin. It's these deposits, as well as oily residues, that lead to the development of persistent smells if left unchecked.

Limber holes between different sections of the bilge can easily become blocked and should be regularly checked and cleaned. Many lockers also have limber holes that connect them to the bilge. On wooden boats these were essential to allow water from leaking seams to reach the bilge, but on a fibreglass boat they can be a nuisance, allowing bilge water to reach an otherwise dry and clean locker. It's worth considering whether your boat would benefit from having them blocked off.

Cleaning lockers

Lockers can quickly accumulate a surprising quantity of unnecessary clutter, which will absorb damp, create dust and add weight that will impair performance. They benefit from being thoroughly cleaned, including washing them out with soapy water at the end of each season, and any non-essential items removed ashore. This is also the ideal time to give them a fresh coat of paint if the existing finish is tired.

Above **Keeping the bilge clean prevents nasty smells forming and ensures there's no debris that could block bilge pumps.**

Left **An annual audit of locker contents is worthwhile. Most cruising boats accumulate many unnecessary items.**

Hull and deck repairs

Removing stains from fibreglass

It doesn't matter how much care and attention you lavish on your boat, any fibreglass (aka GRP, 'glass-reinforced plastic', or FRP, 'fibre-reinforced plastic') will sometimes become stained or marked. The sooner any stains are removed, the easier it will be, and the less time will be required.

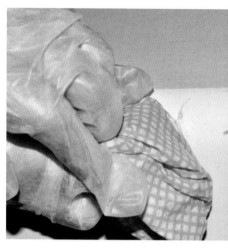

Gel coat

The lamination of glass fibre and resin is given a smooth, shiny outer surface called the 'gel coat'. This is to some extent porous, which means that stains can easily become embedded, so stain removal should be undertaken as soon as possible. One cleaning problem is that the gel coat is usually only 0.02in to 0.09in (0.5mm to 0.8mm) thick, so too much abrasion will wear the surface through to the underlying fibreglass. Another is that some chemicals will react unfavourably with the gel coat.

The best way of preventing stains, or at least making them easier to remove, is to keep the gel coat as smooth and non-porous as possible with a high quality, silicone-free polish.

Below **Pressure washing the hull will remove any fouling but won't remove stains from the waterline.**

Above **Scuff marks are quickly removed using cleaner or polish.**

Right **Exhaust soot stains are easily removed, especially if tackled soon after they occur.**

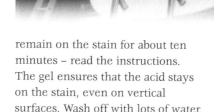

New stains

As soon as you notice a stain, try using a mild, non-abrasive household cleaner to remove it. Avoid bleach and solvent cleaners. If this doesn't work, then something more powerful will be needed.

Non-abrasive chemicals

There are many non-abrasive chemical cleaners on the market, some of which are for specific stains, such as those found along the waterline. These products may or may not work on your particular stain, but should at least be safe to use on your gel coat, provided you follow the instructions to the letter.

There is also a plethora of boat owners' 'I always use' remedies, some of which are no better than old wives' tales. If you really must try one of these, then for the safety of your gel coat, start with a small, unimportant area to check it is safe.

Gel stain removers are painted on with a paintbrush and allowed to remain on the stain for about ten minutes – read the instructions. The gel ensures that the acid stays on the stain, even on vertical surfaces. Wash off with lots of water.

Liquid stain removers are applied with a cloth, normally allowed to dry, and then wiped off with a clean cloth – again, follow the instructions carefully.

Non-abrasive cleaners should be used like a polish. Apply with a cloth and, when dried to a haze, buff with a clean cloth.

Abrasive cleaners

These range from mild bathtub-type cream cleaners to automotive 'colour restorers'. Abrasive cleaners such as Y10 must be used in moderation as eventually they will wear through the gel coat.

✪ **Cream cleaners:** apply with a damp sponge and use pressure to rub the stain away. Dry with a clean cloth.

✪ **Automotive colour restorers:** Apply the restorer to the cloth and rub onto the stain with a circular motion. When the restorer has dried to a haze, buff with a clean cloth. Always follow the manufacturer's instructions.

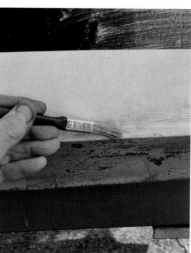

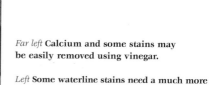

Far left **Calcium and some stains may be easily removed using vinegar.**

Left **Some waterline stains need a much more powerful cleaner, such as Y10. Apply with a brush, following the instructions carefully.**

Polishing fibreglass

The cosmetic condition of the hull and topsides of your boat advertises how much care and attention it gets. Not only that, polish will help keep ultraviolet degradation at bay and enhance the boat's second-hand value when you come to sell.

Gel coat

The cosmetic gel coat on most boats is a polyester resin with an added pigment. The rough and tumble of docking, salt water and general grime will take the gloss off the hull and topsides. Polishing the gel coat will bring back the original gloss and will slow down the soiling process. It may also make any scrapes less obvious, but it will not remove them.

Shallow scratches can be removed by using a cutting compound, which will also remove the chalky appearance caused by ultraviolet radiation.

Above **Minor scratches can be polished out by hand using a cream cutting compound.**

Cutting back the gel coat

Cutting compounds come in various grades of aggressiveness, but for 'polishing' use, you need a high gloss compound. This cuts through grime and light scratch marks to produce a high gloss finish, but removes some of the gel coat in the process. It can be applied by hand, using a cloth and a lot of effort. Once dried to a haze, it can be buffed to a high gloss with a clean cloth. This glossy surface then needs to be protected with a high quality wax polish for best results.

Polishing the gel coat

There are many suitable polishes available, at varying cost and ease of application. But avoid any polish containing silicone, because this will prevent gel coat repairs from being successful and is difficult to remove.

Left **If you're working in an isolated place where there's no mains power available, a generator can power your polisher.**

Right **A mains electric heavy-duty polishing machine, used with a cutting compound, can transform a hull.**

Types of polish

Liquid polishes are applied with a cloth in a circular motion, allowed to dry to a haze and then buffed with a clean cloth. Some have a chemical cleaner incorporated, but others need to be applied on a surface that you have already cleaned.

Hard wax polishes require much more effort to apply and polish, but are much longer-lasting. They must be applied to a clean and dry surface.

Mechanical polishing

Polishing the gel coat mechanically will take some of the hard work out of doing it by hand. There are two types of electric polishers: orbital and rotary.

✪ Orbital polishers are relatively light in weight and inexpensive. The polishing mop doesn't rotate but has an orbital motion. Running at a no-load speed of 3,000 orbits per minute, they are low power and unlikely to overheat the gel coat when you polish. They are not suitable for use with a cutting compound.

✪ Rotary polishers are heavier machines, more expensive and have a true rotary motion. The best have electronic speed control and rev at up to 3,000 rpm. These need more care in use and are heavier to wield, but they are much more effective than orbital polishers. Rotary polishers can be used with a cutting compound as well as for polishing.

Above **A good quality wax polish is the best protection you can give fibreglass.**

Refurbishing wood trim

Wooden trim on a boat will discolour, become watermarked or just start to look tired. Regular cleaning and, where necessary, protection of the wood will ensure that it always looks good. Small areas of damage should be repaired as soon as possible.

Water stains

There are a number of suitable products on the market that will 'brighten' previously untreated wood, and all will have been tested for effectiveness. Follow the instructions carefully both for safety reasons and for best results.

Products of this type often contain oxalic acid, and it is possible to buy this in crystal form and make up your own solution for removing water and rust stains from wood. However, this is a caustic and toxic chemical, so it needs to be used with great care. Follow the instructions on the tub or on the supplier's website, and remember to neutralise afterwards with ammonia or borax.

With varnished wood, the old varnish must first be removed, and the wood is then treated as above before re-varnishing. Varnished veneered plywood, however, needs a great deal of care if you are to avoid damaging the veneer.

The best treatment is, of course, to lightly sand the varnish and apply a fresh coat before any water staining can occur – but assuming the damage has already been done, you will need to use a varnish stripper to get down to bare wood.

If you cannot avoid this, sand in the direction of the grain and be very careful not to sand through the veneer. Remove the watermarks as above, then re-varnish.

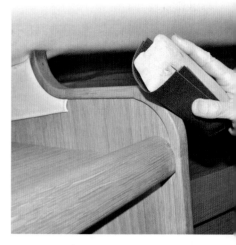

Above **Using a sanding block ensures the whole area is evenly 'flattened'.**

Below: **Watermarks on bare wood can be treated with oxalic acid. If the wood is varnished, the varnish must be removed.**

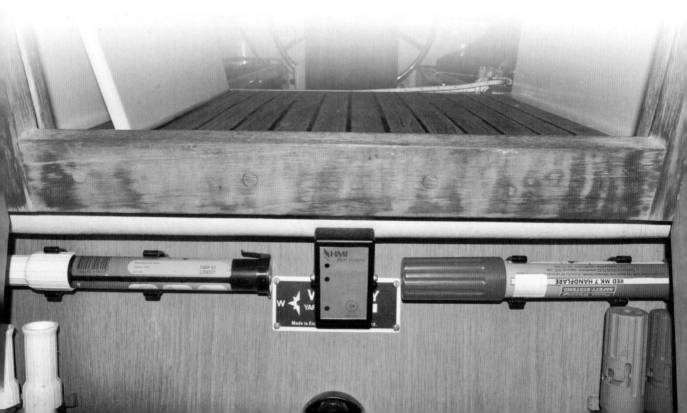

Right **Teak plugs are easily obtained, but you may need to make your own for other woods, using a special drill bit.**

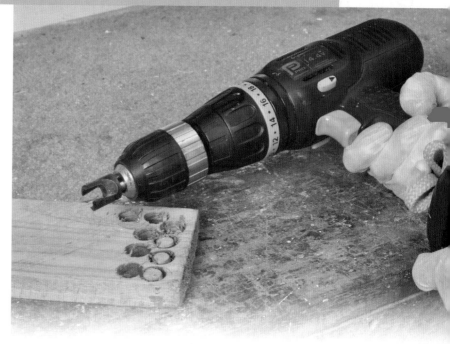

Small areas of localised damage

Small 'bruises' can often be removed by applying water to make the wood swell. Remove any varnish locally and make several applications of warm water, but don't let the damage stay wet or this will cause staining. You may need a little wood-coloured filler to get a fair surface. Sand down and re-varnish.

For damaged edging, the method will depend on the extent of the damage and your woodworking skills. If the area is small and you have some wood-coloured filler, then make good the damage, sand and re-finish.

If you have the necessary skills, a larger damaged area can be removed with a saw and finished off with a chisel. A new piece of wood can be accurately shaped and let in to the gap. Sand the patch and re-finish as required.

Plugging wood screws

Wood screw heads are sometimes hidden behind wooden plugs to make them almost invisible. If the plugs need to be replaced, they will have to be carefully removed. As the plugs are normally only very shallow, a drill bit will usually make contact with the screw head before the plug is drilled out. Special wood bits have small points and sharp, pointed corners and are ideal for this job.

Ready-made teak plugs can be bought in various sizes, but plugs made from other woods are scarce. However, special plug-cutting drills are available, enabling you to cut your own plugs from a matching piece of wood.

Hiding screw heads

Glue in a plug made of the same wood as the furniture, ensuring the direction of the grain is aligned correctly.

Once the glue is set, chisel away the protruding plug. Cut from the side where the grain is closest to the surface.

Finish off with a 'detail' sander, if available, or sandpaper on a block. Touch up with varnish or polish, as appropriate.

Refurbishing deck fittings

Deck fittings have a hard life, and may start to look tired even if they are still working well. If you want your boat to carry on looking good, there may be a way of improving their appearance without having to renew them.

Above **This fitting is looking rather tired, and it may be cheaper to replace it than to have it refurbished.**

What are the fittings made of?

The ease of refurbishing fittings will depend, in part, on the materials used to make them. If the fitting consists of several components, it will have to be taken apart in order to refurbish it. Common fittings materials are:

- ✪ **Galvanised steel:** Regalvanising can usually be done fairly locally. The old galvanising needs to be removed first, so you can have it blasted as a separate job, or get the galvanisers to do it for you.
- ✪ **Anodised aluminium alloy:** Provided there's no underlying electrolytic corrosion, anodising stands up to normal wear and tear very well. If a fitting does need to be refurbished, you should be able to find a local anodising company.
- ✪ **Bronze:** This needs no more than a good application of metal polish.

Below **Traditional bronze fittings look good when polished, but soon tarnish. A continuous polishing routine is needed.**

Above **Fittings may be through bolted, in which case access is required inside the boat to remove the nuts.**

✪ **Chromium-plated bronze:** If the plating has worn away, the fitting can be replated and polished.

✪ **Stainless steel:** Despite its name, stainless steel can rust if oxygen is excluded from the surface. Rust stains can be removed with stainless steel polish, applied with a cloth. If the fitting is badly scratched, the scratches can be polished out professionally, but the fitting will need to be removed in order to do so.

Removing the fittings

Deck-mounted fittings are often difficult to remove because the fastenings are hidden behind panelling in the cabin. A number of different techniques are used to fix and hide the fastenings, so you will need to see how yours are fitted. If you are very lucky, there will be an access panel to inside fastenings, but this is not often the case.

One of the modern boatbuilder's favourite methods is to tap fastening bolts into aluminium plates, because this is cheap and easy. The plate is glassed into the moulding, then a hole is drilled through everything and is tapped with a suitable thread into which the bolt holding the fitting is screwed. Unfortunately the aluminium plate corrodes around the stainless steel bolt, making it very difficult to remove. And, when

Above **You may need to remove the cabin lining to get access to the nuts. This can be re-glued once the fitting is replaced.**

it is removed, the thread often disintegrates.

Sometimes nuts are glassed onto the underside of mouldings. The resin and glass has to be ground away to release the nut, which is often difficult to access.

Head linings often make it very difficult to get at fastenings, so they may have to be removed (or at least peeled back) to gain access.

Refurbish or new?

Refurbishing may be quite expensive, so you may wish to consider whether it's worth spending a little more to get a new item. However, note that the spacing of the holes for the new fitting may not be the same as for the old one.

Left **If the fastenings have corroded, you may need an impact driver to remove them. But only use one as a last resort.**

Re-bedding leaking deck fittings

Water leaking into the inside of a boat can be extremely annoying, and also very difficult to trace. It's probable that it will take time for a leak to be noticed, and the visible dampness may be nowhere near the leak.

Tracing the leak

Finding out where the water is coming from is often the most difficult part of the process, especially if the attachment bolts are hidden behind internal structure or linings. Because water runs 'downhill', the damp patch or signs of water may not be close to where the actual leak is.

If there is no fitting close to the signs of water, look for a fitting above, but note that the water may also run almost horizontally across an intervening part of the structure, so the fitting at fault may not be vertically above the evidence of a leak.

If the lining is easily removable, remove it, as this will make the task much easier. Signs of the leak may now be obvious. If not, spray the area outside the boat with a powerful hose and see what fresh evidence this produces.

Removing the fitting

The fitting may need to be taken apart to reveal the attachment bolts. Page 51 details methods of securing the fitting to the structure, so if necessary, gain access to the nuts. For hexagonal head bolts and hexagonal key bolts, use the correct size tool and unscrew the nut.

If machine screws have been used, it is very easy to damage the slot or cross in the head, so be sure to use the correct size of screwdriver, applying plenty of downforce to stop the blade jumping out of the head.

Where bolts have seized, there are several methods of undoing them. If the bolt is corroded into an aluminium fixing plate, vinegar may break the corrosion. This will take several days to work, so you may need to make a reservoir around the

Below **Most yachts have many fittings and attachment holes, any of which may eventually be the source of a leak.**

bolt to keep the vinegar in place. You may also consider using an impact driver, if you believe the fitting will take the force of a heavy hammer being used on the tool.

Once the fitting, old sealant and any loose dirt have been removed, clean the area thoroughly to leave as smooth a finish as possible.

Applying new sealant and replacing the fitting

- ✪ Mask around the outline of the fitting with masking tape, to make removal of excess sealant easy.
- ✪ Apply a good marine sealant in a ring around the attachment holes. Use a polyurethane sealant rather than silicone, which could prove impossible to remove later.
- ✪ Apply more sealant just inside the outline of the fitting.
- ✪ Apply sealant to the attachment bolts, close under the head and along the top part of the shank.

Above **If you suspect that water is leaking from outside, you may need to remove the cabin lining to find the source.**

- ✪ Replace the fitting and tighten the attachment bolts until the sealant starts to squeeze out from the sides, then stop.
- ✪ Wait until the sealant sets before fully tightening the bolts.

TIP

If the leak has rotted the wooden structure or the balsa core of a deck, the rotten timber must be repaired before you replace the fitting.

Re-bedding a deck fitting

Undo the fastening and remove the fitting. If the fastenings are seized up, a spanner on the screwdriver shaft will allow a lot more force to be applied.

Put a ring of sealant around the screw holes. You can put sealant around the perimeter too, to prevent water sitting under the fitting, but this is not essential.

Tighten the fastenings until you start to see some sealant. Fully tighten only when the sealant is cured.

Repairing seals

In time, the sealant around a porthole or hatch will harden, and flexing of the structure may then cause a leak. It's tempting to dry it and apply some sealant just to the area of the leak, but this rarely works.

Removing a hatch or porthole

This may look like a daunting task, but with patience it can be achieved quite easily, unless the hatch or porthole fastenings are concealed behind non-removable lining.

A number of different types of fastenings are used. Most hatches are fixed using machine screws with nuts on the inside, so you have to remove the trim or even the headlining below the hatch. Open the hatch to reveal the screws, and remove all the nuts. The hatch will now need to be prised away from the deck or coachroof. Use a thin paint scraper and push it under the hatch surround. You will probably need to use a mallet to force it in and work along the seam. This will take

time and patience. Once the seal is broken all round, you will be able to prise the hatch frame away from the structure.

Portholes/portlights may be fixed with self-tapping screws, or machine screws tapped into the inside frame or into 'interscrews' – screws with an internal thread. The screws may be hidden by a removable trim that is part of the frame. Portholes may have a sealing gasket between the frame and the structure, or liquid sealant may have been used. Once the screws have been removed, portholes with a sealing gasket should come away fairly easily. Those fitted using sealant can be removed in the same way as a hatch frame.

Chain plates

Chain plates are subjected to heavy loads, and any weakness in the structure may result in flexing that can cause leaks at the bolts. Sea water in contact with the hidden stainless steel bolts will cause corrosion, leading to possible failure and collapse of the rig. All boats should have easy access to the chain plate fastenings. If yours hasn't, then linings or structure will have to be removed, because the only way to cure the leak is to remove the entire fitting, clean up and re-seal with a high quality marine sealant.

Below **Sometimes the best way to find a leak is to spray water from the outside.**

Right **Having removed the attachment screws, you will need a thin rigid blade to break the old sealant.**

TIP

If you have a portlight that leaks, it's no good trying to add more sealant from the outside. This will look unsightly and is likely to just collect moisture and mould. In most cases, you're much better off removing and re-bedding the offending fitting.

Re-bedding a portlight

Before fitting the cleaned portlight, apply sealant all round the flange - not too much and not too little.

Carefully replace the portlight, making sure it's the right way up and the screw holes line up.

Replace the attachment screws and tighten them almost fully home. Fully tighten them after the sealant has set.

Any excess sealant can be cleaned once it is set, using a craft knife to detach it from the fitting.

Mast gaiters

Boats that have a keel-stepped mast always have a tendency to leak at the mast gaiter (also known as mast 'boot'). Even if the gaiter is a good seal, water can run down inside the mast and exit at the mast step, and there is almost nothing that can be done about this. Ultraviolet radiation and chafe will eventually cause the gaiter to fail, at which point it will have to be replaced. Because the gaiter has to be slid up the mast from the heel, it would be worthwhile considering replacing a worn (if not yet failed) gaiter whenever the mast is removed.

Locating & fitting ventilators

Ventilation below decks is very important in all climates, but frequently boatbuilders don't provide enough ventilators. Boat owners may therefore wish to fit additional ones, which is not a difficult job.

What type of ventilator should you fit?

The most useful ventilator is one that can be left open in all but the roughest conditions and yet not allow water to come below. There are a number of different types like this.

Dorade vents are named after the schooner that first fitted them. They have a scoop (or 'cowl') that can be rotated into the wind, and the air flows into a box with an internal baffle, which prevents water entering the cabin. The box has drain holes at the bottom. Provided ropes can't catch on them, they are the most efficient type. For rough conditions, the scoop can be removed and a blanking plate fitted.

Flush ventilators are very shallow, and so will not snag ropes. Because they are low, they don't catch as much air as a Dorade, but are very neat. They are closed from inside the cabin.

Engine room ventilators are mounted on a vertical surface, with the vents facing downwards to prevent water entering. They rely on forced ventilation, as they don't catch any wind.

Locating a ventilator

You are going to have to drill a fairly big hole in the cabin top, so it's essential that you measure both inside the cabin and on deck from some known reference point, to ensure the ventilator will fit outside (and won't get in the way) and the hole won't hit anything inside.

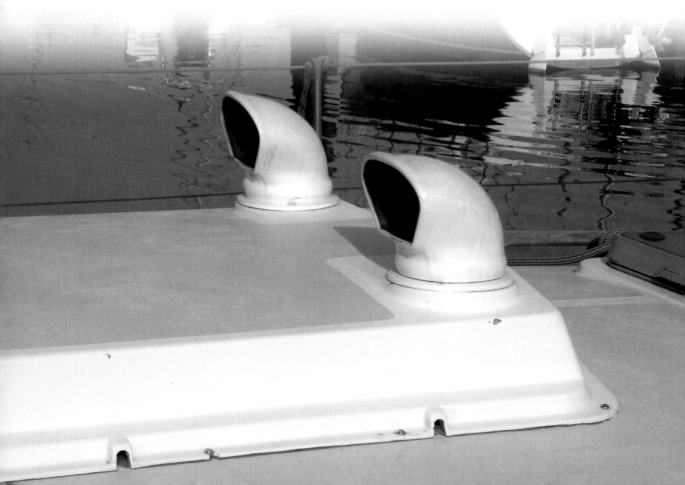

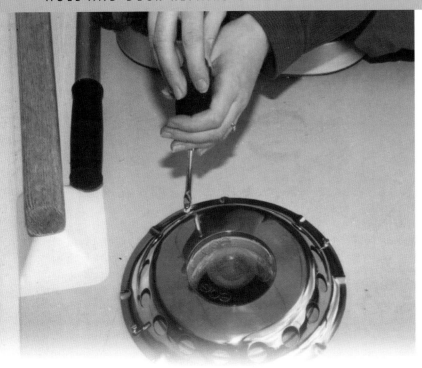

Left **Don't put sealant all around the base, or you'll block the drain holes. Just put a small blob around each screw hole.**

✪ Place the ventilator on the cut-out and mark the position of the attachment screws.
✪ Drill holes for the attachment screws.
✪ If no sealing gasket is provided, put a ring of sealant around each hole.
✪ Fit the ventilator – most use self-tapping screws.

Fitting the ventilator

✪ Measure very carefully where the ventilator is to be fitted.
✪ Drill a very small hole at the centre of the main ventilator cut-out.
✪ Make a template of the cut-out, take it below and centre it on the small hole where it shows on the inside of the cabin, to check that it will not foul any internal structure or damage wiring.
✪ Only make the cut-out when you are absolutely certain that the position is correct. Use a hole saw for a circular cut-out or a jigsaw for other shapes.
✪ If the deck or coachroof has a balsa core, this must be sealed with epoxy to prevent water entering the wood.

Left **Cowl vents such as these are very efficient and can be rotated to maximise airflow. They can also be quite obtrusive.**

Fitting a ventilator

Locate the position of the ventilator by measuring both outside and inside the boat to ensure it will be clear of any obstruction.

Drill a pilot hole from the outside and double-check all your measurements, from inside and out.

Mark a circle around the pilot hole from the inside, and cut the lining away to ensure a clean cut when you drill through.

Drill the main hole using a hole saw. Place the ventilator over the hole, and drill the screw holes.

Resealing through-hull fittings

A leaking through-hull fitting needs to be attended to without delay, as it may indicate an underlying problem such as corrosion. This could lead to rapid and catastrophic failure of the fitting and cause serious flooding.

Types of through-hull fittings

Traditionally, through-hull fittings have been made from bronze – a copper/tin alloy that can suffer from degradation when immersed in sea water. They therefore need to be checked annually. A reddish colour indicates there is electrolytic corrosion, and that the device needs to be changed.

Below **Check the through-hull fittings every time your boat is taken out of the water. It will save heartache later.**

Glass-reinforced polymer resin through-hull fittings are available, and these do not suffer from corrosion. They are fully approved for use below the waterline. Unreinforced plastic through-hull fittings should never be used below or close to the waterline because of their lack of strength and durability.

Leaking through-hull fittings

A through-hull fitting may be leaking due to deterioration of the external seal or because of corrosion. The only satisfactory cure is to remove the fitting, replacing it if necessary, and then resealing it to the hull.

Removing through-hull fittings

Unless a through-hull fitting is mounted well above the waterline, the boat must be lifted out of the water before it can be removed.

Generally, plastic through-hull fittings above the waterline will have no seacock, so only the hose attached to its barb needs to be removed. Unscrew the plastic backing nut, try to break the sealant with a sharp knife, and push the

fitting out from the hull. If the fitting needs to be knocked out it will probably be damaged in the process, and will have to be replaced.

If mounted below the waterline, bronze through-hull fittings will have a seacock attached to them, so the hose and seacock will have to be removed first. Access is often difficult. The fitting's backing nut will have to be removed, and this may have been covered in sealant. There is also likely to be a wooden backing plate glassed to the hull to make a flat, solid surface. Some through-hull fittings are bolted through the hull and backing plate.

Because the fitting will have been screwed down hard, it may well be difficult to break the sealant, and with limited access it may be impossible to drive out. In this case, the outside head of the fitting will need to be ground away with an angle grinder, so that the unit can be driven into the boat from outside.

Marelon through-hull fittings may have a backing nut or be bolted through the hull and backing plate. However, corrosion won't be a factor, so removal of the seacock and backing nut should present no problem.

Re-bedding a through-hull fitting

Clean the hull thoroughly, both inside and out, and use a high quality underwater sealant to re-bed the fitting. Be sure to use the recommended torque on any fastenings.

Removing a through-hull fitting

You will probably need a grinder to cut grooves in the outside of the fitting. Take extra care if you take the guard off.

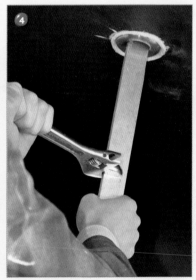

Use a cold chisel to cut between the grooves and remove the outside flange.

With the outside flange removed, the fitting can now be driven in to the inside of the hull.

The new fitting has lugs on the inside, so you can use a flat bar to hold it still while fitting the inside nut.

Replacing anodes

Various combinations of metals may be used externally below the waterline on a boat. Because water acts as an electrolyte, different metals will react with each other, one being corroded away, so a sacrificial anode is used to protect the vulnerable component.

What needs to be protected by an anode?

Any two dissimilar metals will generate a voltage difference between them when immersed in water, and this will cause one of the metals to be corroded away. The difference in voltage depends on the two metals involved, and greater voltage differences cause more corrosion.

Any components made from different metals and mounted near each other are likely to create a requirement for an anode, which needs to be connected to the vulnerable component to protect it.

There may, however, also be a problem with a single component, if that object is made from an alloy. For example, with a bronze propeller, the zinc content of the bronze will be corroded away because it will react with the copper in the alloy. An anode bonded to the propeller will protect it from corrosion.

Above **Check the continuity between the anode and the stern gear. It should read no more than a couple of ohms.**

Below **Propellers may have a special anode to give increased protection.**

Bonding

An anode will work only if it is electrically connected to the component that it's protecting. The connection may be direct physical contact or via an electrical 'bonding' wire. Some authorities recommend that all underwater metal fittings are bonded to a common grounding point, but others argue that long wires and poor connections can lead to voltage differences which will actually promote corrosion.

There needs to be very close to zero resistance between any component and the anode that is there to protect it. This resistance must be checked every time you fit a new anode using the resistance scale on a multimeter.

What size of anode is needed?

An anode will preferably be big enough to last the whole season, so that the boat can remain in the water throughout, and normally this is not a problem. However, sometimes it isn't possible to fit a big enough anode for a particular propeller or sail-drive leg, in which case the anodes will have to be checked and possibly replaced mid-season.

Fresh water or salt?

Fresh water anodes are made of magnesium; salt water anodes of zinc or aluminium. Life is not so simple, though, if your water is brackish or if you move the boat from one type of water to another. The basic rules are:

- ✿ In fresh water use magnesium anodes.
- ✿ In brackish water use aluminium anodes.
- ✿ In sea water use zinc or aluminium anodes.

Above **On some installations, the propshaft is insulated from the engine and a shaft anode is necessary to protect the propeller.**

- ✿ When you take a fresh water boat into sea water, rapid depletion of the magnesium anode will occur. Replacement with zinc is desirable if the boat is going to be in sea water for more than a couple of weeks.
- ✿ When you take a sea water boat into fresh water, a passive crust will build up on the surface of zinc and aluminium anodes and will stop them working. This should be wire-brushed off on return to the sea.
- ✿ Do not use an aluminium anode on a wooden boat because its reaction with the wood will cause the wood to soften.

Left **This anode has some hard crust on it and is about half worn. If you are not going to replace it, give it a very good brush.**

Working with fibreglass

Fibreglass (also known as GRP, 'glass-reinforced plastic', or FRP, 'fibre-reinforced plastic') is an easy material to work with, although care is needed to produce a strong, well-finished piece of work. There are health issues as well, so proper protection is necessary.

What is fibreglass?

A cloth made of glass fibres is used to reinforce a plastic resin. Where extra strength and very light weight is required, other fibres such as Kevlar may be used instead of glass, but this is very expensive. Using a brush and roller, the plastic resin is worked well into the glass cloth, and is then allowed to cure chemically to produce a rigid sheet.

Below **Large sheets of glass cloth can be quite cumbersome and the resin gives off unpleasant fumes, so wear a suitable mask.**

Making a plug

A plug is identical in shape and finish to the final piece of work you are going to make. It may be fabricated from any easily worked material, such as plywood or MDF. The important thing is that the finish is smooth and fair.

Making a mould

The plug is coated with wax, and GRP is laid up over it. If it is large, some reinforcing structure will be needed to ensure that it keeps its shape. Once the GRP has cured, it can be removed from the plug and you have a mould to lay up your piece of work.

Repairing a large hole in a boat

Some form of structure will need to be made, either inside or outside, onto which the GRP can be laid up. You could prepare a plug to temporarily fit to the outside, or something less sophisticated to use inside.

Laying up fibreglass

✪ Wax the surface onto which the GRP is to be laid up, so that the resin won't stick to it.

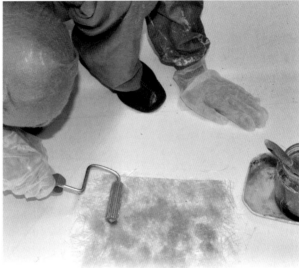

Above **Work the resin well into the cloth —
a stippling action will ensure full penetration.**

Above **Use a grooved metal roller to remove
all trapped air from the resin and cloth.**

✿ If the starting surface is going to
be the 'outside' finished surface,
apply a layer of gel coat with a
brush or roller. Don't work it too
much or it will be too thin.

✿ Once it has started to gel, apply
polystyrene or epoxy to the
surface and then lay the glass
cloth onto it and work the resin
in with a brush or grooved roller.

✿ As one layer starts to gel, keep
applying further layers of resin
and glass cloth to build up the
required thickness, working each
layer in to remove all air bubbles.
A metal roller is best for this.

✿ The work will be hard enough to
enable any supporting structure
be removed the following day,
but won't reach full strength for
a few weeks.

✿ If you have worked from the
inside to outside rather than vice
versa, see pages 66 and 67 for
details of how to finish the surface.

Mixing the polyester resin

Careful measurement of the resin and
hardener is needed, so use a graduated
container for both parts.

Pour the resin into a suitable container so
that it can be mixed with the hardener.

Now add the hardener. For small
quantities only a few drops are required.

Mix the two together using a disposable
stick. Don't mix too much at a time as it
will become very hot.

Cracks, voids & crazing

Small cracks in fibreglass may be no more than cosmetic blemishes, but it is also possible that they may indicate a part of the structure that is under too much stress. If the latter is the case, then the cause of the overstressing needs to be removed.

Stress cracks and crazing

Cracks may be caused by an overloaded structure, as well as flexing due to normal use. Once the cause of the cracking has been determined and (if necessary) removed, the cracking itself can be tackled in this manner:

- ✪ Use a small, high-speed rotary drill with a small engraving cutter to open up the cracks. Ensure that you get to the bottom of the cracking – usually this will mean drilling all the way to the bottom of the gel coat.
- ✪ Drill a small diameter hole 0.04in (1mm) at the extremity of each crack. This acts as a stress relief to stop the crack spreading.
- ✪ Clean the area with acetone.
- ✪ Mask around the area with masking tape.
- ✪ Fill the opened-up cracks with gel coat filler.
- ✪ Once cured, rub down with 'wet and dry' sand paper used wet, starting with 240 grade and finishing with 600 grade on a sanding block. (The masking tape is there to limit the abrasion to the area being repaired.)
- ✪ Refill and rub down again if necessary, until the area is completely smooth.
- ✪ Remove the masking tape.
- ✪ Cut the surface with a finishing compound to make it smooth.
- ✪ Polish with a good wax polish.

Above & left **These stress cracks indicate that some below-deck strengthening is required before making the repair.**

Filling voids

Voids are sometimes found at concave angles in a moulding, usually because an air bubble has been trapped during lay-up. To fix the problem:

- ✪ Use a small, high-speed rotary drill with a small engraving cutter to open up the void, ensuring that all loose material is removed and the whole void is exposed.
- ✪ If the void is large, fill it with epoxy resin.
- ✪ Remove excess epoxy with the rotary tool and cutter.
- ✪ Fill with gel coat filler.
- ✪ Rub down the filler to make a smooth, faired surface. If the void is in a corner with a tight radius, you may need to wrap the wet and dry sandpaper round a suitably sized dowel in order to be able to rub down.
- ✪ Polish the area with compounding paste, and then wax polish.

Colour matching the gel coat

Matching the colour of the gel coat can be difficult, even if it's white, because there are many different tints and shades. Some boatbuilders have their standard colours and they may supply matching gel coat. Some resin suppliers have gel coat colour-matching kits available (for various hues), but it's a trial and error exercise to get a good match. Thin crack repairs don't need as good a match as a larger area.

Treating gel coat cracks

The gel coat needs to be ground out all the way down to the laminate and small holes drilled at the end of each crack before you start filling.

Fill the cracks with gel coat filler of the appropriate colour. Use masking tape to protect any adjacent woodwork or metal fittings.

When cured, rub down the filler with a fine grade sandpaper used with water. Check the gel coat filler is flush, and refill if necessary.

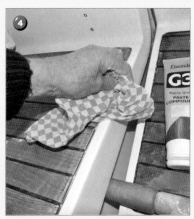

When you are happy that the gel coat is completely flush, cut back with cutting paste to bring back the gloss. Finish off with polish.

Impact & surface damage

Repairs to gouges and blisters can normally wait until a convenient time. However, impact damage, unless it is very minor, will need to be repaired quickly to prevent further damage or even loss of the boat.

Gouges

Gouges that don't penetrate beyond the gel coat are purely cosmetic, and their repair may be delayed to any convenient time. Repair is carried out using gel coat filler as described on pages 64 and 65.

To prevent water penetrating the lay-up, gouges that penetrate into the reinforced layers should be treated as soon as possible by applying an epoxy filler to the gouge. When convenient, remove enough of the surface layer of the epoxy repair so that gel coat filler can be applied, then finish and polish as outlined on pages 65 and 66.

Blisters

Blisters normally occur because of some form of hydraulic pressure under the gel coat. They can be an early indication of osmosis, but may just be caused by an accumulation of excess solvent in the lay-up. If the blister is small and isolated, grind it out and treat it as a void, as explained on pages 64 and 65.

Below **Sometimes shallow scratches can be polished out using a polishing mop and cutting paste.**

TIP

It's tempting to remove as little material as possible when making a repair. But proper repair requires all the damage to be removed before you start to make good.

Impact damage

The impact damage will need to be ground away, and it is likely that the inside surface will require reinforcement, so gain access to the inside of the structure to assess the damage. This may require some internal structure or fittings to be removed. The more that's removed, the easier it will be to carry out the repair and to finish it off so that it's invisible from the inside. Then proceed as follows:

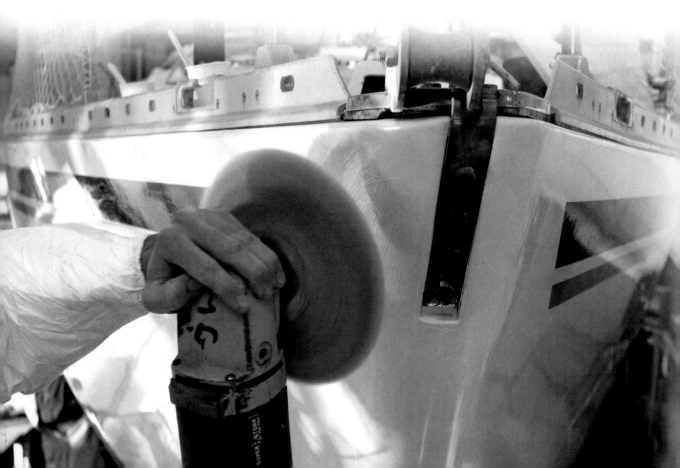

☼ Grind away any damaged lay-up, ensuring that no distressed structure remains.

☼ Chamfer the lay-up so that the layers can be built up gradually. If you chamfer on the inside, there will be a smaller area to fair in.

☼ Clean inside and out with acetone.

☼ Lay up some glass mat on the inside to make a reinforcing layer.

☼ When this layer is stiff, lay up extra layers, each over an area about 2in (50mm) wider than the previous layer. Leave overnight.

☼ On the outside, use a straight edge to ensure that none of the reinforcement is within about 0.25in (6mm) of the finished surface; grind a little away if it is.

☼ Fill the surface until it's just proud of the finished surface, and allow to cure.

☼ Grind the surface back and fill with gel coat, mixing some wax into it, or it won't dry in contact with the air.

☼ Rub down with wet and dry sandpaper used wet to fair the surface, compound it, then polish with wax polish.

☼ Finish the inside with gel coat to complete the repair.

Filling scratches and gouges

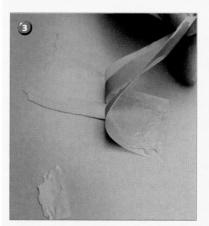

These gouges need to be filled, so first remove any loose or flaking material with a gouge or small grinder.

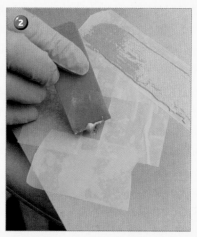

Mask up the area, mix the gel coat filler, and apply with a spatula, ensuring that the filler stands proud of the surface.

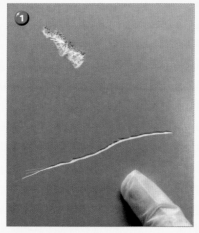

Peel off the masking tape before the gel coat has cured. The raised patches are clearly visible in the picture.

Grind the area flat, refilling if necessary. Then cut and polish the area as described on pages 64 and 65.

Treating osmosis & delamination

Early onset of osmosis indicates either poor build quality or shoddy materials and, unsurprisingly, it is generally considered a catastrophic event. Nor is the treatment cheap – but if it is done properly, the boat will probably be better than it was to begin with.

What is osmosis?

Gel coat is not completely waterproof, so water molecules can diffuse through it to the GRP lay-up. If voids are present in the lay-up, the moisture dissolves any compounds in the building resin that have not cured properly, expanding the cavities. These show up as blisters on the surface. In extreme cases, with many voids, large areas of the hull can be severely weakened and can lead to structural failure.

Diagnosis of osmosis

High readings from a moisture meter alone are not a clear indication of osmosis. Fibreglass hulls will always absorb moisture, but osmotic blisters will only occur if the resin hasn't cured properly. If a blister is pierced and the emerging liquid smells vinegary, osmosis is strongly indicated. Ideally, an experienced boat surveyor should be engaged to diagnose the complaint and prescribe suitable treatment.

Above **Until you explore further, it's impossible to tell if this is paint blistering or osmotic blistering.**

Below **Osmosis isn't the death sentence it once seemed. This yacht has been treated and repainted and looks as good as new.**

Localised blisters

Small blisters can be ground out and washed with clean fresh water to remove any solvents. Ensure that all areas of any delamination are removed back to sound lay-up. Once fully dry, the void can be filled with epoxy filler and the area finished off as detailed on pages 66 and 67.

Treating large areas of the hull

The gel coat will first need to be removed, and this is most easily achieved using an electric gel-plane. Practice is required to ensure that only the gel coat is removed and no deep gouges occur. This will expose the blisters and areas of delamination, which must then be ground back to sound lay-up. If too much material has to be removed, a new lay-up will be required and professional advice should be sought.

Having removed all suspect areas of lay-up:

✪ Thoroughly wash all the ground-back areas with fresh water. Steam cleaning is even better, as it will dissolve and remove any remaining residues and their

by-products. This needs to be done as soon as possible after grinding back.

✪ Allow the old lay-up to dry. This process can be accelerated by using infra-red heating. The aim is to get a moisture content as similar as possible to the unaffected parts of the hull, so you'll need to regularly monitor the hull's moisture readings using a moisture meter.

Above **A moisture meter is used to measure the moisture content of the laminate. This can be compared with a dry part of the hull.**

✪ Prime with two coats of epoxy primer.
✪ Fill and fair with an epoxy filler, sand, and refill any low spots. Continue until the surface is completely fair, checking with a long straight edge (fairing board).
✪ Prime all the refinished area with an antifouling primer, and then antifoul.

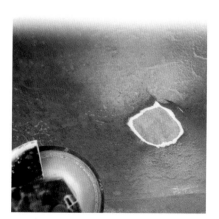

Above **This blister was confirmed to be osmotic, so has been ground out to remove all the damaged lay-up.**

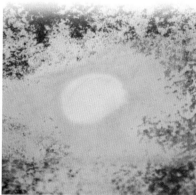

Above **Once the lay-up is dry and free of any remaining traces of solvent, it can be filled and sanded smooth.**

Repairing a centreboard case

A GRP centreboard case should not leak, so any water entering the boat is likely to be from the pivot bearing or from the hoisting mechanism. A wooden centreboard case can leak from its joint with the hull, and removal of the case is normally necessary to effect a repair.

Above **Leaks may occur around the edges of the sealing plate and also at the bearing seal of the lifting pivot.**

Centreboard cases

The forces experienced by a centreboard case are very large, so the structure supporting it must be strong enough to stop the case from deforming or moving. If the design and build qualities are good, no leakage should occur from any structural joint. If a leak does occur, then the strengthening of the structure should go hand-in-hand with resealing.

Below **There is often an inspection panel at the top of the keel box. Any leak here will need the panel to be removed and resealed.**

Centreboard cases in GRP hulls

Depending on the way the hull is moulded, the case will either be bonded to the hull moulding or it will be moulded in two halves, one integral to each half-hull shell. Sufficient stiffening will be part of the design.

Most GRP hulls with centreboards will have an internal lining that will conceal the actual centreboard case. Any leakage from the case itself will be invisible, and any water will find its way into the bilge and be very difficult to trace. Fortunately, any such occurrence is rare in a well-built boat.

Centreboard cases in wooden hulls

The case will be constructed of individual pieces of wood, glued and screwed together, and will then be set onto the hog (or 'inner keel') using a

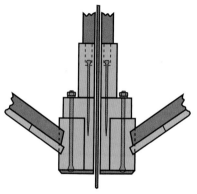

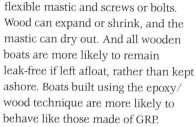

Above **The keel box on a traditional wooden boat uses many interlocking compontents to ensure watertightness.**

flexible mastic and screws or bolts. Wood can expand or shrink, and the mastic can dry out. And all wooden boats are more likely to remain leak-free if left afloat, rather than kept ashore. Boats built using the epoxy/ wood technique are more likely to behave like those made of GRP.

Provided that the support for the centreboard case is adequate, a small leak from the case may be tolerated, because its cure will be time-consuming. Applying some sealant to the leaking area may produce a short term cure.

Rebedding a centreboard case

✪ With the boat ashore and jacked up, remove the centreboard.
✪ Remove sufficient internal furniture and stiffening to gain access to the case.
✪ Remove all the fastenings securing the case to the hog and keel.
✪ Separate the mastic joint.
✪ Lift the case clear.
✪ Clean all the mating surfaces thoroughly and de-grease.
✪ Lay new mastic and rebed the case.
✪ Rebuild the cabin.

Above **This lifting mechanism is open at the top, but as it is in the cockpit any leakage will go out through the drain.**

This is a time-consuming and skilled job, so if in doubt about your ability, have this work done professionally.

Leaks from pivot covers and lifting gear

The centreboard pivot may be above or below the waterline, and may even be below the hull itself. If it's inside the hull, there will be some form of cover plate and any leak should be cured by renewing the seal.

The lifting tackle is normally well above the waterline, but there is likely to be some splashing into its housing when under way. The tackle box should be sealed from the cabin, but any leakage will just require renewal of the seal.

Left **Some lifting keels have their pivot point in an external part of the fixed keel, so this will not be a source of leakage.**

Repairing/replacing wood trim

Wooden trim on a boat may become damaged or start to look just plain tatty. Either way, it makes an otherwise decent boat look unloved, and as most jobs are not too difficult to undertake, it's worth doing something about it.

Repair or replace?

A number of considerations arise when considering whether to repair or replace some damaged woodwork:

- ✿ Is the component's inherent strength important to its purpose? A toe rail's strength would not be important, but a grab rail's would.
- ✿ Is it cosmetic, such as a washboard, or structural, such as a companionway step?
- ✿ If repaired, will the repair be as strong as the original?
- ✿ Will the repair be cosmetically obvious?
- ✿ Can the repair be carried out in situ, or will a lot of disassembly be required?
- ✿ Is new wood for this component likely to be expensive?

Repairing a damaged grab handle

If the grab handle has shattered, it's probably safest to replace it. Chandlers sell or can obtain pre-formed handles in teak, and this is usually the cheapest and simplest course of action. The old ones can be removed, and new ones screwed in place and the holes capped with teak plugs.

Splits can often be repaired safely if done without delay, to avoid contamination of the wood. You'll need to open up the split with wedges and introduce an adhesive.

Below **Most boats have at least some wooden trim in their cabins, and any damage can be very obvious.**

Polyurethane foaming adhesive is good for this because it's both waterproof and gap-filling. Clamp the parts together and leave to set. If necessary, you can use some screws as well, capping with teak plugs.

Repairing damage in the edge of wood trim

Provided any structural integrity can be retained, letting in a patch piece (or 'graving piece') is the easiest course of action. Some care and patience is needed for a neat job, but the procedure is fairly simple:

- ✿ Using a fine-toothed tenon saw, make an angled cut at each end of the damage such that the piece to be removed is longer at the bottom of the patch than the outside edge.
- ✿ Use a sharp chisel to remove the wood between the cuts and to make the ends of the cut smooth. This should now look like a dovetail recess.
- ✿ Shape a new piece of similar wood to fit exactly into the 'dovetail'.
- ✿ Use waterproof adhesive to glue the new wood in place.
- ✿ When the glue has set, clean up and fair the patch to the original piece.

Repairing shallow impact damage

Shallow crush damage can often be removed by the application of wet heat to swell the wood's fibres. One method is to apply boiling water to the crush, and cover with hot wet cloth to retain the heat. Alternatively, use a steamer such as a wallpaper stripper to supply steam to the area, keeping the steam in place with a wooden box or a cloth.

Repairing a damaged grab handle

Drill out the plug to reveal the screw in the cracked hand-hold prior to reglueing.

Reglue and replug using quick release clamps with integral plastic grips to hold the parts together until set.

Remove the excess length of plug, ensuring that you use the chisel in the 'uphill' direction with the grain, so that it shears off proud of the hand-hold.

Finish off with a sander or sanding block, prior to re-varnishing or polishing as appropriate.

Renewing non-skid decks

Decks can be slippery, especially when wet, so builders often incorporate some form of non-skid surface into their decks. Some achieve better results than others, and most will lose their non-skid properties over time.

Moulded non-skid surfaces

This is the easiest non-skid surface for builders to incorporate, as it's part of the moulding and requires no further cost on their part. It's also cosmetically 'invisible'. At best, this can be fairly good as a non-skid surface, but at worst it will be next to useless. Because it relies on sharp edges which will gradually become rounded, the non-skid property will degrade with time.

Once a moulded non-skid surface loses its grip, little can be done that doesn't require a vast amount of effort. The best solution is to apply non-skid paint over it or to fit panels of non-skid sheet in strategic places (see opposite page).

Painted non-skid surfaces

This is invariably better than moulded non-skid, but is more expensive for the boatbuilder and

Above **Small areas can be painted with a brush, especially if there is a concave edge.**

often much less visually appealing. It will also require occasional repainting. To refurbish a painted non-skid surface:

- Remove as much of the old surface as possible. The grit in the paint is often very hard, so you will need very high quality abrasive paper. I use an orbital sander because it has a good combination of speed and a large pad area, and doesn't have any tendency to dig into the underlying gel coat. Unless you are able to control the sander sufficiently so that it doesn't damage the gloss gel coat alongside the paint, mask it up first.
- Degrease the whole area with acetone – make sure you wear protective gloves.
- Use masking tape to protect areas that won't be painted.
- Apply the deck paint to the whole area and, before it goes tacky,

Left **Large areas of non-skid are easier to paint using a roller. Remove the masking tape as soon as you have finished painting.**

generously sprinkle deck sand over the whole area. Don't be tempted to mix the grit into the paint or you will end up with a very patchy result.

❂ Once the paint is dry, brush away loose sand.

❂ Apply a coat of deck paint over the complete area – don't apply any more sand.

Non-skid sheet surfaces

With the possible exception of teak, this is undoubtedly the best non-skid surface. It is expensive and time-consuming to lay, but will last for 20 years or more. Some makes have a diamond pattern, which can be difficult to clean, and eventually edges may start to lift. Re-gluing the lifted edges can be problematical, because it's almost impossible to clean the surfaces adequately.

Replacing non-skid sheet is time-consuming, mainly because it's difficult to remove. This will require the use of flat paint scrapers to work under the sheet to break the bond, which in most places will be sound. Some damage to the underlying surface is inevitable. Once the sheet is removed, you'll need to sand or grind the deck to get a smooth enough surface for the new sheet. If you've gone through the gel coat, you'll need to build it up again with epoxy filler and sand it smooth. Re-laying new non-skid sheeting is the easy part.

Replacing non-skid sheet

Having made a template for the area to be covered, mark the non-skid sheeting and cut out the new panel using a craft knife.

Apply the adhesive to the area to be covered. Don't try to cover too big an area at one time, and ensure good ventilation.

Lower the panel into place with a rolling motion, to avoid air bubbles. Use a roller to firm it in position.

Immediately remove any adhesive from around the edges of the panel using a suitable solvent.

Repairing teak-finished decks

Many fibreglass boats have teak planks laid on top of the GRP deck. In time the seams may open up and plugs may fall out, so some attention will be required to put things right.

How is a teak deck laid?

Strips of teak are bedded on top of the GRP deck using an adhesive. Some builders screw the strips down as well, and cap the screws with plugs. One side of each strip is rebated to half its depth, and the resultant grooves are filled with a flexible mastic.

What can go wrong?

If the owner repeatedly scrubs or pressure-washes the deck, this will remove the soft parts of the grain and the deck will become ridged. Teak decks should be cleaned with a soft brush or a kitchen scrubbing pad, rubbed at right angles to the grain. The deck should be regularly doused in sea water to prevent it drying out.

Another problem is that the mastic can lose adhesion in the grooves, allowing water to penetrate the edges of the strips or even get underneath. Sometimes the wooden plugs over the screws become loose and fall out. This usually occurs because the strips are too thin in the first place or if the deck has been sanded, reducing its thickness and that of the plugs.

Below **A teak laid deck looks good but needs a lot of hard work and care to keep it in good condition.**

Above **Loose sealant should be replaced to prevent moisture getting underneath.**

Dealing with loose mastic in the seams

The loose mastic must be removed. How you do this depends on how much needs repairing. The aim is to remove the mastic without removing any wood. For small areas of loose material, it isn't worth making or buying a special tool just to rake out the mastic:

- Make a diagonal cut through the mastic a couple of inches (50mm) either side of the damaged area, using a very sharp hobby knife (see page 17).
- Cut along the edge of the mastic with the hobby knife, taking care not to cut into the wood.
- Use a sharp chisel the same width as the groove. Hold it vertically, and drag it towards you to remove the old mastic.

For large areas of loose mastic, it will be worth making a raking tool or even buying an electric multi-function tool (the Fein MultiMaster Marine is expensive but versatile) with purpose-designed blades for cutting the mastic and raking out the grooves.

To make your own tool, bend a screwdriver blade at right-angles and sharpen the end. You can then pull it towards you to remove the mastic. You can do the same with a file tang, but in either case you will need to heat the tool with a blowlamp to be able to bend it.

Replacing wooden plugs

- Clean up the hole. An ordinary drill bit won't do, because the tip angle will prevent the bottom of the hole being cleaned. You'll need a 'spur point' bit to clean right to the bottom.
- As soon as possible after the hole has been cleaned, use acetone to degrease the surface.
- Use epoxy wood glue on the new plug, and push it into the hole. Align the plug's grain with that of the deck strip.
- When the epoxy is cured, trim to size and sand.

Replacing deck sealant

Make a diagonal cut across the seam at either end of the section to be replaced, and remove the old sealant.

Clean out the groove with a chisel, taking care not to damage the wood, and then clean up with acetone.

Slowly fill the groove with sealant, taking care not to create any air bubbles.

Smooth off with a palette knife and remove masking tape before sealant sets.

Working with wood

For many people, working with wood is very therapeutic. You don't need to rush, it shows off your skills, and the end result is all down to you. There's good 'job satisfaction'.

Learning the skills

It's worth acquiring a few skills before you start, so practise on some old wood first. The basic skills you need are the ability to use a tenon saw, plane and chisel.

Below **When using a plane, the workpiece needs to be prevented from moving. In this case it's clamped in a portable work bench.**

Tenon saw

- Mark the cut accurately, ideally with a sharp knife to prevent the cut splintering.
- Hold the wood rigidly, either in a vice or by using a bench hook.
- Using a fine-tooth tenon saw, cut slowly and carefully to the correct side of the scored line.
- Do not cut deeper than the end of the line.

Plane

- Use the correct plane for the job: a jack plane for long flat areas, and a shorter smoothing plane for smaller work.
- Secure the work, and ensure that you keep the plane level.
- Use both hands on the plane, and move it steadily backwards and forwards along the area to be planed.
- If the wood grain isn't parallel with the cut, work so that the grain is rising as the plane moves in the cutting direction, or the blade will dig in. Some hard woods have grain which changes in direction, and you may need to reverse the direction of cut at some point.

Chisel

- Accurately mark the area to be chiselled, using a sharp knife.
- Ensure the chisel is sharp.
- Secure the work so that it can't move.
- Place the blade on the wood, at the correct side of the scribed line and use a wooden mallet to tap it gently so that it cuts into the wood.
- Once sufficient wood has been removed, place the chisel in the scribed line to remove the final small amount of wood.

Wood glue

'Weatherproof' glue isn't good enough, except for inside work in a dry, well-ventilated boat. For marine use, the glue should be waterproof. PVA is a white glue that dries transparent, and excess can be wiped off with a damp cloth before it dries. However, even the waterproof variety should only be used below decks. Clamping is required.

Polyurethane (PU) glue is a waterproof glue suitable for on-deck use. It cures using atmospheric moisture and foams as it cures, enabling it to fill small irregularities. The foam is honey-coloured, and clamping is required. Excess glue is best removed after it has cured, using a sharp tool.

Epoxy is a two-part adhesive with good gap-filling qualities. Where panels are joined at an angle to each other, a structural fillet can be formed using a suitable bulking agent such as micro-balloons or colloidal powder. To match existing wood, sawdust can be used to bulk out the epoxy instead.

Clamping

Most work will need to be clamped while the glue sets, unless you are also using screws or panel pins. Wooden blocks need to be used with steel clamps, to prevent damage to the wood, but small plastic clamps are very versatile and shouldn't cause any damage.

Right **When using a chisel, ensure that the workpiece can't move, and keep your hands behind the blade.**

Gluing together two pieces of wood

Make sure the surfaces are clean and dry, and apply the glue, spreading it evenly with a knife or spatula.

Most glues should be applied to one surface only, but read the instructions carefully. Join the two parts together.

If you don't want to use screws to secure the work while the glue sets, clamping will normally be necessary.

Checking & replacing fastenings

The planks of a traditional wooden hull are fastened to the frames using screws or nails, which will in all probability be made of mild steel. These will eventually rust and fail, allowing the planks to become loose.

Detecting rusty fastenings

The screws will have been set into counter-bored holes, so that the screw heads are well below the surface. The counter-bore will have been sealed with a wooden plug about 0.3in (8mm) deep. As a screw rusts, its head will swell, and eventually the swelling will be sufficient to make the plugs protrude from the hull's surface (though you may see rust streaks running down the hull before this). If there's much evidence of rusting fastenings, it's probable that all the fastenings will need to be replaced, and sooner rather than later.

Removing the old fastening

This is the tricky bit, and the sooner you do it, the better the chance that the screw head will still be intact, making the job much easier. The first thing to do is to remove the old plug. If the plug is protruding, it will already have started to come loose:

✪ Drill a hole in the centre of the plug until it comes to the screw, and then stop immediately. The hole should be about half the diameter of your bradawl.
✪ Screw the bradawl into the hole until it stops at the screw and then pull the plug out. With luck it

won't break, and you will now see the screw head.
✪ Carefully clean out the slot in the screw so that a screwdriver will fit properly.
✪ Place a well-fitting screwdriver into the slot. Tap the screwdriver lightly with a mallet to loosen the rust, but not so hard that the screw head breaks off.
✪ Press very hard on the screwdriver, and remove the screw.

Below **This hull needs to be cleaned up and the hull fastenings inspected before work can proceed any further.**

Right **Once the damaged nail is removed, it can be replaced with a bronze screw, which will be easier to replace in future.**

If the screw breaks

One course of action is to drill out the old screw, but this is often easier said than done. Begin by centre-punching the screw right in the middle, then use this start to drill down its centre, using a drill of about half the diameter of the screw.

Next, open up the hole using a drill the same diameter as the screw. The drill is very likely to wander off centre, come off the screw and chew up the wood. In this case, you will need to fill the bottom of the hole with epoxy filler, ready for a new plug.

The alternative to drilling out the broken screw is to leave it where it is and use a different position for the new fastening. This is much easier to do, but do note that the new hole must be positioned along the centreline of the frame, not the plank, so check where the fastenings are on adjacent planks.

❂ Select a new screw made of stainless steel or silicone bronze.
❂ Drill a counter-bore the size of the wooden plug.
❂ Drill a hole the size of the shank of the screw. Use a drill stop to ensure that this hole doesn't go into the frame.

❂ Drill a hole the size of the core of the screw into the frame, using a drill stop so that it doesn't go too deep.
❂ Screw in the new fastening.
❂ Glue in a new plug and finish off.

Replacing a plank fastening

Nails can be difficult to remove. Here a small hole is drilled into the nail's head.

A screw or gripfast nail is then driven into the hole in the nail and a claw hammer used to pull it out.

This bronze fastening is starting to show signs of corrosion where it has turned pink, and will be replaced.

Making & fitting a graving piece

Finding an area of rot on the hull of a wooden boat is always bad news. Rather than replace a whole plank, however, it may be possible to simply insert a graving piece into the affected area.

Finding rotten wood

A sure-fire give-away is blistering, crazing or flaking of paint. Initially this may be due just to moisture under the paint, but do nothing and rot can follow. Tap lightly with a plastic-faced hammer, and you will hear a different sound when you hit soft wood. A sharp-pointed tool can be used to gently probe further for soft spots. Rot is possible both inside and outside the hull planking. Inside, anywhere that allows water to collect is a likely candidate.

Removing an area of rotten planking

It is tempting to remove as little as possible, but old hands would always renew the complete plank. However, if the area of rot is genuinely small and not the complete thickness of the plank, it is permissible to 'let in' a patch, or graving piece. If you need a lot of graving pieces, then renewing the

Below **If the area of rotten wood is only small, a graving piece may be inserted rather than replacing the whole plank.**

plank may be the best option. If the rot is around any fastenings, it may have penetrated deeper than you would like and a graving piece may not make a suitable repair.

- Probe the area to find the extent of the rot.
- Mark out the maximum extent of the rot using a soft pencil or a marker pen.
- Remove all the rotten wood with a chisel.

Right **A graving piece has been let in to replace a section of rotten wood. In time, the whole plank may need to be replaced.**

Making the graving piece
- Measure the depth of the hole you have cut in the hull.
- Plane a suitable piece of wood so that it is slightly thicker than the depth of the hole.
- Cut a shape which is slightly bigger than the area of rotten wood removed, and ensure the sides are straight and at right angles to the front. Graving pieces are traditionally diamond-shaped, but a simple square will work just as well.

Fitting the graving piece
- Offer the graving piece up to the hull and scribe its outline onto the hull using a sharp knife, ensuring it covers the area of removed wood fully.
- Remove the wood from the enclosed area with a chisel, ensuring the sides of the hole are at right angles to the hull and that the hole is of equal depth over the whole area.
- Drive a couple of screws into the outside of the graving piece to act as handles.
- Offer up the graving piece, trim the recess/graving piece to size if necessary and then remove the screws.
- Apply waterproof glue or epoxy to the hole and tap the graving piece into place. Excess glue can escape through the screw holes.

Finishing off
Once the glue has fully set, the graving piece can be faired into the hull using a suitably sized plane.

Fitting a graving piece

Cut a piece of wood to cover the rotten area. Straight sides make it easier to fit.

Chisel out the rotten wood over an area to exactly match the graving piece.

Glue the graving piece in place, tapping it to ensure it's well bedded in.

Once the glue has set, finish it flush using a smoothing plane.

Caulking & paying methods

The planks of a carvel-built hull are not glued in any way, and the only thing that keeps the hull waterproof is the flexible sealing between the planks. In time this will need to be replaced.

How do you know a seam needs to be re-caulked?

If the seam is either opening up or cracking, it needs to be investigated, because it will allow water into the joint and may start the process of rot. If it is opening up, the seam should be re-caulked, rather than just refilled with stopping.

Removing the failed caulking

Great care should be taken not to damage the wooden planking, and improvised tools are more likely to cause damage than a purpose-made one. A proper raking tool has long handles and can be driven with a hammer. The aim is to remove only the caulking, not damage the wood and not drive it all the way through to the inside of the hull. Rake out only as much seam as you can re-caulk in one session. Open seams will dry out rapidly, which means that the wood will shrink, and this will cause trouble later when it swells against the new caulking.

Above **A professional will have several caulking hammers and irons, each used for a specific part of the caulking process.**

Below **Getting into a good, even rhythm is essential for successful caulking.**

Re-caulking the seam

Either cotton or oakum is used for caulking, oakum being more suitable for wider seams. Slightly different techniques are used in different parts of the world, and amateurs may find some things helpful that the pros wouldn't use. The instructions below are not the only way to do the job, but this method has been used successfully by amateurs:

✪ Separate the cotton into strands thick enough to fill the seam.
✪ Twist together the strands you are going to use – you can use a hand drill or a low-speed electric drill to do this.
✪ Make sure the cotton stays clean by keeping it in a box.
✪ Paint the seam with an oil-based primer.
✪ Loop the cotton into the seam and then drive it in with a caulking iron and mallet.
✪ Use a hardening iron, which has a groove in its working face, to drive the caulking deep into the seam, rocking the iron as you go.

✪ You need to fill the seam to about half its depth, so you may need a second layer of cotton.
✪ Again paint the seam with oil-based primer.
✪ Before the primer is fully dry, fill the seam with red lead putty using

Above **The cotton is separated into strands which can be spun together to create a strand thick enough to fill the seam.**

a putty knife. Some amateurs recommend thinning the putty with linseed oil and adding a little grease, to make it easier to squeeze into the narrow seams.
✪ Wet the knife with linseed oil and run it along the seam to polish it.

Relaunching the boat

Once the seams have been re-caulked, the planks will continue to dry out and shrink, so repainting the hull and getting the boat back into the water should not be delayed for too long.

Re-caulking a seam

Once some cotton has been hammered in, gather some more up in a loop using the iron and push it into the seam.

Hammer the cotton into the seam using the caulking iron. Use a hardening iron to 'harden up' the seam.

Refurbishing solid teak decks

General wear and tear, especially that caused by over-enthusiastic cleaning, will dictate whether a boat's deck planking needs sanding down to preserve its looks and even to prevent water penetration.

When is sanding necessary?

If a deck is scrubbed hard and along the grain (rather than gently, and in circles or figure's-of-eight), softer parts of the timber get worn away, leaving ridges. This is particularly true of teak. When the ridges become too deep, the deck will have to be sanded to restore its finish.

General wear of the wood will also leave the flexible caulking standing proud, and this may cause separation between the caulking material and the wood. If the adhesion between the caulking and the wood has failed, re-caulking will be necessary to ensure a waterproof deck.

Below **A variety of tools can be used to remove the old caulking and clean up the the seams, including mallet and chisel.**

CAULKING WITH TAR OR PITCH

Because the deck is more or less horizontal, tar or pitch can be used to seal the deck joint above traditional oakum/cotton caulking, rather than the red lead putty that is used in hull seams. Jeffrey's Marine Glue is almost pure pitch and may be more easily obtainable than tar.

Sanding the deck

Remove as many deck fittings as possible. A belt sander removes wood rapidly, so it needs to be used with care to ensure that no more wood is removed than is absolutely necessary. You will have better control using a floor sander, but it's probable that it will be too big for the space available. If any underlying screw heads are revealed, stop sanding until the screws have been removed.

Removing the screws

If any screws need to be removed:

- Mark the centre of the dowel with a centre punch.
- Drill out the old dowel with a 'spur point' drill bit.
- Stop as soon as you feel the drill bit touch the screw.
- Clean the screw slot and remove the screw with a correctly fitting screwdriver, so that the counter-sinking can be deepened. If necessary use a shorter replacement screw.

Right **A belt sander is an effective tool for cleaning up a deck — but use it with care.**

Deepening the rebates

The easiest way to deepen the rebates is to use a palm router. You may be able to use the remains of the adjacent rebate as a guide, though you may have to devise a tool to do this yourself according to the circumstances. The rebate should be 0.25in (5-6mm) deep.

Re-caulking the planks

If the grooves have been completely removed by sanding, the joints between planks will be revealed and so the traditional caulking between planks may need to be replaced. How to do this is shown on pages 84 and 85.

Re-sealing deck seams

Remove the old sealant. A craft knife is being used here, but a hammer and chisel or bent-over screwdriver can also be used.

A palm router can be used to deepen the rebates. Here, a guide is being used to keep the rebate even.

Having primed the rebate, breaker tape is inserted into the base to stop the sealant sticking to the bottom of the seam.

The rebate is filled with new sealant using a caulking gun. Once cured, any excess will be removed with a belt sander.

Filling the rebates

⊕ Polysulphide is the best, most expensive type of sealant. It takes a long time to cure properly.

⊕ Most compound suppliers recommend the use of bond breaker tape to prevent the sealant adhering to the bottom of the rebate.

⊕ Apply breaker tape to the bottom of the rebate and then fill the rebate with polysulphide or polyurethane sealant to about 0.04in (1mm) above the plank.

⊕ Glue dowels into any screw holes, using epoxy.

⊕ Ensure that you observe the manufacturer's curing times prior to sanding or even walking on the deck. When the compound has fully cured, sand the sealant and dowels to the same level as the rest of the deck.

Repairing wooden rudder fittings

Metal fittings are bolted to a wooden rudder, partly to hold it together and partly to attach it to the hull. These fittings will, from time to time, need to be replaced or repaired.

The wooden rudder

A wooden rudder will be made up of a number of pieces of timber glued and bolted together, but, once it's painted, it will look like one piece of solid timber. Metal straps across the rudder are attached to each other by bolts or rivets passing through the rudder and give added rigidity. These straps sometimes also incorporate the gudgeons on which the rudder pivots on the pintles.

Below **If the rudder fittings are loose, they will need to be refitted, using larger bolts if necessary.**

Above **The transom is marked with a centreline to help position the fittings.**

The metal fittings

The fittings can be made from iron or bronze. Iron fittings can rust and may need to be removed to clean and repaint them. When they are part of the gudgeon on which the rudder pivots, they may also need to be replaced or repaired because of wear and tear.

Removing the fittings

Although it may be possible to undo the bolts, the nuts or heads will sometimes have to be ground away using an angle grinder. This will also be the case if the fittings are riveted. The bolts or rivets can then be hammered through, allowing the fittings to be removed.

Refurbishing the fittings

If iron fittings are badly corroded, it's probably better to replace them with new ones, which can easily be fabricated by a blacksmith or engineering company. Use the old

Right **Drilling the holes for the fastenings of a lower pintle.**

ones as patterns. They should be primed and painted before they are attached to the rudder. Bronze fittings that comprise the gudgeons or pintles can have their bearings refurbished if necessary.

More than two bearings

If there are more than two bearings, the rudder will be stiff to operate unless they are aligned properly. If new fittings are made, it is probable that they will not be identical to the old ones, and having the bearings refurbished may also lead to loss of alignment. In this case it will be better if the old bolt or rivet holes are filled (by epoxying dowels into the holes) and new ones bored when the rudder is rehung.

Refinishing the rudder

With the fittings removed, the rudder can be stripped of paint, and any blemishes filled. If delamination of the wooden sections or corrosion in any bolts is found, further remedial work will be required. Otherwise, simply renew the paintwork. Any straps that are not part of the pivot bearings can be re-attached to the rudder at this stage, as can the upper and lower fittings.

Above **Once the top fittings are done, the rudder is hung to mark off the lower fittings.**

Rehanging and alignment

Rehang the rudder using the upper and lower fittings only, and ensure that operation of the rudder is free and smooth. The lower bearing fittings may need adjustment to achieve this. Then offer up any intermediate fittings, drill holes, insert new bolts and tighten them up, checking rudder friction as you do so.

Below **The rudder of a wooden boat is made up of several planks bolted together and hung using gudgeons and pintles.**

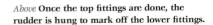

Rudder stock

Bolts

Metal strap

Gudgeon

Pintle

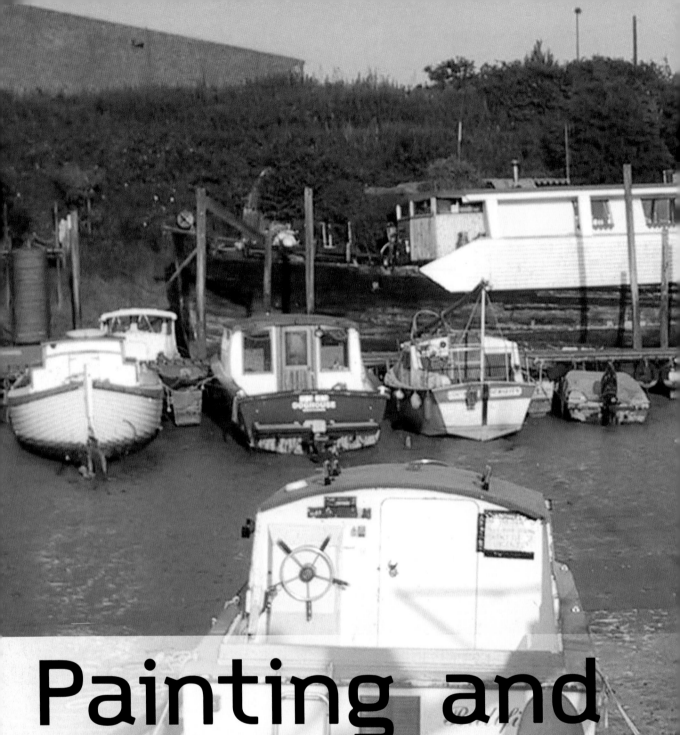

Painting and varnishing

Preparing fibreglass

The secret to a great looking paint job is in the preparation. Applying the final coating is only a small part of the time involved. The better the preparation, the better the finish and the longer it will last.

Chipped and flaking surfaces

One of the most common failures of a new paint system is that it does not adhere to the substrate underneath. Many boats pick up a number of surface chips and dings, and these must be repaired before repainting (see pages 66 to 69).

Areas of chipped or flaking paint must also be dealt with before repainting. Small areas can be removed with a scraper, and the edges of the damage 'feathered' with sandpaper to create a fair finish, but larger areas may need to be stripped entirely.

Most chemical paint strippers will dissolve fibreglass, although a few eco-friendly brands can be used safely. If a suitable paint stripper is not available, the best alternative is sanding with an electric sander equipped with dust extraction. Some professionals use a warm-air electric paint stripper, but these can easily melt fibreglass, and should only be used by someone skilled at the job.

Once the area to be painted is in sound condition, abrade the entire surface with sandpaper to provide a mechanical key for the new paint to stick to.

Above **Stripping paint with a chemical paint remover. Make sure you choose a brand that's safe to use with fibreglass.**

Tools of the trade

Most boat owners end up owning a selection of electric sanders for this purpose. As a minimum, an orbital or random orbit sander is needed to cover large areas, while a small triangular model will enable you to reach some difficult corners. Whatever the type of sander, it's important to keep it moving. It's easy to get distracted and linger in one place for long enough to create a hollow that will show in the final finish.

Left **A large electric sander will help to make quick work of preparing surfaces.**

If a boat's topsides aren't perfectly fair, a new paint finish will highlight this. The high points over a wide area can be removed, without risk of also sanding out the hollows, using a longboard. This is a 3–8ft (1–2.5m) sanding board approximately 4in (10cm) wide and operated manually by one or more people. Its size means that only the high spots are sanded.

Above **Using a longboard to achieve a perfect finish after fairing fibreglass.**

Left **A triangular shaped detail sander is essential for small spaces and for use around fittings and other obstructions.**

ABRASIVE PAPER GRADES

24–50 Coarse and extra coarse, used for very fast removal of paint and fairing compound.

60–100 Medium grit, ideal for initial sanding of bare wood, or surfaces with many imperfections.

120–150 Fine grit, used for preparation for the initial coats of paint.

180–320 Very fine, used to flatten the surface, or provide a key, between layers of paint.

320–400 Extra-fine, ideal to create a perfectly smooth surface when applying the final coats of varnish.

600–2,000 Ultra-fine grits, can be used to polish the finish after applying a number of topcoats, or for polishing gel coat.

Fairing fibreglass

Boats with particularly uneven topside finishes will require more remedial action before they are ready for painting, and all boats need careful cleaning and degreasing. Failure to carry out this step thoroughly will result in the new paint failing to stick securely to the surface beneath.

Fairing uneven surfaces

Larger areas of surface damage may need to be rebuilt through a process known as fairing – applying filler, then sanding until a uniform surface is achieved. There are three options for establishing a level for fairing: you can sand away until the entire area is level with the lowest hollows; add filler until the surface is level with the highest bumps; or compromise, sanding the highest peaks away, then filling the remaining hollows.

The best filler is epoxy resin thickened with PVI micro-balloons until it achieves the consistency of a meringue and is able to stand in peaks. This is very easy to sand, but it doesn't have great water-repellent properties. If used below the waterline, resin should be thickened with glass or phenolic micro-balloons, which are slightly denser and harder to sand than micro-balloons.

Below **Take time when applying masking tape. It has to be positioned accurately to achieve a professional finish.**

POLISH VERSUS PAINT

Paint manufacturers often give the impression their products are the only route to a perfect finish on older boats. However, there can be disadvantages to this approach. Alkyd-based paints are relatively soft compared to gel coat and therefore easily scratched, so polishing the gel coat may be an option worth considering. Hulls that are severely oxidised can be sanded with 400, 600 and finally 800 grit paper to cut enough of the damaged top layer away to reveal shiny material underneath.

The best two-pack polyurethane paints are both tougher and more durable than gel coat, so repainting with these products can give excellent results.

Right **The last step before painting is to give the surface a final clean with a cloth soaked in white spirit – or, if using polyurethane paint, use a tack rag.**

Final preparation

Before painting, surfaces must be clean of dirt, dust and grease. The sanding process can remove a lot of dirt, but if any remains the area should be given a thorough wash with a product such as sugar soap, which does not leave the residues that are a problem with ordinary detergents. This process will also wash away most of the dust.

Alternatively, the majority of sanding dust can be cleaned away with a vacuum or brush, with the rest removed by wiping with a cloth soaked in a solvent such as white spirits or acetone. If using polyurethane paint, clean off using a 'tack rag', a pre-impregnated cloth specially designed for the job.

Sanding between coats of paint is not essential if each subsequent coat is applied within the recommended overcoating time, because a chemical bond forms between the layers.

Masking up

Standard masking tapes gain a tenacious grip over time, especially if subjected to alternate periods of showers and sun. To eliminate the risk of the tape pulling gel coat or previous layers of paint away from the hull, remove masking tape at the end of every day. A better alternative is to use the all-weather masking tape, usually coloured blue, which can be left in place for 14 days.

Above **Avoid the temptation to apply fairing compound too thickly. It's easier to add another layer than to sand excess away.**

1 Sand down to the level of the lowest troughs.

2 Fill surface to the level of the highest peaks.

3 Sand the peaks and fill the troughs.

Preparing wooden boats

The paint finish of fibreglass boats is purely cosmetic, because the gel coat protects the structure, but wooden boats are a different matter. They rely on multi-layer paint systems to prevent the water ingress that will eventually lead to the formation of rot, or delamination of marine plywood.

Regular retouching

Maintaining a wooden boat need not be a hugely time-consuming task, provided the paintwork is given regular attention to keep it in sound condition and prevent water ingress. Regular inspection of the paint will ensure any problems are identified at an early stage. Pay particular attention to the areas around fittings, in corners and at joints between timbers. This is where most problems originate.

Beyond this, there are many similarities with painting fibreglass boats. Exactly the same considerations apply for sanding, masking and final surface preparation. However, small areas of damaged paint need to be dealt with as quickly as possible. Use a scraper to remove loose or flaking paint, then sand the surrounding area to taper the existing paint into the area where the new coating will be applied. A quick-drying primer,

Above **Hand sanding a small area of paint damage. It is crucial to touch up any flaws before water can penetrate the structure.**

Below **Wooden decks are particularly susceptible to rot, and must be kept weatherproofed at all times.**

followed by a thick layer or two of topcoat, will serve as an adequate temporary waterproofing measure until the area can be touched up properly.

It is vitally important to touch up paint in this manner before the onset of winter. Every time water that has found its way under layers of paint freezes, it expands, causing progressively more and more paint to flake away. In a cold winter, the rate at which this can happen is alarming.

Sanding the whole hull

If the majority of the paint system is adhering well to the hull, start by removing any loose, bubbling or flaking paint with a scraper. The whole hull can then be sanded using medium grit paper. This provides a key that will help the new paint adhere to the boat, and it will help to smooth the existing paint. If the surface of the existing paint is very uneven, for example with runs or brush marks, it will benefit from being sanded with a coarser grade – maybe 150 or even 120.

Considerations for wooden decks

Although owners naturally worry about the integrity of their vessels' hulls, the decks of wooden vessels are more likely to develop problems, and therefore demand frequent

Above **Any flaking paint on seams should be scraped away and the area primed and undercoated before recoating with gloss.**

inspection. Problems with decks almost universally stem from rainwater, which lacks the mild preservative properties of salt water, so rot forms more easily. In addition, decks often have a number of places where water can pool, and if the paint system in these areas is not in perfect condition, fresh water will slowly seep into the timber.

Left **A chemical paint remover is the best way to remove old varnish. It is strong stuff, though, so make sure you protect your hands.**

Stripping & repainting wood

Wooden boats with old or badly neglected paint systems will need to be completely stripped and repainted. Before repainting starts it is also important to be sure that the moisture content of the timber is within acceptable limits.

Stripping unsound or suspect paint

With wooden boats there are two main reasons for stripping the entire paint system from the topsides. The paint may be in such poor condition that adding extra coats on top would still not result in a sound paint system; alternatively, if there's good reason to suspect the condition of the timber underneath is unsound, removing the paint will allow a full assessment to be carried out.

Unlike on fibreglass boats, there's no reason why household chemical paint strippers should not be used, although if an adequate electricity supply is available it's usually a lot quicker to use a hot-air gun. If used with care, a gas blowtorch is even more effective and will rapidly remove numerous layers of paint. This method will, however, leave scorch marks on the timber, so it is not suitable if the topsides are to be varnished.

Another option is to sand the layers of paint away with a coarse or ultra-coarse grade of abrasive paper. This has the potential to leave a very fair finish, but on anything other than the smallest boats it is only really practical using a powerful sander with effective dust extraction.

Below **Don't be afraid to strip any suspect paint or varnish. Failure to do so will simply lead to bigger problems later.**

Above **Regularly touching up damaged paint can prevent it becoming a major job.**

Above **A blowtorch is the quickest way of removing large areas of paint, but it should never be used on antifouling. Be sure to wear a suitable mask to guard against fumes.**

Final preparation

Before repainting, it's worth checking the water content of the timber, as the new paint will seal any moisture into the wood. This is easily measured with a moisture meter, which are readily available from builders' merchants. Rot will form if the moisture content of timber is too high. Ideally, water content should be between 15 and 20 per cent when repainting.

Whether the entire paint system has been stripped or the existing coating sanded and any local damage remedied, the entire hull must still be given a thorough final clean before painting.

The number of coats needed will depend on the condition of the underlying paint, but at least two topcoats should be applied. If repainting a bare hull, start with three coats of primer, the first one thinned 10–20 per cent by volume with white spirit to allow it to soak into the timber. Next, at least two undercoats are needed, and perfectionists may add an extra coat or two so that the finish looks brilliant even before topcoats are applied.

If one coat of paint can be applied each day, there's no need to sand down between coats, because a chemical bond will form between layers. A light 'de-nibbing' to get rid of trapped dust will suffice. However, sanding with fine sandpaper will be required if there's a longer time period between coats.

Preparing metal boats

Steel and aluminium boats are inherently strong, and can be very long-lasting. However, without appropriate care they have the potential to quickly succumb to serious rust or electrolysis problems.

Steel boats

Almost all steel boats can be divided neatly into one of two categories: those built after the development and widespread use of highly-effective epoxy paint systems in the early and mid-1980s, and those built before that date.

On older boats, keeping rust at bay can be a continuous process, in the same way as maintaining the paint systems of a wooden boat. Any sign of rust bubbling or staining under paint should be attended to as quickly as possible, as damage can spread quickly. Yachts also have the potential to rust from the inside out, so the interior as well as the exterior of the vessel must be examined for damage to the paintwork.

Rust must be ground away until no evidence of it is left, and bright metal is visible over the whole area. This point is really important, because any residual rust, even if almost invisible, will be a starting point for more corrosion to form. A 4.5in (115mm) angle grinder is ideal for larger areas of damage, although a Dremel type tool is more appropriate for small areas.

The surrounding paint can then be feathered to a smooth edge, the surface cleaned and degreased, and a marine-grade metal primer applied. These processes should be carried out in quick succession, as corrosion starts to form immediately on bare metal. To create a long-lasting repair, it's worth building up a number of layers of primer before adding undercoats and topcoats.

Right **As usual, preparation is key. Power tools make all the difference, but make sure you wear safety gear.**

Boats with epoxy paint systems fare much better, with rust usually appearing only as a result of damage to the paint. If the paint is damaged, the procedure is the same as that for traditional paint systems, with the exception that paint compatible with the epoxy system must be used. In both cases, good atmospheric conditions with low humidity are vital for a long-lasting paint system.

If a steel boat is completely stripped back to bare metal, it's not sufficient to remove just the paint coverings; any rust on the surface must also be removed. This generally involves getting a specialist contractor to grit blast the hull, with the paint removed as part of the process. It's vital to get at least the first couple of coats of primer on as quickly as possible after blasting, because the metal will start to tarnish immediately.

Aluminium boats

Aluminium has excellent strength-to-weight ratio, and does not suffer from corrosion in the same manner as steel, so the topsides can be left bare. However, the material is very susceptible to electrolytic action, so all stray currents must be eliminated from the boat's electrical system, and sacrificial anodes need to be inspected and replaced regularly.

Above **Building up lots of thick coats of paint is the key to keeping corrosion at bay on a steel boat.**

Above **Different considerations apply to steel and aluminium boats, but maintaining an intact paint system is just as important.**

Left **Preparing the hull of a steel boat for repainting. The surface has been extensively faired with filler.**

Repainting

Whether the priority is a perfect finish to rival that of any superyacht, or a faster result that still looks good, it's vital to choose the right paint for the purpose, and to apply it with a good technique.

Types of marine paint

Although relatively expensive, specialist marine paints have important advantages over household and automotive alternatives. In particular they dry to a much harder finish, with better resistance to abrasion and scratching. Marine paints come in both one-pot and two-pot varieties. The former are conventional alkyd resin-based products that are relatively easy to apply, but they lack the high gloss and longevity of two-pack paints.

Applying paint

The two most popular methods for boat owners to apply paint are by brush and by roller. With good technique, brushing has the potential to enable a near-perfect finish to be obtained. Applying paint with a roller is considerably faster, but the finish is not as good.

Painting by brush is a three-stage process, starting with a loaded brush to roughly distribute the paint. Next, strokes should be made at 90 degrees to the first to brush the paint out into an even layer. Finally, the paint is 'laid off' to remove brush marks, using the lightest possible strokes, with only the tips of the bristles touching the surface. These strokes should be in the same orientation as in the first phase. For wooden boats, the strokes in phases one and three should be along the grain.

Large areas need to be broken down into zones that are small enough for the edges to remain wet while the adjacent zone is painted, otherwise joins will be visible in the finished result.

One really effective method of painting boats is to work as a two-person team, with one using a roller and the second following with

Above **A roller is ideal for covering large areas quickly, although the finish is not as good as other methods of painting.**

a brush to lay off the paint, brushing towards the 'wet edge' to create an improved finish. If the paint is polished after being allowed to harden for a few days, the result can be almost indistinguishable from a professional spray job.

Three-stage brush technique

With the brush lightly loaded, apply dabs of paint, working along the direction of the grain, if painting a wooden surface.

Brush this out into an even layer of paint using firm brushstrokes, at right angles to the original strokes.

Use a very light touch to lay the paint flat. The tips of the bristles should barely touch the surface.

Spray painting

Spraying can produce a fantastic finish, but it's a highly skilled operation that few boat owners can master in the less than ideal conditions of most boatyards. The actual spraying is a very small part of the overall task. The bulk of the work is in preparation and masking up. If choosing this option, it usually pays to do the preparation yourself, and then get a professional to do the final spraying.

Whatever method is chosen, a dusty or windy environment can wreck the finish. Before applying the final couple of coats, it's worth checking that nearby boat owners won't be undertaking work that will create lots of dust. To prevent wind-blown dust reaching the paint finish, damp the surrounding area down with a sprinkling of water before starting work.

Above **Spraying requires expertise – and considerable preparation – but results in a perfect finish.**

Preparing & painting decks

Many of the principles of preparing and painting topsides also apply to decks. However, the need for non-slip surfaces introduces a number of differences, and wooden decks require particularly careful attention to prevent rainwater causing rot.

Types of deck paint

Non-slip deck paint comes in two main forms. One is similar to conventional marine paint, but with the addition of fine grit – often made of polypropylene – while the other has a more rubberised consistency. Both can be difficult to remove if stripping is needed.

Below **Non-slip deck paint is difficult to remove from fibreglass. Allow plenty of time for this.**

Owners of wooden boats have an advantage in that a hot-air gun or even blowtorch can be used to good effect. Both of these have the potential to melt a fibreglass deck, although the method of choice for many professionals is to use a hot-air gun, while exercising extreme care. The alternative is a fibreglass-friendly chemical paint stripper, but be prepared for this to be a slow process.

Deck paint is also difficult to sand, but this is rarely a problem, as the textured surface provides an excellent key to which new layers of paint will readily attach. However, this quality also traps dirt and grime, so decks should be given a thorough clean with a pressure washer before the final preparation stage.

Masking up

It's vital to keep deck fittings clean of paint. Even if the smallest amount finds its way onto fittings, the finish will look shoddy. Accurate and effective masking of decks is a very time-consuming task that can easily take a full day on a larger boat. This means it's worth using the all-weather masking tape that can be left in place between coats.

Applying deck paint is a similar process to that for topsides, although spraying is increasingly seen as the key to a top-quality professional finish. Some deck paints are more tolerant of brush marks than standard marine paints, but others show them even more clearly. Before starting work in earnest, it's worth trying the paint you intend to use in a small area, to see how it behaves in this respect.

It takes some time (maybe as much as 24 hours) for deck paint to harden enough to be walked upon, so do not be tempted to step on it when it is only touch dry. And make sure the work is planned so that you can step off the boat without walking on the paint.

Top **Rollers are perfect for applying non-slip paint, as the slightly textured finish is not a problem in this context.**

Above **Masking deck fittings is a fiddly but necessary task. Allow at least half a day, even for a modest size boat.**

Painting other areas

Many small components such as toe rails, hatch surrounds and locker lids look great with a properly applied paint system, especially on older boats, where the original finishes of these items are likely to have been damaged. However, this is a time-consuming process requiring patience and attention to detail.

Preparation

If possible, small items are best removed from the boat. It's much easier to prepare and paint them on a work bench than in the confines of the vessel. The same general considerations apply as for painting larger areas, but attention to detail is even more important. Existing paint systems tend to start to peel at the edges, corners and around other intricacies, and small items tend to have more of these relative to their size than larger areas that need

painting. It's important to allow sufficient time to prepare and paint small items. It can take longer to repaint the cockpit than the entire topsides of the hull.

Before sanding, it's often worth running the blade of a paint scraper along the join between two different items, for instance the coachroof sides and deck, to remove the flaking paint that is often found there. A triangular detail sander (buy the smallest you can find, unless you have a very large boat) will speed up preparation, but some hand sanding is inevitable. A selection of sanding blocks of various sizes and shapes will help to speed up the preparation of awkwardly shaped areas.

Above **Use a sanding block when hand sanding. It's faster and improves the finish.**

Painting aluminium components

Once the anodising on aluminium components, such as hatch surrounds and toe rails, starts to become damaged, they can quickly look very tatty. Unfortunately, paint does not readily stick to anodised aluminium, so do not be tempted to rush this task. A couple of quick coats of paint can all too easily result in a finish that is easily chipped and rapidly flakes away.

Sound preparation starts with sanding the metal with medium grit paper, then thoroughly cleaning and degreasing the surface. An etch primer (also known as adhesive primer) should then be applied as soon as possible, because the metal will start oxidising immediately. This coat helps to bond subsequent coats of paint to the metal, and it can be followed with the first coat of regular metal primer after about 90 minutes.

Below **A small palm-size sander speeds up the preparation of fiddly areas such as the coachroof sides.**

Plastic components

These tend to gradually degrade in
sunlight, and their colour fades.
Ideally they should be covered when
the boat is not in use, but this is not
always practical. It is not wise to
paint them, though. In most cases
the original finish can be restored
simply by polishing with an
automotive polishing paste. This
will remove just enough of the
top surface to reveal undamaged
material underneath, and even
works on steering compasses that
have become opaque due to
exposure to sunlight.

Above **Small areas are impossible to paint
effectively with a roller, so brush painting
is usually the preferred option.**

Left **Aluminium components can look
great if painted, but must first be
meticulously prepared.**

Antifouling

Vessels kept afloat must be antifouled to combat growth of weed, slime and other marine organisms that grow on all submerged surfaces. A wide variety of antifoulings is available, reflecting the many different types of craft afloat. It's important to choose the correct one for your boat.

Types of antifouling

There are two principal antifouling types: those that form a hard surface, and a softer, eroding variety. The former can be scrubbed to a clean finish and is ideal for racing yachts and fast planing powerboats. Eroding types are ideal for displacement motorboats and sailing cruisers.

Over time the top surface wears away, exposing fresh biocides and preventing organisms from getting a firm grip on the hull.

When hauled out of the water, boats should be cleaned with a pressure washer to remove any underwater growth. Any remaining loose or flaking antifoul can be removed using a paint scraper. It is often possible to paint over existing coats with a similar product, but if there's any doubt about whether a new product is compatible with existing layers, an antifouling primer should be used as a barrier coat.

Stripping back

To prevent build-up of too many layers of antifouling, underwater areas should be stripped back to the bare hull every few years. Because of the toxic nature of antifouling, dry sanding should not be attempted, even with dust extraction. The best DIY solution is chemical antifouling stripper, but many owners give this task to a professional.

Before starting work, measure how far the waterline is below the gunwale at 3ft (0.9m) intervals. This information is vital to re-establish the waterline before repainting.

Two types of primer are available for antifouling. Regular antifouling primers offer good performance, but epoxy primers have better adhesion and offer some protection against osmosis. Check the hull isn't already suffering from osmosis, however, before applying epoxy primer.

Left **In tidal areas, scrubbing grids with piles to allow fin keel boats to be dried out are a cheap option for a scrub or antifoul.**

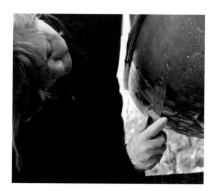

Above Make sure any loose or flaking antifouling is scraped off before the new coat is applied.

Right A keen eye helps to apply masking tape in a perfectly straight line. Stand back regularly to check your handiwork.

Below Never apply antifouling with a brush. A small roller with a long handle is faster, cleaner and much less effort.

Applying antifouling

Application by roller is by far the best method, especially if an extension handle is used with the roller. This allows both hands to be used, and minimises the need to stoop under the boat. Antifouling is expensive, and rollers absorb a lot of paint, so use the smallest that it's realistic to work with. A 3in (77mm) size is adequate for most boats under 33ft (10m). Two complete coats of antifouling should be regarded as a minimum, plus an extra coat around the waterline and the leading and trailing edges of rudder and keel. In locations where fouling is a known problem, at least one additional complete coat is needed.

Maintaining brightwork

Varnish is notoriously difficult to keep in good shape, yet well-kept brightwork looks great on any boat. As with many other aspects of boat maintenance, a small amount of regular attention is the key to maintaining a lustrous finish.

Above **Using a scraper to remove flaking varnish. It's often possible to return even badly neglected varnish to a good finish.**

Preparation for varnishing

Maintaining varnish is not a once or twice a year task. Once water is allowed to penetrate the varnish, it breaks down with alarming speed. Casting an eye over the condition of a boat's brightwork at least once a month, and touching up any problems immediately, greatly reduces the total amount of maintenance needed.

Remove the loose varnish from any isolated areas of damage with a scraper, then sand with a fine grade of paper, and clean/degrease as for painting. The first coat of varnish on bare wood should be thinned with 10–20 per cent of white spirit. Two further coats will be an adequate temporary measure to keep the area watertight, but another three or four coats are needed for a longer-term finish.

If the entire varnish system is to be re-coated, prepare the areas in a similar manner, sanding all of the varnish with a fine-grit sandpaper before starting work. If existing varnish is in poor condition and needs to be stripped, chemical strippers and electric hot-air guns are both very effective.

Below **A natural finish on teak. Left to its own devices the wood takes on a silver-grey colour which is easy on the eye.**

Above **Sanding the same area of wood in preparation for the first, thinned, coat of varnish.**

Right **A scrubbed teak finish is easily achieved, but slowly erodes the thickness of a teak deck.**

Care of teak

There are three primary options for looking after teak on a boat: leaving it in a natural state, regular scrubbing, and oiled finishes. The first minimises the amount of maintenance needed, and arguably maximises the life of the timber. Over time it will gain a silver-grey appearance, with the wood's natural oils providing adequate protection.

A scrubbed finish can result in a fabulous classic appearance. One of the key active ingredients in teak cleaners is oxalic acid, which bleaches the timber to an attractive shade. However, this appearance comes at a cost, as repeated scrubbing wears the material away at up to 0.04in (1mm) per year, hastening the time at which it will need to be replaced. Oxalic acid in its pure form is highly poisonous and should not be used.

Oiling the wood after cleaning and scrubbing it will maintain an attractive appearance for longer than scrubbing alone, but the process must be repeated every two or three months to keep the boat looking at its best.

Painting over varnish

If water damage has started to blacken timber, a remedial option is a painted finish. However, the varnish should be removed first. Even if it has been thoroughly sanded to provide a key, paint will never adhere well to varnish. For interior areas with low wear, it may be acceptable to paint without first stripping the varnish, but this is never the case for exterior brightwork.

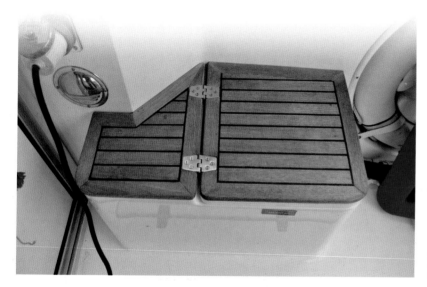

Left **Freshly oiled teak looks great on any boat, but requires regular work to keep it in good shape.**

Varnishing

The secret to a superb, long-lasting varnished finish is to choose the right product and apply a number of coats with great care. The exact procedure to follow varies, depending on the product used.

Types of varnish

There are several types of marine varnish on the market, all with different properties. Traditional solvent-based one-pot alkyd varnishes are relatively soft, and have enough flexibility for timber that expands with the wet in winter and contracts in dry summer weather. Normally, one coat is applied per day. After application, they can be sanded with progressively finer grades of sandpaper to achieve a perfect finish.

Polyurethanes are a harder option, with good wear resistance, but they lack the flexibility of alkyds. They are available as both one-pot and two-pot products, the latter giving a faster cure, allowing multiple coats to be applied in a day. Flexible polyurethane varnishes such as Coelan are a more recent innovation that can last twice as long as traditional varnishes, but at a comparatively high price. Coelan is a two-part product and a number of coats can be built up in a day.

Applying varnish

Varnishing is more difficult than painting simply because it's a transparent coating and is therefore difficult to see. The solution is to put your head close to the work, so that you are looking obliquely across the surface. Areas with too much or too little varnish are then clearly visible.

Beyond this, there are a number of factors in achieving a perfect finish. The varnish must be expertly laid off, and a large number of coats are needed – up to a dozen for traditional products. The first coat on bare wood should be thinned using around 30 per cent white spirit by volume, and the next couple with 10–20 per cent of white spirit. This allows the varnish to penetrate the timber, providing greater protection and adhesion of subsequent layers. Sanding with progressively finer paper between coats, working up to 600–800 grit, helps to create a perfect flat finish.

Flexible polyurethanes use a separate primer for the initial coats. Subsequent coats can't be sanded between applications, but these products are easier to apply in an even coating than traditional varnishes.

Protecting varnish

Sun and frost are the biggest enemies of a varnished finish. Large areas of exterior brightwork, such as the cockpit of a wooden boat, therefore benefit from a cover that provides shade from the sun.

Right **Good weather is essential for varnishing, so don't schedule it for short winter days.**

Achieving a perfect finish

Before applying the final coat, sand the surface lightly with fine wet and dry paper.

Finish with light brushstrokes that lay the varnish off in the direction of the grain.

The final result – a perfectly smooth surface – is worth the time spent.

General mechanics

Fresh water system

Unless the boat is very small, it will have a fresh (that is to say, potable) water system. The bigger the boat, the more complex this system is likely to be. The system will require annual maintenance to be sure that it remains clean.

Fresh water tank

The boat's fresh water tank is filled from the mains water supply. It will usually be rigid and made from stainless steel, plastic or even fibreglass. Some boats use flexible plastic tanks, which can easily be removed, but may suffer from abrasion.

Primary filter

The filter prevents any solids in the water flow from damaging or clogging the pump and is sometimes mounted on the pump itself. The filter needs to be cleaned at least annually, and should be checked if the water supply fails.

Water pump

An electric water pump is used on larger systems, so that water under pressure is supplied at the turn of a tap. Regular maintenance is not required.

Below **Most larger yachts have pressure systems which deliver fresh water at the turn of a tap.**

Accumulator

Without an accumulator, the pump will cut in and out repeatedly if the tap is opened only partially. An accumulator stores water under pressure, so that the pump runs only when the accumulator needs to be 'topped up'. This results in less wear on the pump.

Calorifier

A calorifier takes cold water from the tank, uses waste heat from the engine's cooling system to heat this water, and stores it. A mains electricity heating element can also be fitted to heat the water.

Pressure relief valve

Because there is a rise in pressure when water is heated, a relief valve is fitted to prevent the calorifier from bursting. Any replacement fitted must be of the same pressure setting.

Pressure relief drain

Each time the pressure relief valve operates, water will overflow into the bilge, so it is usual (and a good idea) to run a pipe from the valve to an easily emptied container.

Hot and cold water taps

Domestic-style taps are generally used to supply hot and cold water to the galley sinks and heads compartment wash basins. They require no routine maintenance.

Manual pump

A hand- or foot-operated pump may be used to supply cold water when the electric pump fails – or where there is no pressurised water system fitted to the boat. Some boats have a manual pump supplying sea water to the galley sink for washing pots and vegetables, thus saving fresh water.

Isolation valves

Isolation valves make maintenance and isolating faults much easier, but are not always fitted by the boatbuilder. A leak in the water-heating part of the system would render the engine inoperable, so the ability to isolate the engine from the system is very desirable. And a leak in the hot or cold water pipes could rapidly empty the fresh water tank.

It is therefore recommended that you should fit these three valves, as a minimum, if they are not already present in the system.

Above **A bacterial filter will make fresh water from almost any source suitable for drinking. Change the filter as recommended by the manufacturer.**

Below **The freshwater system on a small boat will contain some or all of these components.**

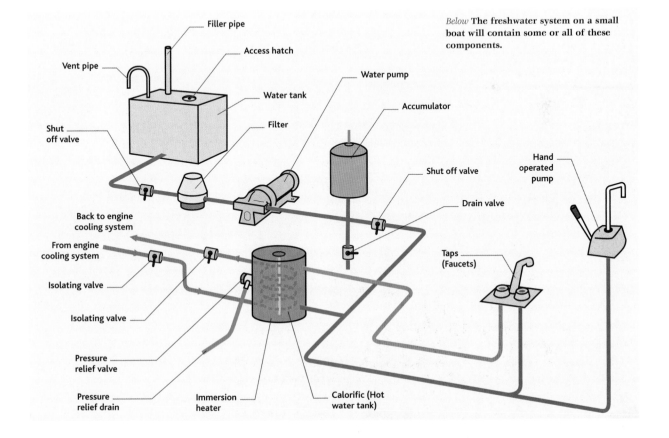

Filler pipe
Access hatch
Vent pipe
Water pump
Water tank
Accumulator
Shut off valve
Filter
Hand operated pump
Shut off valve
Drain valve
Back to engine cooling system
From engine cooling system
Isolating valve
Taps (Faucets)
Isolating valve
Pressure relief valve
Pressure relief drain
Immersion heater
Calorific (Hot water tank)

Fixing a water pipe leak

Water leaks can be notoriously difficult to locate, and small leaks from the water system often go unnoticed for a long while. Generally, the first thing you will notice is some water in the bottom of a compartment or in the bilge, so test it to see if it's fresh water.

Finding the leak
Any leak is more likely to be from a loose or badly joined fitting, rather than a hole in a pipe – unless you have driven a drill, screw or nail into it. If you have recently done some 'fixing', that's the place to start looking. Otherwise, pressurise the system by switching on the pump, then check the nearest pipe joints above the collected water. Run your fingers around each joint, and around the pipe just below it, looking for any signs of water. If you aren't immediately lucky, then work 'uphill' checking other joints. If the leak is between the tank and the pump, switching the pump on won't be necessary, but you may need to fill the tank completely to give more chance of finding it.

A leaking joint
The first action will be to check the tightness of the connector using two spanners – one to hold the joint, the other to tighten the nut. Don't apply too much force or the seal may distort, causing a bigger leak. If tightening doesn't cure the problem, separate the joint, remove any sealant, check that the olive or seal isn't distorted (replacing if necessary) and remake the joint.

If the coupling is plastic, rather than metal, you may be unable to tighten it or take it apart. In that case the coupling will need to be cut out and replaced with a new one. There will usually be sufficient slack in the pipe to allow for a small amount of shortening. If not, you'll need to splice in a new piece of pipe with two couplings, or temporarily use a piece of flexible hose and a couple of Jubilee clips.

Below **The plumbing may be quite complex but can be easy to follow if neatly installed, like this professional example.**

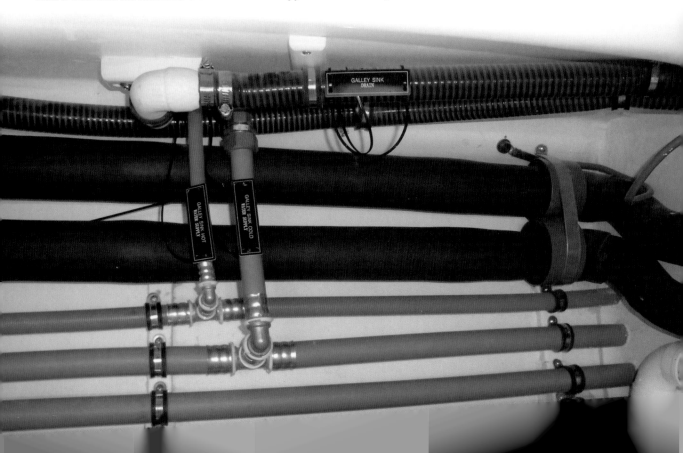

A leaking pipe

The leak will have to be repaired by cutting out the damaged portion and replacing it. If the leak is in an inaccessible place, you will need to cut out a much larger piece of pipe and thread a new piece through the inaccessible area.

Most boatbuilders use either semi-rigid plastic water pipe or flexible plastic water pipe. Semi-rigid pipes are joined by permanent plastic connectors, reusable plastic connectors or standard brass plumbing connectors (see page 123). Semi-rigid pipe should be cut using a special pipe-cutting tool available from a plumber's merchant.

Flexible plastic pipes are joined by barbed plastic connectors, using hose clips to clamp the pipe. A hobby knife may be used to cut flexible pipe.

Below **The components of a compression joint. These joints can be undone and remade whenever needed.**

Making a compression joint

The components of a copper compression joint. Once made, this can be taken apart and reassembled during any future work.

The copper tube should be cut using a pipe cutter, not a hack saw which leaves a jagged edge.

Fit the nut and olive onto the copper tube. You can use semi-rigid plastic tube as well, provided you fit a pipe support (see pages 122 and 123).

Push the tube into the compression fitting as far as it will go, then loosely tighten the nut. Repeat the process for the other side of the joint.

Use two spanners to tighten the joint. Don't overtighten: one half turn after encountering serious resistance should do the trick.

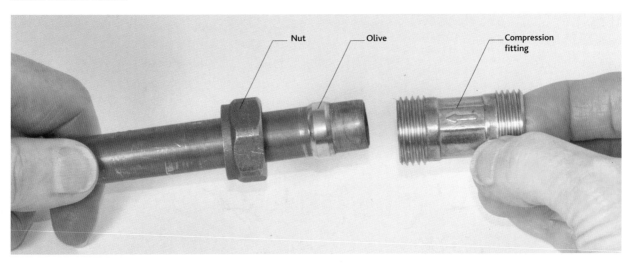

Nut   Olive   Compression fitting

Fixing a leaking tap

A leaking tap is an annoyance, but on a boat it can also waste precious water. On many modern boats, the water taps are very similar to, or even the same as, domestic taps. Older and smaller boats may have taps supplied with water by a hand or foot pump.

Taps with rubber washers

With use, the rubber washer becomes deformed or even perishes, causing the tap to drip. As a temporary cure, a deformed washer may be reversed – but spares are very cheap, so you should always have some available.

Taps with ceramic cartridges

Ceramic cartridges have no replaceable parts, so these must be changed as a complete unit when the tap starts to drip.

Below **A leaking tap washer will waste water and may stain varnished surfaces, so should be replaced as soon as possible.**

All taps

The shaft on which the ON/OFF knob is mounted is sealed to the body of the tap by means of a 'gland'. The packing inside the gland will harden or wear with time, and may need to be squashed up a bit more or replaced if water starts to leak from just under the tap's knob.

Removing the knob

First of all, depressurise the system by switching off the pump and opening the tap. There may be a grub screw in the lower part of the knob, securing it to the shaft – in which case, remove it. Alternatively, there may be a nut under the knob's cap, in which case you may need a very small screwdriver to prise off the cap before you can undo the nut and pull the knob off. Occasionally the knob will be simply push-fitted, and all you will need to do to remove it is exert a strong upwards pull.

Tightening the seal

Use a spanner to tighten the top nut – although in an old tap this may not stop the leak. In this case the packing will need to be replaced. A cartridge unit will need a new O-ring.

Removing the gland

Use a spanner to unscrew the top nut and then pull it up the shaft. This will reveal if it has an O-ring or packing.

Removing the cartridge or washer

Undo the lower (largest) nut, which will unscrew the mechanism from the tap to reveal the cartridge or washer.

TIP

If the leak is annoying and you can't fix it straight away, keep the water pump turned off unless you actually want to run some water.

Changing a washer

Prise off the cap. A slim bladed screwdriver will do the job for many taps. Often there is no visible fixing.

Remove the knob. Some just pull off, with a bit of effort, but this one has a screw underneath the cap.

The tap valve should now be visible and, in most cases, can be unscrewed from the base using a spanner.

The washer is at the base of the valve and may be held in place by a small screw. If you don't have a replacement, the washer can be turned as a temporary cure.

Changing the washer

The washer may be held in place with a small nut or by a spigot with a bulbous end. Remove the washer and replace it with one of the same size.

Changing the cartridge

The complete tap mechanism is replaced – this contains the cartridge, seal and gland.

Manual pump spout

The spout usually swivels, using an O-ring seal at its base. Often the spout just pulls out to reveal the seal, but sometimes there is a nut that needs to be undone first.

Changing contaminated water pipes

Water pipes can become coated internally with fungal or algal contamination that may be harmful to health. Opaque pipes are less readily contaminated, but any contamination remains unseen. Transparent pipes are more easily contaminated, because light passing through the pipe wall encourages contaminant growth – but at least you can see it.

Water tank filler pipe

This is usually transparent and, although it runs inside the hull from the filler cap to the tank, there is often sufficient light to accelerate fungal or algal growth. With the pipe being transparent, the build-up is readily seen, and you should change the pipe when contamination becomes evident.

Because the pipe is usually about 1.5in (38mm) inside diameter, it isn't too easy to thread from the tank filler to the tank. However, the new pipe will be much more flexible than the old. Make all the compartments

you need to work in as accessible as possible, then remove the pipe clips at both ends of the filler pipe.

If there are places you can't get at, you can pull the new pipe through as you remove the old one. Join the two together using a barbed plastic pipe connector rather than pipe clips, which may get stuck as you pull the new pipe through. Two people may be needed, one to pull, the other to push the pipe.

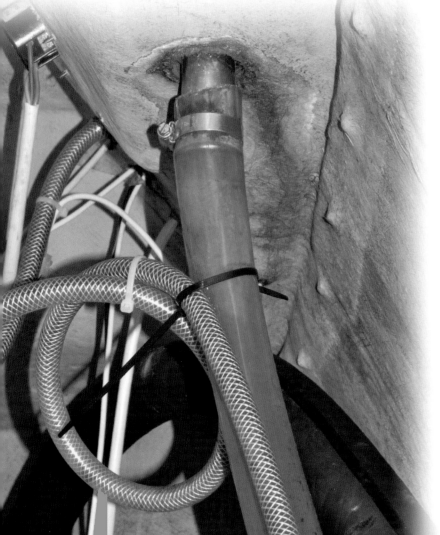

Above **Use a hot air gun on low heat or a hair dryer to remove the pipe from a fitting if necessary.**

Left **A contaminated water tank filler pipe. This will need to be replaced or it will spoil the fresh water.**

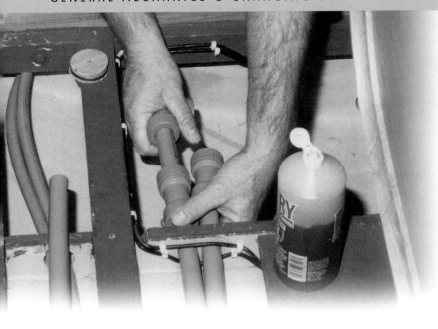

Water system pipes

The system pipes are normally opaque and of drinking water quality. They are normally full of water. Provided the tank and water system is cleaned annually, these pipes will not normally need to be replaced because of contamination. However, if they do become contaminated, use the same technique as outlined previously.

Left **Assembling semi-rigid pipework joints. If you think you might need to take the joint apart again, use the more expensive reusable type (below).**

Once the pipe is in place, it can be trimmed to length and attached to the tank and filler, and the pipe clips tightened.

Water tank vent pipe

This is replaced in the same manner as the filler pipe, but it's usually only 0.5in (12mm) diameter, so is much easier.

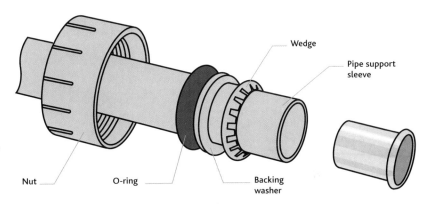

Wedge

Pipe support sleeve

Nut

O-ring

Backing washer

Making a semi-rigid joint

The components of a reusable plumbing connector joint in semi-rigid plastic pipes.

Cut the plastic pipe using a pipe cutter, not a saw, which leaves a jagged edge. A smooth cut makes a better connection.

Make sure you have all the components in the correct order and the right way round. It won't work otherwise.

The support sleeve is necessary to ensure that the pipe is not squashed when you tighten the joint.

Cleaning a contaminated water tank

Water tanks can become contaminated with bacteria, fungus or algae, and should be cleaned at least annually for the protection of your health. The process of cleaning the tank will also clean the complete water system. A bacteriological filter will ensure water from your tank is safe.

Annual cleaning

Routine cleaning requires nothing more powerful than water sterilising liquid or tablets (many people use baby bottle steriliser). Drain the complete water system. If you have an electric water pump, open all taps, both hot and cold, and let the pump run until the system is empty.

If you have a manual pump, then try to drain the tank using a drain tap – if necessary into the bilge, using the electric bilge pump to pump the water overboard. Otherwise try to set up a siphon system or use a portable electric pump.

Follow the instructions on the sterilising agent to calculate the amount required, and put it into the filler pipe. Now refill the water tank. After allowing sufficient time for the tablets to dissolve, open each tap in turn to allow the complete system to fill.

Top up the tank and leave for a day or so. Drain the system once more, and refill with fresh water.

Above **A bacterial filter, although expensive, is the best protection against water contamination.**

Below **This plastic water tank has an access panel to enable it to be cleaned, although it's not very accessible.**

Severely contaminated tank

If the water tank becomes severely contaminated, then more drastic action is required. If the tank has an access hatch, removing it may allow you to clean the inside. However, internal baffles may prevent thorough cleaning. If this is the case, steam cleaning may be an option, especially if the tank can be removed.

Fully flush the tank with fresh water as much as possible. Set up a steam generator (a wallpaper stripper unit works well) so that steam enters at a high point and

TIP

If your tanks are big, the pump will take quite a large amount of current from your batteries, so if you can do this with shore power available, so much the better. To prevent the pump overheating, don't run it for longer than about ten minutes before giving it a rest.

Left **Steam is passed through a suspect tank using the steam generator of a wallpaper stripper.**

Above **A clamp-on thermometer monitors the incoming steam.**

waste hot water exits at the low point, then steam for as long as possible. Make sure the generator doesn't run dry. Flush with fresh water and repeat the process until the tank is clean. Reinstall the tank, and clean the system with sterilising agent. Flush and refill.

Water filters

The majority of water filters will not make water safe to drink. Filters using activated carbon can improve taste and remove odours, but bacteria can build up inside them so they must be changed annually. These filters are popular when sterilising agents are used to clean the tank. Filters that remove bacteria, viruses and hydrocarbons are available, but the very fine filter element needed to do this reduces flow rate considerably. These filters are expensive but do produce potable water. The element needs to be changed only when the flow rate reduces to an unacceptable level.

SAFETY TIP

Annual cleaning will normally avoid the need for high-strength sterilising agents, but if you do need to use a strong steriliser, follow the instructions to the letter, and if necessary wear protective clothing and a face mask. After you have finished cleaning, ensure the system is flushed fully to ensure no trace of the steriliser remains.

Below **This tank is ready for removal from the boat. Often the tank is installed in such a way that its removal is not possible without dismantling some structure.**

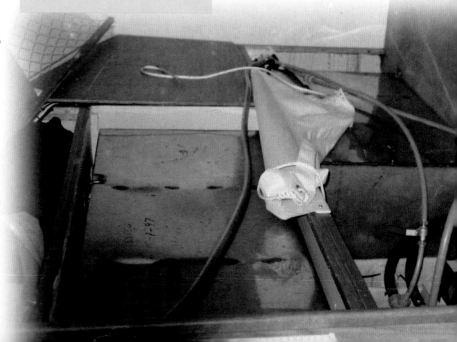

Servicing the water pump

Even if you have an electric water pump, ideally you will have a manual pump as a back-up in case the electric pump fails. Routine servicing is not normally required, other than checking the pump filter and recharging the accumulator, if fitted.

Priming

Any leakage between the tank and the pump, seals or valves will prevent the pump from self-priming. So if the pump operates but no water flows and the filter is not blocked, this is the place to start looking for the leak. Check that all joints are tightened, then turn your attention to the pump itself. Hopefully you will have kept the leaflet detailing how to take the pump apart!

Manual pumps

These are operated either by a hand lever or a foot pedal. Inside the pump body will be the diaphragm or piston that pumps the water, and the seals or valves that control the flow. If it doesn't work, you will need to take it apart. Clean or renew any worn parts, reassemble and check its operation. Simple piston pumps may not be repairable and, in any case, are not expensive to replace.

Electric pumps

An electric motor operates the pump, which usually has a pressure cut-out switch. Some pumps run at a constant speed, using the switch to detect a pressure drop in the pipe between the pump and the tap when a tap is opened. The pressure switch then turns on the pump. When the tap is closed, the pressure builds up and stops the pump. Other pumps may have a variable speed and use

Below **This water pump is installed neatly in an accessible position, making inspection or removal easy.**

a different type of pressure switch, responding to how much the tap is opened.

If the pump doesn't run
✪ Check its fuse, and check that power is available at the pump, using a multimeter.
✪ Check that the pump impeller is not seized, which can occur due to freezing or infrequent use.
✪ Check that the pressure switch is not stuck in the 'off' position.

If the pump runs but doesn't cut out
✪ Check that the pump has primed.
✪ Check for a leak between the pump and the tap.
✪ Check that the pressure switch is not stuck in the 'on' position.

If the pump keeps cycling on and off
✪ Check that the pressure in the accumulator is correct.

The accumulator
The accumulator stops the pump cycling on and off when a tap is opened. It is pressurised with air or nitrogen, and when the pump runs, water is forced into the accumulator as a store of pressurised water. The initial gas pre-charge can leak away and may need to be restored occasionally. Simple accumulators have no diaphragm, and you need to follow the instructions to recharge them. Accumulators with a diaphragm are pumped up to the specified pressure using a tyre inflation pump and pressure gauge.

Right **The pump's pressure contacts can best be tested using a multimeter set on its resitance scale.**

Pressure switch

If the pump is not working and you have checked the electrical supply, the pressure switch will need to be checked next.

Undo the screws to remove the switch unit. An internal spring will push the switch unit away from the body.

Carefully remove the switch unit from the pump body. Take care not to lose the spring and other components.

Make sure the contact is free to move. If in doubt, check with a multimeter that the contacts are closing correctly.

The gas system

Liquid Petroleum Gas (LPG) is stored in a gas bottle to supply a cooker, space heater or water heater. LPG is an explosion hazard. Because it is heavier than air, any leakage will cause gas to accumulate in the boat's bilges, from which it can't escape.

Above **The regulator's vent hole may become blocked. If the gas flame is low, check this.**

The gas bottle

Gas bottles are filled with either butane or propane, according to the operating temperature, and are usually available on an exchange basis – although in some countries bottles can be refilled at a service station. When changing a gas bottle, ensure that it is first turned off.

Disconnect the bottle from the system, replace it with a new one, and ensure that the connector is properly secured.

Below **Replacing an empty gas bottle. Not all gas lockers are so conveniently located.**

The regulator

The gas is stored at such a high pressure that it is liquefied, and a special regulator is required to reduce the pressure so that it becomes a gas for use in the system. Different regulators are required for propane and butane, and these are not interchangeable. The regulator or the coupling to the LPG bottle is fitted with an ON/OFF control, which should be turned off when the system is not in use.

A diaphragm in the regulator has one side open to atmospheric pressure, and a blockage in this will cause the gas flame to be very low or even to go out. In this event, the breather hole in the regulator casing should be checked. The regulator will have a date code stamped on it, and regulations may require it to be changed at specified intervals. In any case, change the regulator if it looks corroded.

Gas bottle locker

The bottle and regulator should be installed in a self-draining locker so that any leaking gas cannot accumulate in the boat. This drain must be kept clear of any blockage. If a gas leak detector and an electrical shut-off solenoid are installed on the boat, these should also be within the self-draining locker.

Right **If you have a 'bubble' leak detector fitted, it should be checked when you open the gas bottle valve.**

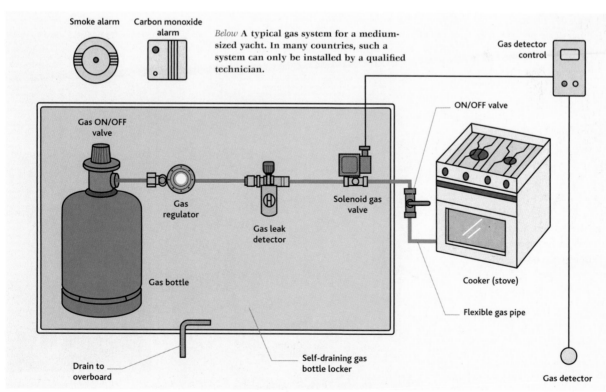

Smoke alarm   Carbon monoxide alarm

Below **A typical gas system for a medium-sized yacht. In many countries, such a system can only be installed by a qualified technician.**

Gas detector control

Gas ON/OFF valve

ON/OFF valve

Gas regulator

Gas leak detector

Solenoid gas valve

Gas bottle

Cooker (stove)

Flexible gas pipe

Drain to overboard

Self-draining gas bottle locker

Gas detector

The gas system 2

Above **Fit an electronic gas leak sensor as low as possible, but clear of bilge water.**

Gas leak detector

A 'bubble' leak detector can indicate even extremely small leaks in the system. Following its instructions on a regular basis will show if the system is gas-tight.

Solenoid shut-off valve

The solenoid valve can allow the system to be shut off remotely, either by a manual switch or by a gas alarm if an accumulation of gas is detected. They usually have a screwdriver-operated valve so that the gas can be turned back on in case of electrical failure.

ON/OFF valve

Any gas appliance must have an ON/OFF valve located where it can be reached in case of fire. This should be kept closed at all times unless the appliance is in use.

Flexible gas pipes

Any flexible gas pipe must be checked for wear and deterioration annually, and replaced if needed. Regulations may require it to be changed at specified intervals, and a date marking will be found on the pipe.

Gas appliances

All appliances should be serviced, at least annually, as specified in the installation/operating instructions. They should have flame failure devices, and if these are not working, they should be replaced.

Gas alarms

Because of the explosion hazard of LPG accumulating in the bilge, a gas alarm should be fitted. The detector should be mounted in the bilge or at floor level, because LPG is heavier than air. Most detectors do not tolerate being wet and will occasionally fail, especially if the bilge area contains water. Failure

Right **To test for gas leaks, paint joints with water mixed with washing up detergent. A leak will cause bubbles to appear.**

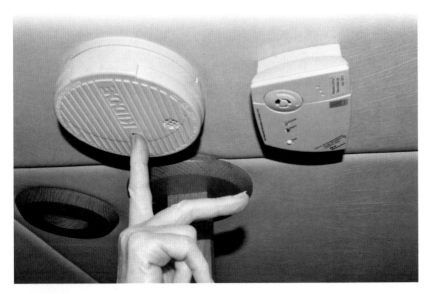

Smoke alarm

Not strictly part of the gas system, this gives an indication that there is smoke in the air, and therefore that a fire may be in progress. A smoke alarm's audio and visual indications should again be checked regularly for safe operation.

Above **If the smoke alarm is fitted near the galley, you may need to press the 'cooking' button to desensitise it when cooking.**

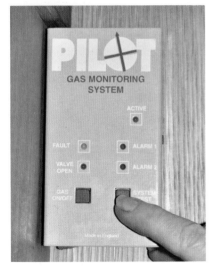

Left **The gas detector alarm can be tested using the test button. Some allow the gas bottle to be turned on and off remotely.**

Checking for gas leaks

A detector will indicate you have a gas leak, but will not show you its location. Any time a component in the gas system is disturbed or replaced, a leak test must be carried out. The easiest way to do this is to paint a mixture of washing up liquid and water on to any joint, with the gas turned on. Any leak is indicated by bubbles at the joint.

Carbon monoxide detector

In a poorly ventilated environment, the operation of any gas-burning appliance can cause levels of carbon monoxide to rise, possibly to a dangerous level. A carbon monoxide detector will alert you to this well before the level becomes a hazard. Regularly check any audio or visual indications made by the device to check it is working correctly.

will usually cause a continuous false alarm, and if the alarm is connected to a solenoid, it will also cut off the gas supply. In the event of a failure, you will have to switch the alarm off and operate the solenoid valve manually to turn the gas on. Expensive waterproof detectors are available. Normally the alarm should be switched on at all times, and the solenoid should be switched off (if it has a manual control), except when an appliance is in use.

Replacing gas piping & fittings

Gas installations need to be carefully examined at least once a year for leaks, and any worn or chafed component must be replaced. Flexible gas piping and some fittings have a finite life and need to be changed on a regular basis for safety reasons.

Rigid copper tubing

Some authorities require that all gas pipes are rigid copper tube, with flexible pipe used only at the gas bottle and at a gimballed cooker. Rigid copper tubing should be run in continuous lengths, with no joins except at each component. Where the tubing passes through a bulkhead, either a specialised bulkhead fitting should be used, or a grommet fitted to prevent chafe. The tubing must be supported regularly along its length; the spacing of the supports may be specified by national regulations. Some regulations require that the pipe can be visually inspected for its whole length.

Flexible piping

Flexible piping must be specified by the manufacturer as suitable to be used with LPG, and the date of manufacture should be printed on the cover. It may be connected to the barbed connector of a fitting or directly to the correct size of copper tube. In both cases, it must be secured with pipe clamps. It is also available in specific lengths with special end fittings to suit particular applications, such as direct fitting to a gas bottle.

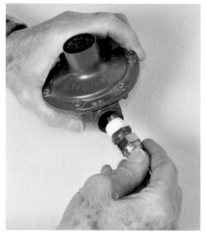

Above **Screwed fittings are best sealed using PTFE tape.**

Below **The gas supply pipes must be supported regularly, and an isolation valve fitted close to any appliance.**

Armoured flexible pipes

These come in specific lengths and have several different types of end fitting. They are used where chafe may occur, such as when connected to a gimballed cooker.

Pipe connections

Apart from where flexible pipes are attached to the system, all pipe connections must be compression fittings. These comprise a nut and an 'olive' that (when compressed by tightening of the nut) is forced to make a gas-tight seal between the tube and the fitting. Once compressed, the olive cannot be removed from the tube, but the joint can be separated from the fitting.

Making a joint

Use a pipe cutter to cut the tube to length (don't use a saw, or you will make a ragged edge that will not seal properly), and then de-burr the cut using a fine file or a deburring tool such as a reamer. Clean the tube with wire wool to remove tarnishing and dirt, then slide the nut onto the tube with the screwed end towards the join. Slide the olive onto the tube, push the tube fully into the fitting and tighten the nut.

No sealing compound is required when first making a joint, but if one is made and then undone, a small amount of LPG-compatible sealant may be used when the joint is remade. All joints should be leak-tested when made. The joint should not be over-tightened or the olive may be deformed and cause a leak; however, insufficient force will leave the olive loose on the tube.

Making a joint

Compression joints in copper tubing must be carefully made to avoid leaks. The beauty of this method is that the joints can be undone and rejoined as required.

Cut the tube to length using a pipe cutter, not a saw which will will leave rough ends.

Use a reamer to tidy the end of the pipe, which will have been squashed by the cutter.

The olive should be squashed onto the tube after fully tightening the nut.

Do not apply too much joint sealant; this is all that is required.

Push the tube into the fitting. The olive should be flush, leaving no gap.

Tighten the nut onto the fitting with a spanner, but do not tighten too hard.

Servicing heads

Unlike a domestic toilet, a boat toilet requires more than just cleaning to keep it serviceable. It is therefore essential that everyone on board knows how to use it properly and that at least one person understands how to maintain it.

Operating the heads

Marine toilets have small diameter waste pipes and several rubber valves, any of which can become blocked if anything other than human waste and soluble toilet paper are put into the bowl. Unblocking the heads can be a messy and unpleasant chore.

Below **A manual toilet is simple but prone to seal wear, so having a knowledge of how it works and a set of spares is a good idea.**

Anti-siphon valves

Where the toilet is mounted below or near to the waterline, anti-siphon valves are normally fitted to prevent sea water siphoning into the bowl. These valves need to be inspected and cleaned annually, but on many boats they are hidden away and it may take some exploration to find them. On electric toilets, these may be operated electrically.

SAFETY TIP

When servicing any toilet, wear protective gloves. Keep the gloves and toilet cleaning materials separate from any other cleaning kit for health reasons. Ensure the seacocks are closed when servicing the toilet. Failure to close the seacocks when the heads are not in use leaves the boat open to flooding if the anti-siphon valves fail.

Manual toilet with integral pump

Most production boats have a manually-operated toilet with an integral piston pump. The pump is used both to flush the toilet and to empty the bowl. When operating the piston in one direction, water is sucked into the bowl, and in the other direction the bowl is emptied. A lever selects whether the pump is used to simultaneously empty the bowl and flush it, or just to empty it (by holding the inlet non-return valve closed).

Servicing a manual toilet with integral pump

To avoid trouble, the toilet should be serviced annually. A service kit will be available, containing all the valves and seals required, and should always be carried on board in case attention is needed between services. Make sure that the kit matches the make and model of your unit. The kit will contain full service instructions.

Manual vacuum toilet

These toilets rely on a good seal between the lid, seat and bowl to allow a vacuum to be formed within the bowl when the external pump is operated. The external pump is of the diaphragm type and, when operated, the contents of the bowl are emptied, while the vacuum caused by this sucks flushing water into the bowl.

Servicing a manual toilet

Annual servicing of your toilet will help ensure trouble free operation. Combine this with strict rules about what goes into the toilet and you should have no problems.

A complete spares kit should be available for your toilet. Ensure you have the correct kit for you model.

Remove the valve unit from the toilet pump. This contains the macerating/non return valve which should be replaced.

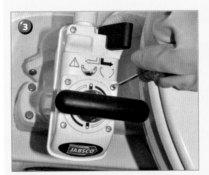

Undo the screws securing the top of the pump to the pump body. Ensure the flush lever is in the position shown above.

Remove the flushing pipe from the rear of the unit, then carefully pull the handle to lift the top off the pump cylinder.

Check the piston sealing and replace it if it shows any sign of wear or damage. Lubricate with petroleum jelly.

Replace the valves and gasket. Note which way round the gasket/valve assembly is fitted so the new one is replaced properly.

Servicing a manual vacuum toilet

On the toilet itself, only the seat seals need any attention. These need to be kept clean to ensure proper sealing, and when they become hardened with time, they will need to be replaced.

The size of the vent hole in the inlet anti-siphon valve controls the level of water remaining in the bowl after flushing, so keeping it clean is important. If you enlarge the hole while cleaning it, this will have a detrimental effect on the water level.

Maintaining the pump is a simple job, requiring the removal of the face plate to access the two non-return valves, which should be replaced annually. Spares kits are available, but the diaphragm itself will not need frequent replacement. These pumps are usually identical to a manual diaphragm bilge pump (see pages 142 and 143 for full servicing details).

Left **A vacuum toilet, like this Lavac, has a seal under the lid which, when the pump is operated, creates a vacuum in the bowl. The anti-syphon valve and pump are both visible in the locker behind.**

Right **The sea water inlet pump and strainer of an electric toilet. The strainer should be checked regularly in case there is an accumulation of weed.**

Electric toilets

Electric toilets come in a number of different forms:

✿ Very similar to a manual toilet with integral pump, but in this case the pump is electrically powered. The flush/empty control is on top of the pump body.

✿ A vacuum toilet with an electric diaphragm pump – so there's just an ON/OFF switch.

✿ An electrically-pumped toilet on which the pump and valves are hidden under the ceramic bowl. Control is achieved using an electronic unit and a control panel. These are normally supplied with water from the boat's fresh water system for flushing but may use sea water instead, in which case an extra sea water pump is required.

Servicing an electric toilet

As with manual toilets, servicing kits are available. The installation manual and the service kits will contain detailed instructions, and these should be followed. Those most similar to a manual toilet will require annual maintenance to replace valves and seals, while others may require less frequent servicing – see the user manual.

Where sea water flushing is provided, the sea water pump impeller will need to be changed occasionally, as will the motor's shaft seal.

Troubleshooting an electric toilet

Failure of the electrical supply will prevent the toilet from being used, so if the pump fails to run, first check the fuse or circuit-breaker. If these are OK, the control switch or electronic control will need to be investigated. If the toilet fails to flush, the fresh water or sea water pump may have failed. Follow the troubleshooting guide in the user manual.

Servicing an electric toilet

The mascerator pump is usually mounted at the base of the toilet, so servicing may require the toilet to be removed.

Some electric toilets use a turbine pump mounted under the ceramic bowl which will also need to be removed for servicing.

Clearing blocked heads

A blocked toilet usually requires at least partial dismantling of the toilet pump and valves, which is a messy and unpleasant job. This is an entirely avoidable situation, provided certain simple rules are followed. All crew and visitors should be fully briefed on how to operate the toilet correctly.

Avoiding a blocked toilet

Put only bodily waste into the toilet. If toilet paper has to be put into the toilet bowl, use only a type that dissolves easily, and use as little as possible.

In the event of a blocked toilet

Do not continue pumping. Attempting to clear a blockage by forcing the pump is likely to cause damage or a messy burst. Check that the discharge and inlet seacocks are open. If the unit is definitely blocked, before dismantling any of it, get a bucket to put the parts in. Wear suitable protective gloves.

Clearing a blockage in a manual toilet

The blockage is probably in the discharge pipe, somewhere between the toilet bowl and the macerator non-return (joker) valve, but if there is any foreign matter visible in the bottom of the toilet bowl, remove it by hand and try a quick pump to see if this has cleared the blockage.

If not, close both seacocks. Follow the instructions for servicing the pump and remove the pump and the non-return valve in the discharge pipe. There will be a leakage of foul water onto the floor. Clear any debris from the pipework between the bowl and the non-return valve, and clean the non-return valve itself. Next check the pump. If there is no obvious sign of blockage here, the problem is in the fixed pipework between the toilet and the outlet to sea or the holding tank.

> **TIP**
>
> It's always a good idea to have a full set of spares for the toilet on board, ready to hand. Spares from this kit can then be used when reassembling the toilet, if needed, after clearing a blockage.

Below **A well maintained manual pump gives an excellent flushing action and is less likely to get blocked.**

Remove the pipework from the diverter valve, if fitted, and check the valve for blockage. If the valve is clear, the fixed pipework will need to be cleared using a flexible drain-cleaning rod, or all the pipework will need to be removed and cleaned as necessary.

Reassemble everything, ensure all pipe clamps are secure, open the seacocks and pump the toilet. Clean up the mess!

Clearing a blockage in a manual-style toilet that has an electric pump

The procedure is the same as for a manual toilet.

Clearing a blockage in a vacuum toilet

Check the exit from the toilet bowl and clear as necessary. Remove the cover plate from the diaphragm pump and remove any debris. Check and clean the inlet and outlet non-return valves, and reassemble. If the system is still blocked, proceed as for a manual toilet.

Clearing a blockage in an electric toilet

Follow the instructions for servicing the toilet to find the blockage.

Macerating the waste

In a manual toilet, the waste is macerated by the rubber non return valve at the base of the toilet or in the diaphragm pump. This maceration is only partially effective so blockage is a little more likely than in an electric toilet with an electric macerator pump which chops up all the waste into a slurry.

Clearing a blockage

A blockage in the toilet will require the pump to be dismantled – so be prepared to have foul water spilling onto the floor. (See Tip on page 141.)

Remove the outlet from the base of the pump. There is a rubber valve in the outlet fitting which must be removed and cleaned.

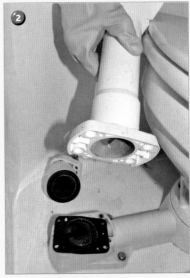

Undo and remove the screws from the base of the toilet pump, and then remove the pump itself from the toilet base.

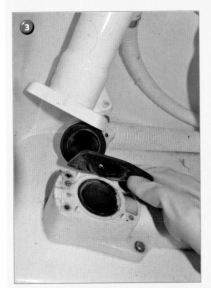

Remove the rubber valve from the toilet base, check and clean. Ensure there is no debris inside the bottom of the pump.

You may need to remove the drain valve from the toilet base to push any blockage through. Reassemble in the reverse order.

Black water systems

It is not always a good idea to discharge toilet waste directly overboard. Indeed, some authorities prohibit this, either by locking the overboard discharge valve or by the threat of very heavy fines. Many boats therefore have a holding tank to store the black water.

Holding tank system

There are a number of options when a holding tank is fitted:

- All waste is pumped to the holding tank.
- Waste may be pumped either overboard or into the holding tank, using a changeover valve.
- The tank may be emptied only from a deck-mounted discharge point.
- The tank may be emptied either through a deck-mounted discharge point or by gravity when the discharge valve is opened.
- The tank may be emptied either through a deck-mounted discharge point or by means of an on-board electric discharge pump.

Emptying and cleaning

Holding tanks require regular emptying, and ideally they should be flushed out with clean water to remove any build-up of solids. Some systems have a flushing-water filler on the deck, so they can be flushed while being emptied at the dockside. The tank should be flushed with clean water as frequently as possible.

Some systems are fitted with an odour filter in the tank vent system, and this will need to be changed annually. Otherwise, apart from regular emptying and flushing, the holding tank will require no routine maintenance.

Above **This small holding tank is translucent, allowing the contents to be checked, but cleaning is difficult unless the tank is removed.**

Below **An easily accessible inspection hatch on this holding tank makes cleaning easy. Not all builders are so considerate.**

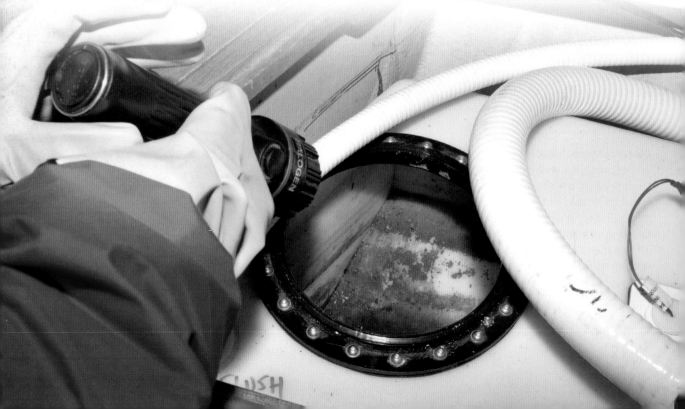

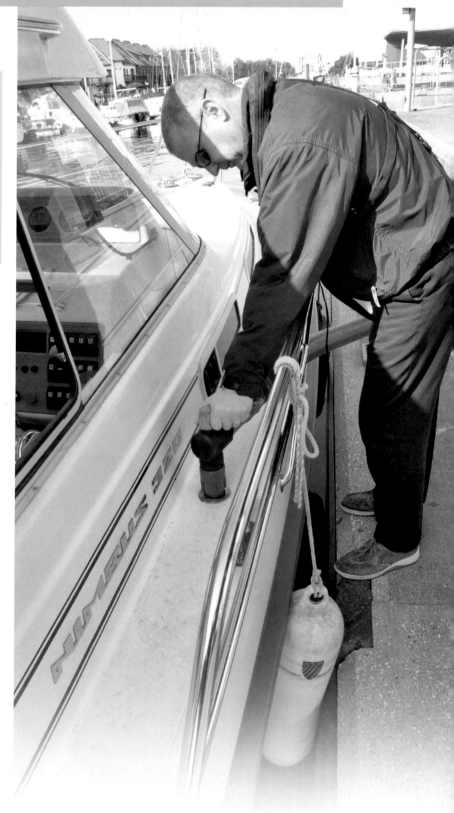

Right **The most satisfactory method of emptying the holding tank is at a marina pump out facility.**

On-board discharge pump

Where the holding tank can be emptied overboard in suitable open water, a discharge pump will be fitted unless it is a gravity-drop system.

A hand-operated diaphragm pump has non-return valves and a diaphragm, which may need occasional cleaning or replacement (see pages 142 and 143)

An electric macerating discharge pump usually has a stainless steel rotating blade and a rubber impeller pump. The impeller will need occasional replacement and a spare should be carried on board.

Cleaning the holding tank

Occasionally, it may be necessary to clean the inside of the holding tank, and there will normally be an inspection cover to allow access to the inside. Empty and flush the tank several times before removing the access panel. Inspect the inside of the tank, and clean it if necessary.

Servicing bilge pumps

Unwanted water in the boat as a result of damage, failure or a storm is evacuated using a bilge pump. Bilge pumps usually lie hidden away and forgotten until an emergency arises, and then the boat owner hopes that they will work and are big enough to save the boat.

Emptying water from the bilge

Water will accumulate in the lowest part of the boat, though the boat's structure will often form barriers to the downward flow of water. 'Limber' holes are usually arranged to allow the water to flow out of these compartments to the main bilge. A water strainer (often called a 'strum box'), placed at the lowest point, stops rubbish entering the bilge pump. Easy access to the strum box is essential so that it may be cleared of debris if necessary.

The bilge pump draws water from the strum box and pipes it overboard above the waterline. The pump may be either manual or electric, and ideally one of each will be fitted. A manual bilge pump is usually a diaphragm pump, and must be mounted in the cockpit in such a position that is comfortable to use for a long period. Putting a small quantity of water in the bilge will enable either type of pump to be tested.

Maintaining a manual bilge pump

These are normally very simple to maintain. The pump will have either a large screwed face plate that is rotated to release it or else a very large pipe clip that needs to be loosened to remove the flexible

Above **Regularly check the automatic float switch of an electric bilge pump.**

Below **Don't take your bilge pump for granted. Check it's working frequently, and keep the handle in an accesible place.**

rubber cover. A spares kit will have a diagram showing how to proceed. The diaphragm will need to be replaced only if it is perished or holed. There are two non-return valves, and these will lose their flexibility, so will need more frequent replacement.

Maintaining an electric bilge pump

Electric bilge pumps will be either diaphragm or centrifugal, the latter requiring no maintenance. An electric diaphragm pump is maintained in the same way as a manual one. In addition, you should be aware that failure of its electric motor is most likely due to corroded connections.

Automatic bilge pump switch

Electric pumps may have a switch that allows either manual or automatic operation. Float switches sometimes jam, so the float occasionally needs to be lifted up by hand to ensure it works. And because its wiring to the pump is in a damp area, any connections in the bilge need to be checked regularly for corrosion.

Bilge pump size

It is well worth noting that a 1.5in (38mm) hole, 1ft (300mm) below the waterline, will flood the boat at a rate of about 1,500 imperial gallons (6,750 litres) per hour. A manual bilge pump in a comfortable position

Above **Diaphragm bilge pumps usually have an inspection cover allowing any blockage to be cleared.**

is unlikely to shift more than about 400 gallons (1,800 litres) per hour. Most electric pumps are rated in US gallons per hour (a US gallon = 0.8 imperial gallons), and a commonly fitted 750 US gallon per hour pump will not keep pace with a 1in (25mm) hole in the boat.

Servicing a manual bilge pump

The pump's diaphragm can be changed after removing part of the casing.

The two non return valves should be checked and replaced if necessary.

Servicing seacocks

All 'through hull' skin fittings below or close to the waterline must be fitted with a seacock, a valve which allows the opening to be closed, to prevent leakage into the boat should a component fail or siphoning occur.

Different types of seacock

There are a number of different types of seacock in use:

☼ Traditional seacock

Also known as 'Kingston valves' or 'Blake's seacocks', these are integral with the skin fitting and made from bronze or DZR (dezincification resistant) brass. They have a tapered plug in a tapered seating, and a port is opened by rotating the handle through 90 degrees. These require annual servicing.

☼ Ball valves

These are made of marine bronze or glass-reinforced plastic. A handle is rotated through 90 degrees to open or close a spherical valve. Generally these cannot be serviced or repaired, so any problems will require the valve to be replaced.

☼ Gate valves

A 'gate' is raised or lowered by a sliding action when a control wheel is rotated through several turns. These can jam, and the user has no

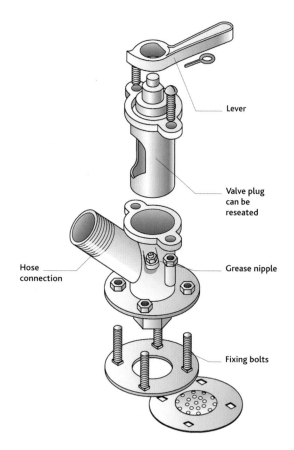

Lever

Valve plug can be reseated

Hose connection

Grease nipple

Fixing bolts

Above **This ball valve seacock is made of glass reinforced plastic. It's corrosion-free and approved by certification authorities.**

Left **A Blakes traditional seacock may be taken apart and serviced. Newer versions have a grease nipple.**

Right **This gate valve seacock has a cylindrical water stainer and is linked to the boat's anode system.**

visual clue as to whether the valve is open or closed. Although many of these valves can be serviced to replace the shaft seal and to grease the mechanism, they really have no place in a below-waterline application.

Servicing a traditional seacock

The tapered plug is either in line with the skin fitting or at right angles to it. Because these are specialist items, the manufacturer will provide installation and maintenance instructions. The tapered plug is 'lapped' to the mating housing (see below). To service, first take the boat out of the water. Following the instructions, remove the tapered plug, then clean the housing and plug with de-greasing agent. Lightly coat the plug surface with a lapping compound (cutting paste), push the plug back into the housing and rotate by hand backwards and forwards about ten times.

Withdraw the plug and inspect to check that the paste is evenly spread around the mating surfaces. If there are bare patches, recoat with paste, insert the plug, assemble the retaining plate and tighten gently. Continue this lapping process until all the mating surfaces fit properly, then thoroughly clean the valve, coat it with seacock grease and reassemble, following the manufacturer's instructions.

Replacing a seacock

Remove the pipe. If the through-hull fitting moves when you unscrew the seacock, it will also have to be removed.

With the through-hull fitting removed, clean the surface and remove any sealant from the inside of the hull.

Once a new through-hull fitting is in place, attach the replacement seacock, replace the hose and the hose clips.

The new fitting is in place. Check for leaks as the boat is relaunched and before the slings are removed.

Cooking equipment

Liquid Petroleum Gas (LPG) is still the most common fuel used for cooking on leisure boats, but there are alternatives, such as diesel, spirit and paraffin cookers. If you're connected to shore power, electric cooking is also a possibility.

LPG-powered hobs and ovens

On gas appliances with flame failure devices, if the device fails, it will need to be replaced. As this is connected directly to the gas supply for its burner, this work should only be undertaken by a qualified person.

If there's no ignition spark on a burner, first check that the burner base is clean and that there's no carbon on the igniter. Either of these will prevent the spark from jumping the gap. Piezo electric ignition uses a semiconductor to give a spark each time the ignition control is pressed. These need no maintenance unless the unit fails, when it must be replaced.

Above **The choice of fuel for your cooker depends on what type of boat you have and what energy supply is available locally.**

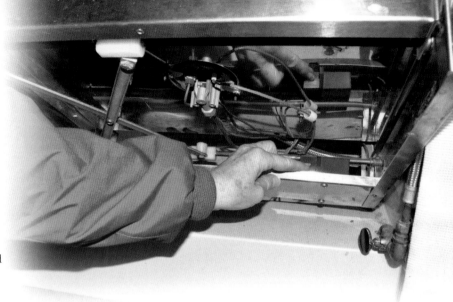

Right **Gas cookers often have a built-in ignition system. They may have a battery that needs occasional replacement.**

On units where a battery supplies power to an electronic ignition circuit, the battery will need occasional replacement, so check the user manual for details.

Because many of these appliances are not specifically designed for use in a marine environment, if you are experiencing ignition problems, the electrical connections may also need to be checked for corrosion.

Diesel-powered cookers

Some diesel cookers have quite complicated electrical control equipment powered by the boat's battery system, and all of them will require at least some disassembly of the unit for routine maintenance or repair. It is essential that the user handbook is followed to ensure safe and proper maintenance.

Left **Don't take your cooker for granted. Service it regularly, or it might break down just when you need it most.**

Paraffin-powered cookers

Paraffin (kerosene) cookers may have electronic ignition and an external flue, or need to be preheated using a 'denatured' alcohol such as methylated spirit before opening the paraffin valve. Maintenance should be carried out according to the manufacturer's instructions

Spirit stoves

Spirit stoves have a wick in a reservoir of alcohol. No routine maintenance is required.

Mains cooking appliances

The mains hook-up is likely to be limited to 13 or 15 amps, which rules out anything more than 3.5 kilowatts at 240 volts. Even with a generator, the available power is limited, so it's most likely that the boat owner will restrict any such use to small appliances such as microwaves, grills, toasters, kettles and the like. Even then, selective use of more than one at a time will be required so as not to trip the mains supply.

As these will be normal domestic appliances no user maintenance will be required other than keeping them clean. Apart from replacing a blown fuse, a failure will usually mean replacing the unit.

Changing the ignitor

To clean or replace the ignitor, you'll need to remove the burner cover.

The ignitor can then be removed. Clean it if it's sooty or replace it with a new one.

Refrigeration

Refrigeration is quite power hungry so careful thought needs to be given to its use and power supply. The power requirement for air-conditioning is more than the boat's battery system can cope with, so a hook-up to shore power or an on-board generator is a necessity.

Refrigerators

In a compressor refrigerator, the compressor pressurises gas and this causes the gas to heat up. Energy is removed by a heat exchanger, using either air or water to take the heat away. The now cool compressed gas is then allowed to expand rapidly, and it gets dramatically colder as it does so. This cold gas is what is circulated through the cold plate in the fridge.

Above **The failure of the fridge to cool down, even though the compressor is running, probably indicates the need for the gas refrigerant to be recharged.**

Compressors

Boat fridges may be fitted with either electric or engine-driven compressors. The first type is driven by an electric motor, powered by the boat's battery. Maintenance entails ensuring that the electrical connections are clean and secure.

In the second type, an electronic clutch allows the compressor to be driven by the engine when it is running. The electrical connections, belt drive and clutch all need to be checked periodically for correct operation.

Air-cooled heat exchangers

In these, an electric fan blows air through a cooling matrix, through which the refrigerant passes. The matrix needs to be kept free of dust, and the electrical connections must be checked periodically. The airflow path needs to be kept unobstructed, and the air must be drawn from a compartment separated from the outlet.

Left **A fridge helps keep food fresh and beer cool but does make heavy demands on a boat's battery.**

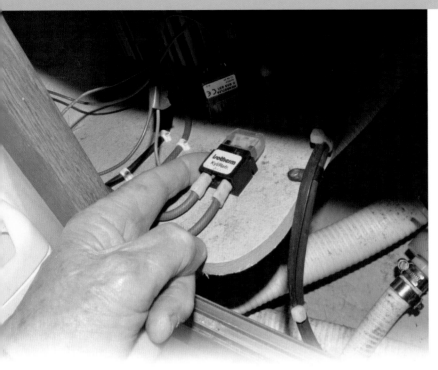

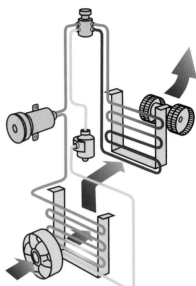

Above **If the refrigerator won't run, check its fuse. The resistance of the fuse itself may be high enough to set off the fridge's own low-voltage cut-out if the battery voltage is low.**

Above **The fridge's compressor and heat exchanger will need to be cleaned of dust and dirt occasionally.**

Water-cooled heat exchangers

In this type, heat is extracted by pumping sea water through a heat exchanger mounted inside the boat, or by allowing the refrigerant to flow through a heat exchanger mounted in the water outside the hull. The sea water pump may be engine- or electrically driven, and either type will require appropriate annual maintenance.

The refrigerant

Over time, refrigerant may leak out of the system. Although the fridge appears to run normally, it will not become cool enough, and ice may never form on the cold plate. Maintenance requires the refrigerant to be topped up or replaced. The best practice is to drain the refrigerant completely and replace it with dry refrigerant. This is a job requiring specialist equipment.

Above **Air-conditioning works in a similar way to a refrigerator, allowing cooled dry air to be circulated around the boat.**

▮ Low pressure gas
▯ High pressure liquid
▨ High pressure gas
▮ Low pressure liquid

Air-conditioning

Air-conditioning uses the same principles as refrigeration. The units are much larger and require mains electrical power, either from a shore hook-up or an on-board generator. The unit will need to be maintained according to its user manual, and for most people this will mean it requires professional attention.

Servicing cabin heaters

If the boat is going to be used in the cooler seasons, cabin heating will make life much more comfortable, especially overnight. Heaters, whatever their type, are not entirely maintenance-free and, for safety reasons, they need to be serviced annually – as well as having any faults fixed if they occur.

In-cabin heaters

A heater may be situated in the saloon, in which case it needs a flue to vent combustion gases overboard. As most use up oxygen from within the cabin, sufficient ventilation must be provided at all times the heater is lit. There are two main types of in-cabin heating:

⊛ **Solid fuel** These stand on a fireproof base and maintenance consists of keeping the flue clear of soot and ensuring the integrity of the flue. The flue vent design should ensure that the fire 'draws' properly and prevents backdraughts down the flue.

⊛ **Drip-feed diesel or paraffin (kerosene)** These may have a gravity-fed fuel system from a tank mounted close to the heater or they may be pump-fed from the boat's diesel fuel tank. There are electrical supplies to the pump and fan, if fitted. Manufacturer's instructions must be followed with respect to maintenance.

Heaters mounted outside the cabin

These draw their combustion air from outside the accommodation, and vent exhaust fumes overboard. Using a heat exchanger, hot fresh air flows around the accommodation, usually by means of 4in (100mm) flexible ducts with fan assistance. Some systems heat water in a heat exchanger and this hot water is pumped through small bore pipes to heat radiators or fan matrix heaters,

Left **The metering valve and the burner of a drip-feed diesel heater. With the covers open, inspection is easy.**

Right A diesel cabin heater has an electronic ignitor which lights the burner when the heater is started. The ignitor may fail and need to be replaced or cleaned.

SAFETY TIP

If your heater uses cabin air for combustion, fitting a carbon monoxide alarm is a wise precaution, because CO is invisible, odourless and, most importantly, poisonous.

and may also heat the domestic hot water. Diesel fuel, paraffin (kerosene) or Liquid Petroleum Gas (LPG) may be used for combustion.

Maintenance of external heaters

External heaters will have an electronic control system, fuel pump for liquid fuel, an ignition plug and a circulation fan or pump. Maintenance and accessibility to the working parts will vary, so it is important to follow the manufacturer's maintenance instructions.

Failure of external heaters

Infrequently used heaters are much more prone to failure than those in regular use. Make a point of firing up the heater frequently, even in the summer. Running the heater for ten minutes on your way home will reduce the chance of ignition failure and seizure of motor and fan bearings.

Servicing a diesel heater

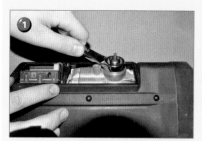

Remove the casing as necessary. Disconnect the electrical connector, and unscrew the ignitor plug.

Remove the ignitor plug and inspect its condition. Clean it if it is sooted up, or replace it if it is damaged.

The fuel pump is mounted in the fuel supply pipe. If you can't find it, switch the heater on and listen for a clicking sound.

Check the fuel pump electrical connector, which may become corroded, and clean it if necessary. Reassemble in reverse order.

Servicing steering systems

Probably the most important system on the boat is its steering. It is also one of the least inspected and the most taken for granted. Although most steering systems need little maintenance, they must receive regular inspection. An emergency tiller should always be available.

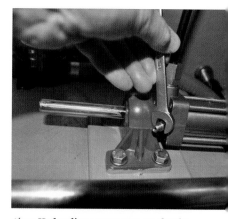

Transom-mounted rudders
With the rudder bearings mounted externally, inspection is easy. 'Pintles' are the pins attached to the transom on which the rudder pivots, while the bearings mounted on the rudder are known as 'gudgeons'. The pintles and gudgeons eventually wear and need to be replaced or repaired. If new ones are not easily available, a good marine engineer may be able to make copies.

The pivot of a lifting tiller will also wear. Boring out the holes and using a larger pivot bolt may be the easiest repair. A suitable piece of wood carried on board could make an emergency tiller if the old one breaks.

Above **Hydraulic systems may need to be bled if the steering is spongy or there has been a fluid leak.**

Hull-mounted rudders
The rudder shaft is mounted in a tube containing several bearings and a watertight seal at the top. Whenever the boat is dried out, the bearings should be checked for wear by pushing and pulling the rudder sideways at its tip. Renewal will require the rudder to be dropped clear of the boat.

The water seal is mounted above the waterline, so at rest no water should leak into the boat. Any leakage observed under way (due to heel or waves) must be investigated, and with care this may be done with the boat afloat, provided that the top of the tube is well above the waterline.

Wheel steering with cables
The cables must be inspected at least once a year, looking out especially for broken strands, which will require replacement

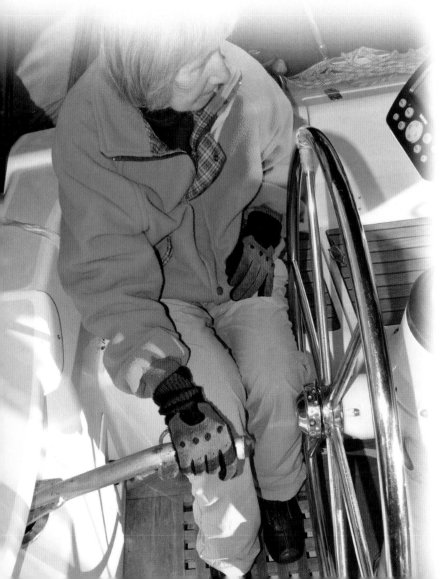

Left **Ensure that the emergency steering is tested at least annually.**

of the cable. All pivots, connections, split pins and adjusters need to be checked, and the cable tension adjusted. Cable adjusters should be tightened by hand to avoid over-tensioning, but ensure that lock nuts are fully tightened by spanner.

Push-rod steering

There are bearings at the end of each rod, which have length adjusters with lock nuts. The condition of the bearings and the tightness of lock nuts need to be checked at least once a year.

Hydraulic steering

A hydraulic ram moves the rudder, and is connected to the steering pump using hydraulic pipes. The pump may be mounted directly within the steering wheel, or remotely operated by rod or cable from the wheel.

A reservoir containing hydraulic fluid supplies the system. The level of this fluid needs to be checked frequently. Spare fluid (check the user manual) must be carried on board, and any leak must be found and remedied.

At least once a year (and immediately a leak is suspected) check the hydraulic rams for leaks. Check all pivots for wear and all locking devices for security at least annually.

Pivots and bearings

Carry out inspection and lubrication at least annually.

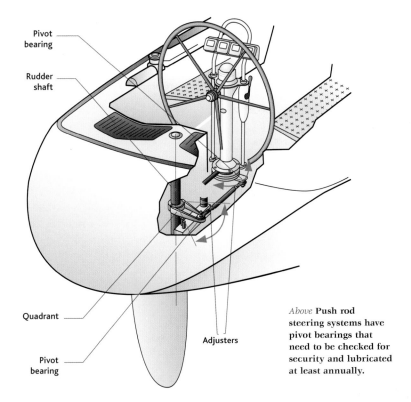

Pivot bearing

Rudder shaft

Quadrant

Pivot bearing

Adjusters

Above **Push rod steering systems have pivot bearings that need to be checked for security and lubricated at least annually.**

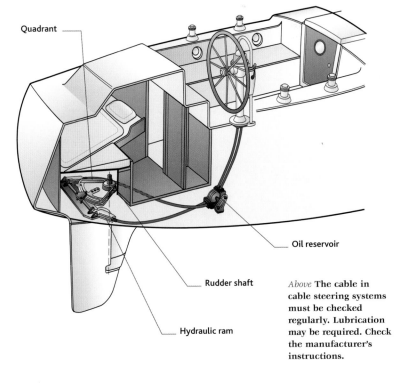

Quadrant

Oil reservoir

Rudder shaft

Hydraulic ram

Above **The cable in cable steering systems must be checked regularly. Lubrication may be required. Check the manufacturer's instructions.**

Anchor windlasses

The bigger the boat or the less physically able the crew, the more need there is for an anchor windlass. An adequate anchor, together with its chain, requires quite a lot of effort to haul in, so if you do much anchoring, a manual or electric windlass may be a necessity on your boat.

Manual windlasses

These are mounted above deck and usually have a horizontal axis, with a chain gypsy on one side and a warping drum on the other. They are operated by a long lever, using a back and forward motion. Some models have a vertical axis, with the gypsy and drum on top, and are operated by a winch handle.

Maintaining manual windlasses

A clutch enables the anchor to be let down under gravity, and this requires regular and frequent maintenance to ensure that the clutch and manual release do not seize. The clutch also allows the warping drum to operate without rotating the gypsy.

TIP

Never let the anchor loads be taken by the windlass because in heavy conditions the shaft can fail due to excessive loading. Once the anchor is set, take the chain or rope and make it fast to a strong cleat or Samson post.

Below **Vertical axis windlasses are becoming increasingly popular, for use both on sailing yachts and powerboats.**

To service, engage the pawl to stop the gypsy rotating, then use the operating handle to release the clutch. If necessary, use a lever inserted between the gypsy and the windlass to move the gypsy out along its shaft. Apply a grease gun to the shaft nipple until grease emerges along the shaft. Then tighten the clutch ready for re-use.

The gear-case contains oil, the level of which will need to be checked annually – and, if it looks milky because it has been contaminated with water, it will need to be changed. The handbook will give the specification and quantity of the lubricant.

If there is a warping drum, this is often made of aluminium and, when mounted on a steel shaft, corrosion can make it very difficult to remove when you need to, unless it has been removed and cleaned annually.

Electric windlasses

Electric windlasses may have a horizontal axis or a vertical axis (in which case they should be properly called a 'capstan'). The electric motor may be mounted either above or below deck. In the case of a horizontal axis unit, manual operation is achieved in the same way as the manual windlass, whereas vertical axis units use a winch handle to release the clutch and rotate the gypsy in manual mode. Because the winch handle is not geared, vertical units require a great deal of effort when used manually.

Servicing a manual windlass

A manual windlass should be serviced annually to ensure it runs smoothly. Your handbook will tell you exactly what's required, but this is a typical sequence.

The gypsy's clutch must be lubricated through the shaft nipple with waterproof grease.

Loosen the clutch ring by rotating it counter clockwise. Note that the pawl should be engaged, not open as show.

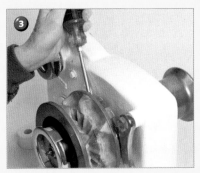

Ensure that the gypsy can be slid sideways to release the clutch cone.

Undo the retaining bolt securing the warping drum.

Slide off the warping drum, ensuring the key doesn't fall out and get lost.

Remove the key, clean the key-way groove and re-grease. Reassemble components.

Anchor windlasses 2

Maintaining electric windlasses

The clutch of a horizontal electric windlass will operate in the same manner as a manual one, and the same maintenance considerations apply. With a vertical windlass, if there is a manual override, it should be used frequently to ensure that the clutch disengages. Any maintenance required will be specified in the user manual.

For both types of electric windlass, an annual check of the gearbox oil level is required, topping up the level as necessary or changing the oil if it is contaminated. If oil is leaking from the shaft seals, they will need to be replaced.

Electric motor above deck

Many manufacturers recommend that the seal between the motor casing and the windlass body is replaced annually. To do this, remove the securing nuts or bolts from the casing, then carefully remove the casing. Examine the motor and electrical connections, cleaning and re-protecting them as necessary. Spray the motor and connections with a water repellent.

Next, replace the seal between the case and the body, cleaning the mating surfaces if required. Replace the casing and tighten the fastenings. Finally, check the tightness of the bolts securing the windlass to the deck.

Electric motor below deck, in the chain locker

This is the most vulnerable position for the motor, and it needs to be checked at least once a year. The motor casing will get very damp and will remain so, as will the electrical connections. The chain may also hit the unit. To maintain it:

- ✪ Check the tightness of the bolts securing the windlass to the deck.
- ✪ Regularly dry and clean all the components in the chain locker.
- ✪ Check the electrical terminals for corrosion and remake them if required.
- ✪ Repaint damaged parts.
- ✪ Treat all surfaces with a water-repellent product.

Above **Windlass motors mounted in the chain locker are subject to condensation and should be checked regularly.**

Electric motor below deck, not in the chain locker

In this position, the motor and electrical connections are protected in a dry environment. To maintain, simply check the tightness of the mounting bolts and of the electrical connections, and tighten up if necessary.

Up and down controls

Deck-mounted switches are vulnerable to corrosion if their waterproof membranes are damaged, so check these switches at least annually for their condition. Cockpit-mounted switches are probably less vulnerable, but also need to be checked for damage and operation.

Servicing an electric windlass

Remove the cover, following the handbook instructions. Check that the sealing gasket is not damaged and replace it if necessary.

Check the motor and electrical connections for corrosion and clean as required. Apply silicone grease to the connectors annually.

Windlass battery isolation switch and fuse or circuit breaker

Normally these need no maintenance, but if the fuse keeps blowing or the circuit breaker keeps tripping, the cause needs to be discovered and rectified.

Windlass battery

The windlass may be powered from the service battery, engine battery or its own dedicated battery. The current taken by the windlass is very high, and all connections need to be clean and secure to avoid excessive voltage drop. Unless maintenance-free, the battery level needs to be checked at least every three months, and topped up if required.

At least once a year, check all electrical connections for security and cleanliness. Then, after ensuring that the battery is not being charged – engine not running, battery charger off – check the battery voltage against the following values (the 24-volt system is shown in brackets):

❂ At rest and fully charged, the reading should be 12.8 volts (25.6 volts).
❂ With the windlass running, the reading should not be less than 10 volts (20 volts).

The voltage should quickly recover to 'at rest' value after running the windlass. If voltages are much lower than expected, the connections need to be rechecked, and if they are good, the battery will need to be replaced.

Right **This windlass is mounted above deck where it can be checked, hosed down and maintained easily.**

Testing & marking ground tackle

The anchor and its chain or rope may be something you use only in an emergency, or it may form part of your normal boating lifestyle. All the 'ground tackle' needs to be maintained in good condition and marked in such a way that you can use it easily and confidently when required.

What is ground tackle?

Ground tackle consists of the anchor and everything connecting it to the boat:

- The anchor itself.
- The connector that joins the anchor to the rode.
- The rode.
- The connector that joins the rode to the boat.

Sometimes the length of anchor chain is relatively short, with the extra length made up of rope. Collectively the chain and rope (if any) is known as the 'rode' or 'cable'. The connection between the rode and the boat must be of rope, securely attached to the boat and long enough to be easily accessible on or from the deck. This is so that it can be cut in an emergency – something that can't be done if a chain-only rode is shackled or bolted directly to the boat.

Marking the rode

To minimise the chance of dragging your anchor, a minimum length of rode is required according to the depth, weather conditions and whether the rode is all chain or chain and rope. The length of rode that you let out can be measured by a chain counter, but more commonly it is assessed by marking the rode in some manner. An alternative, if you have no windlass, is to lay the necessary length out on deck before 'letting go' the anchor.

Above **You can use cable ties (or coloured cord) to mark individual lengths. The number of ties represent specific multiples of metres (or feet).**

Below **Spray-painting the chain at intervals will give a good visual cue to the amount of chain let out.**

There are a number of methods that may be used to mark the chain:

✪ Paint the chain at predetermined lengths, say every 15ft (5m).
✪ Use proprietary chain markers.
✪ Use electrical cable ties. These are cheap, easily replaced and can be felt in the dark. A different number of ties can be used at each point to indicate the length.

Rope can also be marked with cable ties through the 'lay'. Whether you decide to use multiples of feet or metres for your marking intervals will usually depend on the units in which depths are marked on the charts for your usual cruising areas.

Ground tackle maintenance

At least annually, all the rode should be laid out on the ground and inspected. Carefully check the connector between the anchor and the chain for any defect, including corrosion. Also check the general state of the chain, including the galvanising – if the anchor and the chain are galvanised and the connector is stainless steel, galvanic action may remove the galvanising.

If part of the rode is rope, check the chain-to-rope splice for condition, and remake if necessary. Check the condition of the rope, throughout its length, and check the condition of the rope connecting the rode to the boat. Make sure that it is long enough and that it is securely fastened both to the rode and the boat.

Making a chain/rope splice

The splice joining the chain and the rope is subject to a lot of wear and must be able to pass around the gypsy. Here is a well-established method of making a durable splice.

Wrap insulating tape around the rope at least 15 times the diameter of the rope from its end and unlay the three strands.

Pass two strands through the first link from one direction, and the other through the link from the opposite direction.

Pass one strand through the lay of the rope and pull tight, twisting the strand to tighten its lay.

Pass the second strand under the lay and over the first strand.

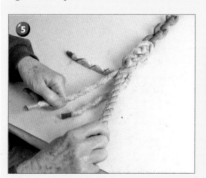

Repeat with the third strand. Remove the tape binding the rope and pull the three strands tightly to remove any slack.

After making at least five tucks, smooth and tighten the splice. Trim the ends to length, and heat seal each one.

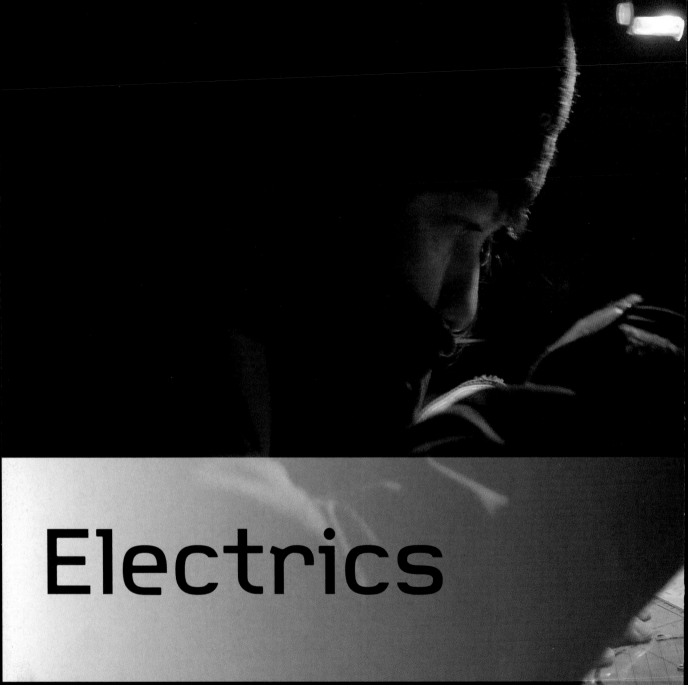

Electrics

6

Wiring system & earthing

Modern boats rely heavily on electrical systems, both for domestic functions and for operating the boat. Unless you are adding new circuits, maintenance consists mainly of checking the security and cleanliness of all connections.

Low voltage system

Like a car's, a boat's normal electrical system is low voltage (usually 12 volts, but sometimes 24 volts on larger boats) direct current (DC), powered directly from the boat's batteries. The batteries are charged by running the propulsion engine, using an on-board generator, or connecting to a mains-powered charger. Although the voltage is low, currents can be very high, and incorrect installation or inadequate maintenance can easily cause a fire.

The battery

The battery stores electrical charge so that it is available when required. Compared with household electrical consumption, its storage capacity is pretty small, so owners need to be strict about rationing the use of electrical equipment unless their boats are frequently hooked up to a mains supply.

Battery capacity is measured in amp hours. Simplistically speaking, this means that a fully charged 100 amp hour battery should supply 100

TIP

✪ The engine start battery should be isolated from any domestic loads so that there will always be sufficient battery power to start the engine, even if the domestic battery has been flattened.

✪ When adding new equipment or troubleshooting an electrical fault, a wiring diagram can prove an invaluable aid. Boatbuilders often fail to provide a proper wiring diagram, and subcontractors rarely supply one, so the boat owner ends up at a loss. If at all possible, make a proper wiring diagram for yourself.

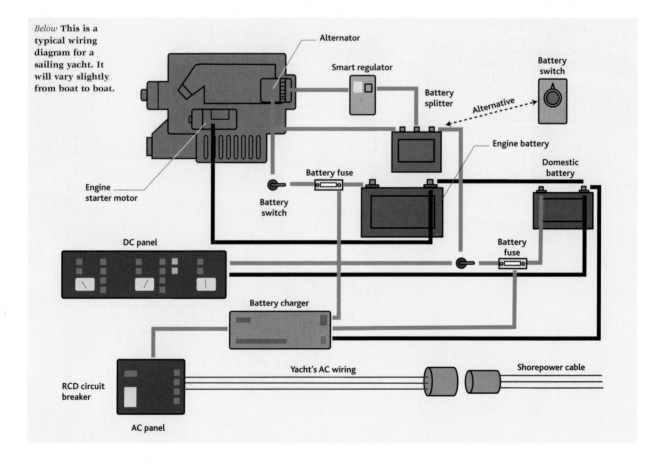

Below **This is a typical wiring diagram for a sailing yacht. It will vary slightly from boat to boat.**

Alternator

Smart regulator

Battery splitter

Battery switch

Alternative

Engine battery

Domestic battery

Battery fuse

Engine starter motor

Battery switch

DC panel

Battery fuse

Battery charger

Yacht's AC wiring

Shorepower cable

RCD circuit breaker

AC panel

amps for one hour, or one amp for 100 hours. (In reality, using 100 amps would discharge more quickly and one amp more slowly.)

Current is only part of the story, because equipment is rated by its 'power', which is measured in watts and is obtained by multiplying the current (in amps) by the voltage. Thus a 25 watt, 12 volt navigation light bulb draws a current of slightly over 2 amps, and would fully discharge a 100 amp hour battery in 48 hours.

Batteries may be connected in groups, or banks, to increase either capacity or voltage, and there may be more than one bank. For example, there may be one bank of batteries for 'domestic' services and another for engine starting.

Right **Batteries must be firmly secured to prevent them falling out when heeling.**

Below **A twin-engine motorboat will have two individual systems, which may have a battery link switch.**

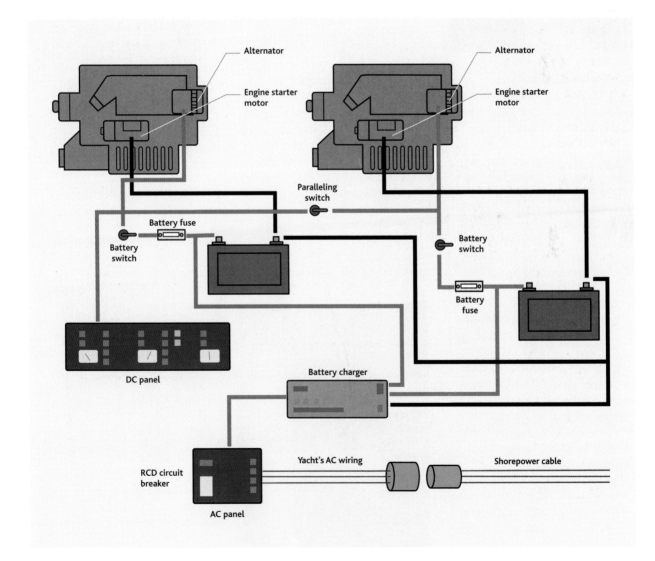

Left **Some sensitive electronics may require a noise filter.**

runs via the fuse/circuit breaker panel, while the negative wire returns to one of several terminal blocks connected directly to the battery.

Battery charging system

The battery is charged by an alternator attached to the engine. When the engine is running, the battery is being charged. Additionally, a mains-powered battery charger may be fitted so that the battery can be charged when connected to shore power.

Twin-engine installations

Where there are two engines, each will have its own batteries to charge. Often one engine's battery bank will be larger than the other's, and this will be used for domestic services. It is usual for a battery link switch to be fitted, enabling both engines to be started even if one battery is flat. Boatbuilders may well have their own methods of supplying the various services from the two battery banks, so owners will need to

Battery isolation switch

It is essential that a battery can be isolated from all of the electrical circuits, and this is done by the battery isolation switch. There are two reasons for this: so that the battery can be isolated from all the circuits in case of a fault; and so that it cannot be inadvertently discharged by accidentally leaving a circuit switched on. If there is more than one bank of batteries, it should be possible to isolate the banks from each other as well as from their individual circuits. This is achieved by a single multifunction switch or by several individual switches.

Low voltage distribution system

In order to restrict the effect of any circuit faults to only a few items, the distribution system consists of separate circuits, each served by its own fuse or circuit breaker. These are normally mounted on a centralised panel, and have indicator lights to show when the circuit is switched on.

Low voltage circuits consist of two wires. Usually (though not invariably) the positive supply is the one that

familiarise themselves with the user manual.

Mains voltage system

Many boat owners fit accessories that require mains electricity (alternating current, high voltage, also known as 'line power'), and so cannot be supplied directly from the boat's battery. In this case, there will be a separate wiring system, powered by connecting to a dockside supply. As with all mains electricity, inappropriate use of this supply can be lethal.

If mains power is required when not alongside, it is possible to

Left **If there are two nuts on a connector stud, use spanners on both to prevent the stud rotating and causing internal damage to the unit.**

Above **A battery monitor will enable the state of charge to be displayed.**

Right **An efficient charging system will incorporate a charge controller.**

convert low voltage DC power into mains voltage AC. However, this makes heavy demands on the battery, so some owners fit a separate engine specially to charge the batteries and supply mains voltage. This is commonly known as a 'gen-set'.

Mains distribution

Power enters the boat from a cable connecting to the dockside supply. The mains cable consists of three wires: live (aka 'hot'), neutral and earth (or 'ground'). The first component in the system must be a special circuit breaker that detects

any fault and trips in a small fraction of a second to isolate the mains supply. Its test switch should be operated frequently to check the action. Mains power is then distributed via circuit breakers to mains sockets (outlets) as in a normal house installation.

Below **Each circuit will be supplied from the electrical service panel.**

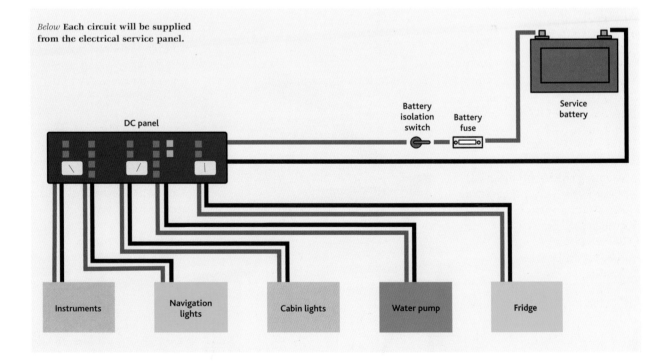

Fuses & circuit breakers

If a wire's insulation breaks down or a connection comes adrift, it is possible that positive and negative wires may come into contact with each other in a short circuit. A fuse or circuit breaker quickly cuts off the power to prevent overheating or a fire.

Circuit protection

Circuits should be protected by either fuses or circuit breakers. A fuse is a device containing a short length of thin wire. If the current rises above its rated value, the wire overheats and breaks. Fuses are rated according to how much 'over-current' they allow and how long they take to 'blow'. A blown fuse should be replaced with one of like value and type.

Circuit breakers visually indicate that they have 'tripped' and this occurs at a current a little more than its rated value. Some operate thermally and some magnetically. Circuit fuses and circuit breakers must be able to withstand the maximum total current flowing in their respective circuits. Failure of the fuse (or tripping of the circuit breaker) will disable all the equipment in that circuit.

Ideally every length of wire, including the heavy battery cables, should be protected. This requires that, as well as all the small fuses in the various circuits, a high-value fuse should be connected very close to the battery terminal, though many builders don't do this.

Above **Panel-mounted circuit breakers with indicator lights are ideal.**

Below **Fuses can be tested with a multimeter set to 'resistance'.**

Right **Inevitably, some individual fuse holders will need to be fitted. Make sure you know their location.**

Equipment protection

Individual equipment fuses protect the devices from further damage if a fault occurs 'within the box'. They may be mounted internally or there may be a fuse holder in its individual supply wire. Failure will disable only that piece of equipment.

Troubleshooting

⊙ If only one piece of equipment has failed, check its fuse.

⊙ If more than one item fails to work, check that circuit's fuse or circuit breaker.

⊙ Blown fuses can be found by removing them and checking them visually or with a test meter.

⊙ Tripped circuit breakers are identified visually, for example, the light goes out.

New installations and maintenance

All new equipment and its wiring must be protected by fuses or circuit breakers. Installation instructions will indicate the rating and type of protection required.

To maintain circuits, periodically check all connections for corrosion and security.

Where connections are exposed to potentially corrosive conditions, you should protect them by coating with petroleum jelly or silicone gel.

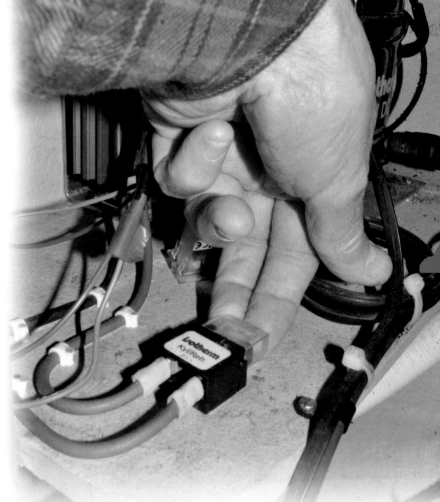

Above **If at all possible, keep all the fuse holders in an accessible position, and preferably in one place.**

TIP

⊙ All circuit protection fuses should be easily accessible, not hidden behind panelling.

⊙ Some items of equipment, such as refrigerators, have quite a high starting current. If the wiring is inadequate, or the battery voltage is low, the added resistance of a fuse may well cause the electronic control to shut down the unit or even prevent it starting, because the voltage at the unit is too low. Replacing the fuse with a surge-tolerant circuit breaker may solve a persistent problem of this type.

Soldering & replacing connectors

Most electrical connections never see the light of day, yet the integrity of these connections is essential for the reliable operation of the boat's various electrical systems. Vibration, rough handling and corrosion due to the marine environment all contribute to a gradual deterioration of connections, which may result in equipment failing to operate.

Avoiding connector strain

Four types of electrical connector are commonly found on boats – soldered, crimped, screwed and clamped – all of which are examined individually below. However, connectors of any type must never be placed or left under mechanical strain, otherwise they may fail. Therefore it's essential that the wiring on either side of a connector is fully supported.

Soldered connections

Soldered connections have excellent mechanical strength and, if the soldering work is carried out properly, have almost zero electrical resistance, even if the surface is corroded. The correct way to make soldered connections is as follows:

✪ Strip the insulation to expose just sufficient wire core.
✪ Clean the tip of the hot soldering iron and melt a small quantity of flux-cored solder onto it – 'tinning' the iron.
✪ 'Tin' each wire/connector by heating it with the hot soldering iron and applying the flux-cored solder to the wire (not the iron).
✪ Place the two components together and apply the iron to them to heat up the components so that the solder melts and combines.
✪ Remove the iron, holding the components absolutely still until the solder hardens.

Wires that are to be joined can be first twisted together to increase mechanical strength – but be aware that this makes subsequent disassembly more difficult. When joining two wires, you should insulate the join. If you intend to use sleeves or 'heat shrink' tubing to do this, remember to thread them onto the wire prior to soldering.

Crimped connections

The connector is mechanically squeezed onto the wire using a crimping tool. Mechanical strength is good provided sufficient compression is applied by the tool. Ratchet tools supply much more compression. Electrical conductivity is good, given sufficient compression, but corrosion can occur between the connector and the wire over time. The correct method of making these connections is:

Soldering connections

Strip off the end of the plastic sheathing using a wire stripper.

'Tin' (i.e. apply solder to) each component separately.

Bring the wires into contact and apply heat with the soldering iron. This will melt the solder so that the components join without any need for additional solder.

The two components are now joined. If you won't need to dismantle the joint, the two wires can be twisted together and tinned and soldered as one component.

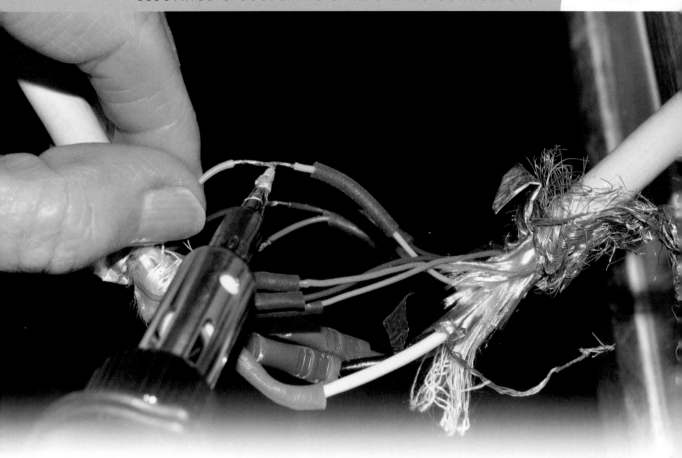

- ✪ Use the correct (colour coded) size of connector for the wire diameter.
- ✪ Strip just sufficient insulation from the wire to enter the connector sleeve.
- ✪ Insert the wire into the connector.
- ✪ Match the crimping tool anvil to the connector size by its colour.
- ✪ Use the ratchet crimping tool to squeeze the connector to its full extent.

Screwed connections

Screwed connectors allow easy dismantling of the joint. However, they don't inhibit corrosion, so should be liberally smeared with silicone sealant. The correct method is:

- ✪ Strip the insulation to expose just sufficient wire core.
- ✪ Insert the wire into the connector.
- ✪ Tighten the clamping screw securely.
- ✪ If the connector is exposed to corrosion, coat it with silicone sealant.

Clamped connections

Instead of using a screw, security is achieved by a lever clamp. These are neater and often smaller than screw clamps, and can be soldered to a circuit board.

Above **Soldering is best done with a gas soldering iron. Ensure that each joint is insulated from the others using a sheath.**

Below **A heavy-duty crimping tool can be used with a hammer or in a vice.**

Battery installation & maintenance

For most boat owners, batteries form an essential adjunct to life aboard. However, they tend to be hidden away, forgotten and often abused, leading to slow deterioration until they suddenly fail completely. Proper installation, good maintenance and knowledgeable use will prolong battery life significantly.

Battery types

The construction and technology of a battery is dictated by the type of use it will get and how much money you are prepared to spend. Engine starting requires a very high current for a very short time, and is easily satisfied by a reasonable quality lead-acid battery. If used for no other purpose, these can last for six years or more.

Supplying domestic services requires a relatively low current that can be maintained for a long time.

Above **A strong wooden batten is often the best way to secure a battery.**

Service batteries can be wet lead-acid, absorbed glass mat (AGM), gel or, at the most expensive end of the scale, nickel-cadmium (NiCd/nicad). Apart from dual-purpose lead-acid and some AGM types, they are not suitable for engine starting.

If a long service life is required from them, lead-acid batteries must not be discharged by more than 50 per cent of their capacity before being recharged.

Battery capacity

Battery capacity is measured in amp hours (see page 162) and a typical boat battery will be around 100 amp hours – anything more will be too heavy to lift. Depending on how much electricity you use when on battery power, you may need to join several batteries into a 'battery bank'. Batteries may be connected in two ways:

Left **These batteries are well secured in a dedicated battery box. Note the white ventilation hoses at the far left of the box.**

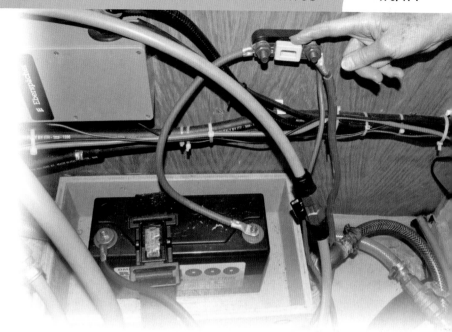

Right **All battery wiring should be protected with a battery fuse, though often this is omitted by builders.**

✪ Series connection – negative to positive. What is added together here is the voltage of all the batteries, so two 12 volt, 100 amp hour batteries connected in series will supply a voltage of 24 volts but the same 100 amp hours as a single battery.

✪ Parallel connection – positive to positive and negative to negative. What is added together here is the capacity of all the batteries, so two 12 volt, 100 amp hour batteries connected in parallel will supply 200 amp hours, but the same 12 volts as a single battery.

Groups of batteries

Ideally, the system will comprise an engine start battery and a service battery that are separated from each other except when they are being charged. The service battery may well consist of several batteries connected together as a bank of batteries, because it will need much more capacity than the engine start battery.

Single-engine boats

Both the engine start and the service batteries are charged from an alternator fitted to the engine, with some form of isolating arrangement between the banks, so that the engine start battery always remains fully charged.

Twin-engine boats

Each engine charges a separate battery bank. It is normal for one engine to have just an engine start battery and the other to have a combined engine start/service battery. So that the 'service battery' engine can be started if its battery becomes discharged, a link switch should be provided to allow it to be started from the other battery.

Securing the battery

Batteries must be securely held in position. They are very heavy and can cause a great deal of damage if they break free in rough conditions. Ideally they will be fitted in an acid-proof tray, so that any spillage cannot spread. The battery can be secured using strong straps or a heavy wooden batten. The battery restraint needs to be inspected at least annually to ensure that it has not become loose or weakened.

TIP

✪ If the battery terminal connector is of the 'clamp' type, trying to lever it off may pull the terminal post out of the battery case. Having loosened the clamp bolt, use a screwdriver to prise the clamp apart so that it can be pulled off without the use of force.

✪ To clean up battery cases or battery acid spills, use a bicarbonate of soda solution. If acid is present, the solution will 'fizz' as it neutralises it.

✪ A carbon monoxide alarm may be activated by hydrogen venting from a battery that is being charged vigorously. This may indicate a faulty battery that is past its prime.

Battery ventilation

Wet lead-acid batteries give off the explosive gas hydrogen when they are under charge. Hydrogen from each cell is collected in a system discharging at a vent in the upper casing. Some batteries are supplied with a tube to connect to the vent so that the gas can be discharged safely. No naked flames must be used near a battery under charge, and the best installations pipe the battery vent outside the cabin, or at least close to an opening port.

Battery maintenance

Unless they are of the 'maintenance-free' type, wet lead-acid batteries need to be topped up with distilled

or de-ionised water, because water can be lost through the vent system when under charge. Battery water level needs to be checked regularly – the more often the batteries are charged, the more frequent the checks required. Clean and dry the battery case afterwards. Other types of battery can't be topped up.

The 'state of charge' can be checked by measuring the battery's specific gravity using a hydrometer. The hydrometer will be calibrated to show how well charged the battery is, but this will be affected by the temperature of the electrolyte and what was put in the battery in the first

Top **Unless the battery is truly 'maintenance-free', it will need regular topping up with distilled (de-ionised) water.**

Left **Because batteries give off hydrogen gas when being charged, the battery or its compartment must be provided with ventilation.**

Above **Some boats have a single, four-position battery switch, allowing the selection of OFF/Battery 1/Battery 2/or BOTH batteries.**

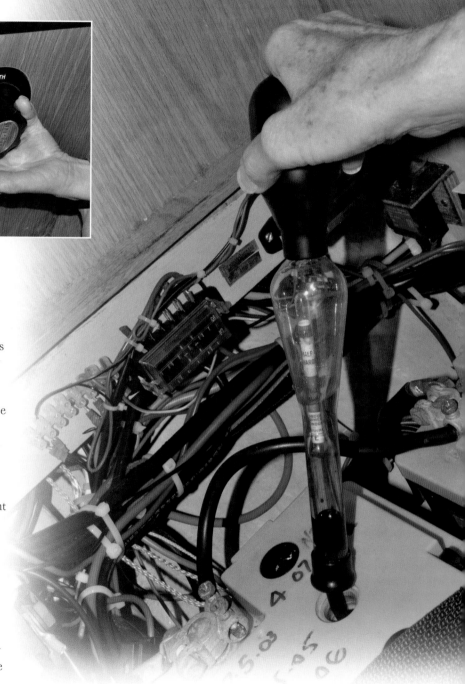

place, so is not absolutely reliable. It's best if the specific gravity of the new battery is checked after full charging so that you have a reference.

All battery connections need to be checked for tightness, cleaned and coated with petroleum jelly at least annually.

Battery replacement

Replacing a battery can often present a dilemma. Ideally all batteries charged by the same source should be of the same type and age. As a boat ages and has more electrical systems added, the battery system gets out of balance – the service battery gets bigger, but less able to start the engine. A compromise will have to be made, usually dictated by cost. Often the best solution is to use medium-cost general purpose batteries for both starting and services, especially if you don't make heavy demands on the batteries.

Above **The only accurate way to determine the state of charge of a battery is with a hydrometer.**

Charging the batteries

Battery charging is much more complicated than is often imagined. If you regularly spend time away from a mains electricity supply and rely on your batteries for domestic services, it is unlikely that the standard charging system fitted to your boat will be able to keep up with the demand.

The alternator regulator

A standard regulator will never charge the batteries above 70 per cent of their full charge in any reasonable engine running time. As the batteries should not be discharged below a 50 per cent state (to prolong their life), this means that only 20 per cent of the rated capacity is available for use. Fitting a 'smart' regulator will enable the batteries to be charged to at least 90 per cent of full charge quite rapidly, so that at least 40 per cent of the batteries' capacity is available. (Charging the battery from 50 per cent full to 80 per cent takes much less time than charging from 90 per cent to 95 per cent.)

Alternator output

If you fit more batteries, you may need to increase the size of your alternator. As a rule of thumb, the battery capacity in amp hours should be no more than four times the alternator output. So if the alternator output is 50 amps, the battery bank it is charging should be no more than 200 amp hours. The engine starting battery may be discounted, as only a small amount is taken out of it to start the engine.

Below **Moisture in the AC circuit breaker can cause annoying 'trips', and this one is very poorly sited in a wet locker.**

Above **The mains power circuit breaker panel should have a 'RCD' which must be tested regularly.**

A mains-powered battery charger

When mains power is available, the batteries can be charged using a mains charger. A marine 'smart' charger is desirable to ensure that the batteries are fully charged and can remain connected without fear of overcharging. Because there is more time available to charge the batteries (say overnight), the output needed may be only about one tenth of the capacity. In other words, a 200 hour battery bank could be recharged overnight by a 20 amp battery charger.

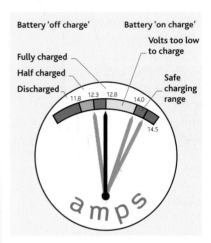

Above **Understanding battery voltage values is invaluable. Note that a fully discharged 12-volt battery at rest still has a voltage of about 11.8 volts.**

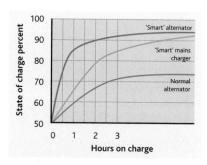

Above **Relative charging performance. A standard alternator regulator can never fully charge a battery in any reasonable time. Using a smart charge controller reduces charging time and increases effective battery capacity.**

Dynamo output

Old engines may be fitted with a dynamo rather than an alternator. These produce direct current, but are very inefficient for charging batteries. Engines that are even older may use a 'dynastart', which is a combined starter motor/dynamo.

On-board generators

If an on-board generator (commonly called a 'gen-set') is available, this can supply the mains charger to charge the batteries at the same time the gen-set is running to supply other mains appliances.

Shore power connections

The hook-up cable gets pretty rough treatment, and so the connectors at each end need to be inspected frequently to ensure that the cable is secure. Also inspect the cable for damage along its length.

A fast-trip fault-detecting circuit breaker must be fitted on the boat to protect people from electric shock should a fault occur in the cable or on the boat. This must be fitted in a dry place if it is to be reliable, and must be tested frequently – preferably every time you hook up.

Maintaining the charging system

The security and cleanliness of all connections should be checked at least annually. If the batteries don't appear to be charging correctly, check the output from the alternator using a clip-on ammeter, or preferably a battery charging monitor. Also consider the possibility that one or more batteries are coming to the end of their life.

Above **The AC power circuit breaker 'trip' should be tested regularly, and the polarity checked every time you connect to shore power.**

Above **This mains cable sheath has pulled out of the plug and must be re-secured.**

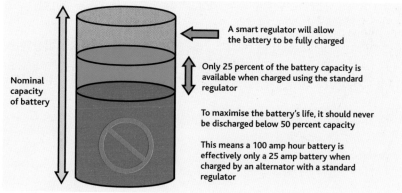

Nominal capacity of battery

A smart regulator will allow the battery to be fully charged

Only 25 percent of the battery capacity is available when charged using the standard regulator

To maximise the battery's life, it should never be discharged below 50 percent capacity

This means a 100 amp hour battery is effectively only a 25 amp battery when charged by an alternator with a standard regulator

Above **Charging output of a smart regulator in comparison with a standard regulator.**

Cabin lights

Mellow cabin lighting is wonderful for just relaxing. If you need bright task lighting, then something better than a low-wattage festoon bulb will be needed. Fortunately, there are many different types of low voltage light fittings available, though some are quite expensive.

Fluorescent lights

Fluorescent lights have the advantage of low current consumption. Also, because they are popular in the caravan (trailer) market, 12 volt units are not expensive. The cheaper fittings are not marinised, so corrosion may be a problem, in which case the cheapest form of maintenance is to replace the unit with a new one.

The downside of fluorescent lights is that cheap units may produce electromagnetic emissions that interfere with navigation and entertainment electronics.

Filament lights

Filament lamps are very inefficient as most of the energy ends up as heat. They tend to be relatively cheap, but the bulbs have a comparatively short life. And when the filament fails, it may trip a sensitive circuit breaker. To maintain filament lamps, simply check the bulb contacts for corrosion.

Halogen lights

Halogen lamps give more light per amp than filament lamps and are very good for task lights. The bulbs are more expensive than filament

Above **If a fluorescent light fails, first change the tube. If that doesn't work, the whole unit may need to be replaced.**

Below **Cabin lights are essential for comfortable living aboard. LED lights make far less demands on the boat's battery.**

lamps, but you can save a lot of money by purchasing them from an electronics supplier.

Some deck lights use halogen lights with bare pin contacts. These corrode, and cause the lamp to fail and become seized in the socket, so remove and clean them at least annually. Do not handle the glass portion of halogen lamps with your fingers. Skin oils will coat the bulb and cause premature failure.

Light emitting diode (LED) lights

LEDs have a long life expectancy and use very little electricity. Individually, they are not very bright, but they can be mounted in multiples to give good light intensity. High-power LEDs give quite a lot more light but are relatively expensive. White LEDs are bluish in colour, so the light is quite harsh and cold – not very good for background lighting. Warm white lights are available, but are much more expensive. No general maintenance is required.

Oil lights

Traditionalists love the warm ambiance of oil lamps, and of course they make no demands on battery power. They do require a little maintenance, though. The wick needs to be trimmed regularly to remove the burnt edge and keep the flame in a good shape.

Above **If an LED light fails, there is often no other solution than to replace the complete unit.**

Night lighting

It takes up to 30 minutes for the eyes to see well in very low light, so watch-keepers need to avoid bright lights to preserve their night vision. Traditionally red light is used as night lighting, but it is the dimness rather than the colour that is important. In fact, tests have shown green to be better than red – and aircraft just use a dimmer control on their standard lights. An oil lamp turned well down gives good background lighting at night.

Left **Halogen bulbs need to be handled with care, as contamination with oils from your skin will reduce the life of the bulb. Hold the bulb in a tissue.**

Navigation lights

The regulatory requirements for navigation lights vary according to the size and speed of the craft and whether it is used at sea or on inland waterways. Various combinations of lights are required in different circumstances, so the owner must be familiar with the regulations.

Visibility and bulb type

In order to have the correct colour, angle of visibility and range from which it can be seen, it's essential that the correct bulb is used in the unit and that the supply voltage is adequate. The design of the navigation light ensures that the arcs of visibility for the various colours are correct. If you use the wrong type of bulb, the alignment of its filament may produce the wrong cut-off angles, while incorrect wattage will affect the distance from which you can be seen.

Voltage drop

Navigation lights are often a long way from the battery, so there can be a large voltage drop due to the resistance of the long cable run. If the cable is undersized or the contacts dirty, voltage drop will be excessive and the light output of the bulb will be considerably reduced. No more than a ten per cent voltage drop should be tolerated, to ensure you will be seen from a distance.

Below **If you are going to navigate at night, international regulations require the correct navigation lights to be used.**

Above **This old bulb has corrosion around its collar. As this is a two-pin bulb, it will have no effect, but if this was one of the conductors, the bulb would need to be cleaned or discarded.**

Right **Some deck lights have exposed bulbs to keep them cool but suffer badly from corrosion, making a failed bulb very difficult to remove.**

LED navigation lights

LED lights need much less power than filament bulbs for a given light output. LED lamps specifically designed as navigation lights are tested to ensure that they comply with the relevant regulations and they are sealed for life. However, LEDs that are not designed for the purpose are likely to be non-compliant, even though they may fit comfortably into standard navigation lights.

For one thing, the red, white and green colours of the LEDs may not comply with those required by the regulations. Also, the angles of visibility of the colours may also not comply with the regulations when used in the standard navigation light. So care is required in the selection of LEDs if they are to be used as replacements for filament bulbs.

MAINTENANCE

At least annually, you should service your navigation lights by:

◆ Removing the bulbs and cleaning their contacts.
◆ Cleaning the inside of the navigation lights, especially the lenses.
◆ Checking the wiring connectors for corrosion and security.
◆ Using silicone grease to protect all wiring connectors once they have been cleaned.
◆ Ensuring that the lens seals are intact.
◆ Ensuring that any drain holes in the casing are not blocked.
◆ Checking the voltage at the bulb contacts with the light switched on and the bulb removed – don't short the contacts together, or the fuse will blow.

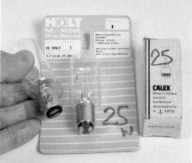

Above **The wattage of bulbs is very difficult to read in poor light, so clearly mark the packaging or the bulb itself.**

TIP

If you are checking the masthead navigation light, you might just as well change the bulb for a new one to save an unscheduled climb if and when the used bulb fails. Keep the old one as a spare.

Navigation equipment

A boat's navigation equipment may vary from a hand-held GPS to a complex fully integrated system. Normally everything works well and needs little routine maintenance. The apparent failure of a particular piece of kit often requires no more than switching it off and switching it back on again to make it work.

Paddlewheel log

This is the only part of the system that needs regular maintenance. If it is not retracted when out of use, it will become fouled with weed and baby crustaceans. Pull in the paddlewheel every time you leave the boat unattended, remembering to replace it with its blanking plug.

Also remember to pull in the log when the boat is lifted, to avoid it being damaged by the strop.

Anemometer

Whenever you are at the masthead, inspect the wind unit to ensure it is secure and rotates freely.

Above **The paddlewheel of the log will become fouled, so keep it retracted when not in use. It can be cleaned with an old toothbrush.**

Radar

Run the radar for five minutes whenever possible, to ensure that the scanner bearings are kept free and that the heat from the magnetron helps to remove condensation. Make sure your head (and the rest of you) is at a safe distance from the operating scanner. This may be as much as 16ft (5m), depending on the radar's power.

Left **The helm and navigation station of a small motor cruiser needs little servicing. Typically, there will be a combined radar and chartplotter, an autopilot, speed and depth sounder and magnetic compass.**

Instrument displays

The instrument displays may be all of one make, or a mixture. They can be made to 'talk' to each other, though if they are of differing makes, some form of connection interface will be required. This needs to be considered when troubleshooting or if adding a new instrument. For maintenance:

✪ Chartplotter screens can be cleaned with PC screen cleaner.
✪ Most displays are waterproof only if the back is sealed against the bulkhead/pod.
✪ Don't use solvent or abrasive cleaners.

Replacing a failed instrument

If a replacement is available from the same manufacturer, then swapping the display or transducer is no problem – just plug the new one onto the existing cable. Because they have a good life expectancy, you may find that spares are no longer available, and a different make or incompatible unit will be needed as a replacement. If that's the case, there are several options:

✪ If the instrument is 'stand-alone' and not networked, it doesn't matter that it can't 'speak' to the rest of the system, so fit any instrument of your choice.
✪ If the instrument is networked with others, check to see if they have a standard NMEA output. The North American Marine Electronics Association has designed protocols so that

instruments of any make can 'talk' to each other. There are several NMEA standards, including NMEA 0183 and NMEA 2000. The new instrument must use the same NMEA protocol and can then be connected to the old network, but may need extra cables to be installed. NMEA is an international standard devised in the USA and applicable worldwide.

Above **Cables can be threaded through conduits using a threader. This coil was pushed all the way up a 49ft (15m) mast.**

✪ There's a limit to how many instruments can be networked using NMEA 0183, so you may wish to install a data combiner into the system. This may also be used to network NMEA 0183 and NMEA 2000 systems together.

Installing a new chart plotter

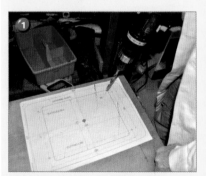

Stick the template provided with the instrument to the panel, and drill a hole in each corner.

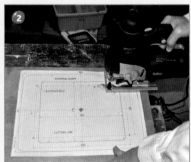

Cut along the template with a jigsaw to form the cut-out for the plotter. Assemble in a suitable position.

Solar panels

If your boat spends most of its time without access to shore power, its battery will slowly discharge, even if not in use. With use, the battery will quickly become discharged, and one way of keeping this more under control is to fit solar panels as a means of charging the battery.

Types of solar panel

There are a number of different types of photovoltaic (PV) solar panels, but they all convert light directly to DC voltage electrical current. As a PV panel heats up, its output is reduced, but technology is improving, and the efficiency with which solar panels convert solar energy into electrical power (currently 8–16 per cent) is constantly increasing. The types of panel respond variously to different wavelengths of light, so while some give a smaller maximum output than others, they may perform better than their rivals in dull conditions.

Rigid panels

Many rigid panels use crystalline technology that gives greater efficiency in strong sun (up to 16 per cent), but their output falls dramatically in dull conditions. And just one cell in shadow causes a drastic reduction in output of the whole panel.

Semi-rigid and flexible panels

These use three very thin layers of amorphous semiconductor. Although having less efficiency in strong sun (eight per cent) they are up to 1.3 times as efficient as rigid panel types in dull conditions. And one cell in shadow causes a relatively small loss in output.

Below Flexible panels on long leads can be laid in a position out of any shadows and moved as required. Shadows falling on a solar panel reduce its output considerably.

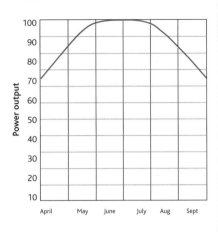

Above **A solar panel will not achieve its full output at all times of the year. Mounting it so that it can be tilted towards the sun will improve its output.**

Angle to the sun

Maximum output is achieved when the panel is at right angles to the sun's rays. If mounted horizontally, output can fall by as much as 15 per cent. To obtain the best results, the panel would need to be fitted on a swivel mount that can always be aligned to the sun – but this is rarely practical. A flexible panel can be draped in a good position, but a rigid panel should at least be mounted on a tilting frame.

Above **A semi-rigid panel can be mounted permanently on deck.**

Output factors

Full output from a solar panel is achieved for only about an hour either side of midday. In full sunlight all day, the average output across the daylight hours is about 75 per cent of maximum, and winter output is half that of summer. Dull conditions reduce output by 70 per cent. Even the shadow of a halyard can cause a 20 per cent reduction in the panel's output, so you should try to keep the panels completely clear of shadows.

Voltage regulation

If the PV panel is to be left connected unattended, or if the battery is small in comparison to the panel's output, a voltage regulator should be fitted to stop the battery being overcharged.

Maintenance

❂ Keep the panels clean, washing them with fresh water.
❂ Ensure that all electrical connections are clean and secure.

Left **A rigid panel on a tilting frame can be aligned to the sun.**

Wind turbines

Wind power can be used to generate electricity on your boat. Given a high enough output, it can keep your boat self-sufficient for some time, and can be very useful on a cruising yacht. And unlike a solar panel, it can work at night.

Vertical axis turbines

The blades are in the form of a cylinder, rotating about a vertical axis. They have a very low output, are quiet in operation, are less likely to strike a person and are really suitable for trickle charging the battery of an unattended boat. They are simple in operation and require virtually no maintenance.

Horizontal axis turbines

The blades look like aircraft propellers rotating about a horizontal axis. Their power depends on their diameter and blade design, and they can be quite noisy. Provided that they are big enough, they can contribute a large portion of a boat's electrical power requirement. Because the blades must always face

Above **A vertical axis wind turbine is suitable only for trickle charging the battery when the boat is unattended.**

the wind, they must be able to rotate about their pole, which makes transmission of their electrical output more complicated, and this adds to the maintenance required.

Power output

The rated power output can be misleading. The start-up wind speed is 6 to 8 knots, when their output will be very low, typically 1 amp or so at 10 knots. Only with wind speeds of 30 knots will they produce their rated output. To prevent the turbine from over-speeding in high winds, it will need to be tethered or have an electronic brake to stop rotation.

Left **'Propeller' turbines produce the most power, but check the output in average wind conditions before you buy one. Often they produce only one amp at 12 knots.**

TIP

Wind turbines are fairly heavy and mounted at height, so routine maintenance may be difficult. If you mount the pole on a pivot, it can be lowered to deck level and supported, making maintenance easy.

Regulation of power output

Horizontal turbines are capable of overcharging a boat's batteries. Normally a regulator will be used that senses the load on the electrical system and the state of charge of the battery, and regulates the output accordingly. The regulator needs no maintenance other than occasionally checking the state of any connectors.

Maintaining a horizontal turbine

The blades need to be inspected regularly for damage and the security of their fastenings. The turbine's bearings may also require routine maintenance – the handbook will give details.

There may be brushes to pick up the electrical power from the turbine, depending on its design, and there will be brushes to transmit the power down the pole on which the turbine assembly rotates to keep it facing into wind. The handbook will detail the maintenance required on any particular model.

Above **If the pole is pivoted at its bottom, it can easily be lowered by one person for servicing.**

Servicing a turbine

Check the brushes and connections, and use a spray lubricant if necessary.

Check the blades are secure and free of defects, as they revolve at high speed.

Engine maintenance

Servicing the engine

Servicing the engine according to the manufacturer's schedule is essential to its reliability, and therefore to safety. On many boats, proper maintenance is not always easy, because priority is given to the living space over the needs of accessing the engine.

Above **A suitable filter removal tool makes life much easier.**

Annual servicing

Most engines in leisure use will not operate for sufficient hours to warrant more than annual servicing. This should be carried out according to the engine manufacturer's service schedule. This schedule will not include items that aren't fitted to the engine (such as stern gear, fuel primary filter, exhaust and so on), all of which also need to be checked and serviced annually. If a professional service engineer is employed, then ensure that all these extra items are covered in the service – otherwise they may not be included.

Lubrication system

- ✪ Change the oil. If the specified oil for older engines is no longer available, use the nearest API (American Petroleum Institute) specification or contact your dealer for advice.
- ✪ Change the oil filter.
- ✪ Top up the oil level to the dipstick mark after the engine has been run for a few minutes.

Transmission / Gearbox

- ✪ Change the lubricant if scheduled (transmission lubricant may not need to be changed annually).

Cooling system

- ✪ The coolant should be changed every two years, because the corrosion inhibitors gradually lose their effectiveness.

Fuel system

- ✪ Change the pre-filter (agglomerator) and clean the bowl. If it's dirty or contaminated, the fuel tank will also need to be cleaned.
- ✪ Change the engine fine filter.
- ✪ If starting has become difficult or there is white, grey or blue smoke in the exhaust, consider having the diesel injectors serviced.
- ✪ Bleed the fuel system to purge it of air (see pages 190 and 191).

Engine mounts

- ✪ Carefully inspect all parts of the engine mounts for wear or damage.

Air system

- ✪ Clean the air filter/silencer.
- ✪ Carefully inspect the exhaust water injection bend for corrosion/cracks.

Valve gear

- ✪ As specified by the manufacturer, check and adjust the valve clearances.
- ✪ If the camshaft is belt driven,

Below **The full right side view of a diesel engine, showing the lubrication system and fuel pump.**

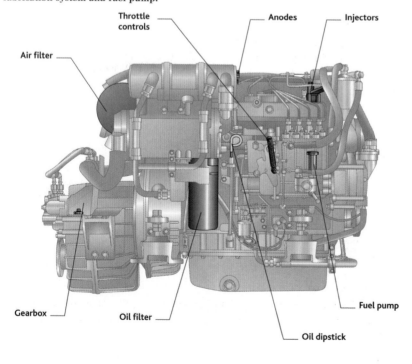

Throttle controls — Anodes — Injectors

Air filter —

Gearbox — Oil filter — Fuel pump

Oil dipstick

change the belt, idler and pulleys at intervals specified by the manufacturer (roughly every 800 hours).

Ignition system (petrol/gasoline engines)
⊙ Inspect, adjust and change as necessary the spark plugs, plug leads, contact breakers, distributor and distributor cap.

Miscellaneous
⊙ Carry out any other work as specified by the manufacturer.

Outdrive units and saildrive legs
Outdrive and saildrive units need careful annual servicing to ensure that corrosion is prevented, that the steering and trim mechanisms (if fitted) are in good order, and that the rubber bellows/seal are in good condition (see pages 218 and 219).

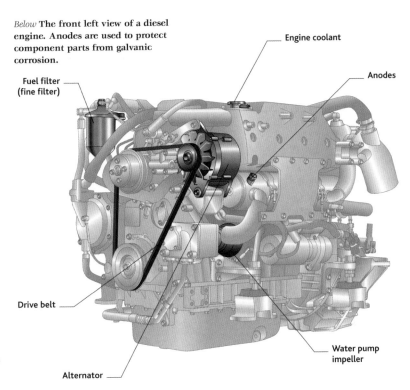

Below **The front left view of a diesel engine. Anodes are used to protect component parts from galvanic corrosion.**

Engine coolant

Anodes

Fuel filter (fine filter)

Drive belt

Water pump impeller

Alternator

Adjusting the valve gear

Periodic adjustment of the valve gear is required as specified by the manufacturer. Undo the rocker box retaining bolts.

Carefully remove the cover without damaging the sealing gasket. Note which way the gasket should be reassembled.

Check the valve clearance with a feeler gauge, 'turning' the engine so that the gap is at its maximum. Adjust for a tight fit.

Bleeding the fuel system

If air has been admitted to the fuel system – because you have serviced the fuel system, run out of fuel or have developed a fuel leak – you will need to 'bleed' or 'purge' the fuel system to remove any air. Bleeding the system is often seen as a daunting job, but it needn't be.

Diesel engine fuel system

A fuel pump on the engine sucks fuel from the fuel tank, via a primary filter/water separator, and delivers it under low pressure to the engine fuel filter and then to the fuel injection pump. The fuel is then pressurised, measured into very small quantities, and sent to each of the fuel injectors at exactly the right time. The amount of fuel delivered is determined by the governor controlling the rpm of the engine according to the load.

Below **The new filter being inserted prior to bleeding the system.**

Petrol (gasoline) engine fuel system

Fuel is delivered to the engine in the same way as in the diesel engine. It is then mixed with air in the carburettor, where it enters the inlet manifold. On some engines there is no carburettor, but the fuel is injected straight into the inlet manifold instead, where the mixing with air occurs.

The primary fuel filter

This stops fuel tank debris reaching the fuel pump and separates any water from the fuel, prior to delivery to the engine.

The fuel pump

This transports the fuel from the tank to the engine. It is also used manually when bleeding the fuel system.

The engine (fine) fuel filter

The fine filter prevents very small dirt particles from reaching the fuel injection pump (diesel engines) or the carburettor/injection system (petrol engines).

The fuel injection pump

This pressurises, adjusts the quantity and times the fuel to the injectors. Excess fuel is returned to the tank.

The fuel injectors

These inject the fuel to the individual cylinders. Fuel leaking past the injector is returned to the tank or fine filter.

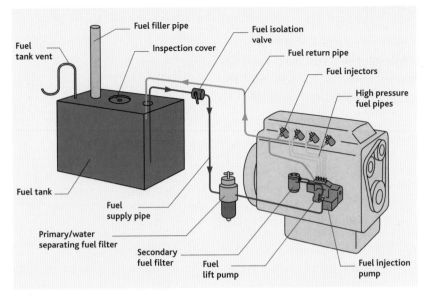

Fuel filler pipe
Fuel isolation valve
Fuel tank vent
Inspection cover
Fuel return pipe
Fuel injectors
High pressure fuel pipes
Fuel tank
Fuel supply pipe
Primary/water separating fuel filter
Secondary fuel filter
Fuel lift pump
Fuel injection pump

Above Ensure that any sealing rings are properly installed to prevent the filter leaking.

Left A typical diesel fuel system. Older boats may have the fuel supply from the bottom of the tank.

Bleeding the fuel system

- ◉ Turn the fuel supply on.
- ◉ If the primary filter is lower than the fuel level in the tank, open the filter bleed screw. Pressure due to gravity will force any air out of the pipe. When fuel is running from the bleed screw, close it.
- ◉ If the primary filter is above the fuel level in the tank, do not open its bleed screw.
- ◉ Open the bleed screw on the engine fine filter.
- ◉ Use the manual fuel pump lever/ plunger to pump fuel through the system. If the primary filter could not be bled, this may take some time, as the primary filter bowl will have to be filled as well as the fine filter.
- ◉ When fuel runs continuously from the bleed screw, close it.
- ◉ It is unlikely that the injectors will need bleeding.

Bleeding the engine

The engine will not run without fuel, so ensure that it's turned on before you bleed the fuel system. Have a container ready to collect any fuel released.

If the pre-filter is lower than the level of fuel in the tank, open the bleed screw until the fuel flows out. Close the bleed screw once any air bubbles have gone.

There is a bleed screw on the filter body to allow trapped air to escape. Undo this about two and a half turns and let the fuel flow until all air bubbles have gone.

Pump the priming lever (or plunger) on the fuel pump until the fuel runs from the bleed screw without air bubbles, then close the bleed screw.

Adjusting the belt drive

An engine has one or more rubber belts driving the alternator and sometimes the raw water pump. If the belt fails, there will be no electrical output from the alternator – and if the raw water pump stops working, the engine will overheat in a matter of minutes, rendering it unusable.

Types of drive belt

The most common drive belt is of fabric-reinforced rubber. Generally these are quite adequate. If a heavy duty alternator is fitted, a heavy-duty drive belt should be used – these often have notches in their contact face.

Measuring belt tension

A slipping belt will cause rapid wear, so it is important that the belt is under sufficient tension. It is often recommended that, to test tension, the belt is pressed as hard as you can halfway between the pulleys. The deflection should be about

Above **On some engines, the water pump is driven by a separate belt. This must also be kept tensioned correctly.**

Left **Adjusting the alternator belt often requires a lever to tighten the belt while the adjustment clamp bolt is tightened.**

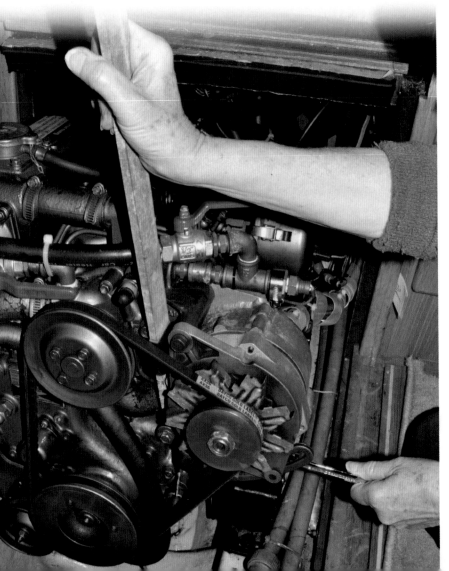

Left A correctly adjusted belt should twist through approximately 90 degrees.

0.5in (12mm). Possibly an easier and more reliable method is to grip the belt, at its mid-position, between your thumb and forefinger and twist. If properly tensioned, it should twist approximately 90 degrees.

Adjusting belt tension
Most engines have a very unsophisticated method of adjusting belt tension:

- ☯ Loosen the adjustment bolt and the pivot bolt on the alternator or water pump.
- ☯ Use a long, strong lever to force the alternator or pump away from the engine, first ensuring that the two bearing points of the lever are not resting on any part that could be damaged by the strong force that you are going to apply.
- ☯ While still applying the strong force with one hand, tighten the clamp bolt with the other.
- ☯ Tighten the pivot bolt.
- ☯ Check the belt tension and readjust if necessary.

Drive belts with screw adjusters
- ☯ Slacken off the clamp and pivot bolts.
- ☯ Screw the tensioner in the required direction.
- ☯ Check the tension.
- ☯ Retighten the bolts.

Rubber cam belts
Some engines are marinised versions of car engines, and these may have rubber cam belts. Failure of these will result in very expensive damage. Cars normally require cam belts and their associated tensioners to be changed at 50,000- to 80,000-mile intervals, which equates to about 1,000 engine hours. Usually beyond the DIY mechanic, this essential maintenance should be undertaken by a professional.

Below Once the belt has been tightened, the adjustment bolt is tightened, followed by the alternator/water pump bolt.

Water pump maintenance

Most marine engines are water cooled, and use a pump with a rubber impeller to pump the water through the system. Failure of the impeller will render the engine unusable, so you need to be able to change the impeller yourself in case it fails.

How a water pump works

The majority of engines use a pump with a flexible-bladed rubber impeller rotating in a chamber. During part of each revolution, the blades are squashed by a fixed cam, so that the volume between consecutive blades is reduced. This reduction causes water to be forced out of the exit port. As the blades recover their normal shape and the volume increases, water is sucked in through the inlet port.

Priming the pump

These pumps are self-priming, provided that there are no air leaks in the 'suction' pipe and that the pump is no more than 15ft (5m) away. If the pump is reluctant to prime, check that the water strainer cap is fully tightened and, if necessary, fill the strainer with water.

Below **This flow of water from the exhaust pipe shows that the sea water pump is operating correctly.**

TIP

Its position on the engine does not always make the water pump easily accessible. Also there are a number of small screws to remove to gain access to the impeller.

✿ It is sometimes easier and quicker to detach the pump from its mounting (you don't need to remove the hoses) when changing the impeller.

✿ Fitting True Marine's 'Speedseal' in place of the original faceplate will allow the pump's faceplate to be removed using no tools, and makes the job very quick and easy.

Impeller failure

The impeller is a tight fit in the casing to prevent leakage, resulting in a lot of friction and therefore heat. The impeller and casing are cooled by the water that is pumping. If no cooling water flows, the impeller will rapidly overheat, causing it to disintegrate.

Changing the impeller

⊕ Close the cooling water seacock.
⊕ Remove the screws holding the faceplate in place.
⊕ Remove the faceplate, endeavouring not to damage the sealing gasket.
⊕ Withdraw the impeller from its shaft – this may require partial withdrawal at first, to expose a set screw, which can then be removed.
⊕ Insert the new impeller, having first coated the blades with washing up liquid or grease.
⊕ Clean the mating surfaces of the faceplate, renewing the gasket if necessary.
⊕ Replace the faceplate and screws.

Changing the impeller

If the pump is inaccessible, it might be easier to unbolt it from the engine first.

Loosen the retaining bolts on the front of the pump and remove the faceplate.

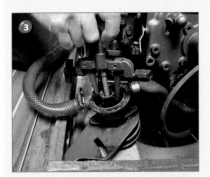

It's best to use a specialist tool to remove the impeller, otherwise use screwdrivers.

Check the impeller for cracking at the blade roots. This one needs to be replaced.

Use a cable tie to pre-shape the blades into the correct position to make insertion of the new impeller easy.

Insert the new impeller in the pump, and slide the cable tie out. Reassemble in reverse order.

Servicing the transmission

The gearbox on a boat engine serves two purposes: it reduces the speed at which the propeller rotates, so that it can operate more efficiently; and it allows selection of forward, neutral and reverse gears.

Types of gearbox

There are a number of different types of gearbox – epicyclic, twin-shaft, bevel gear and lay-shaft – and each may be operated manually or hydraulically. Manually operated gearboxes are generally restricted to smaller horsepower engines. The operating clutches rely on hand power for gear selection. Hydraulic gearboxes operate the clutches using the augmented power of the pumped lubrication system.

Manual clutches

The gear selector lever moves either the forward clutch or the reverse clutch into engagement to drive the output shaft. Once the clutch starts to engage, the internal mechanism

Above **Check the gearbox oil dipstick every week. There should be no change in the colour of the oil.**

Left **The gearbox oil in a saildrive is drained from the bottom of the leg.**

may cause the clutch to engage with more force. On these engines, if the propeller shaft is locked by engaging gear when sailing, it may be difficult to select neutral when re-starting the engine. In this case, start in gear, slipping the lever into neutral as the engine starts.

Maintenance

Ensure that the selector mechanism is correctly adjusted according to the handbook, or the clutches may slip under load, causing overheating and failure.

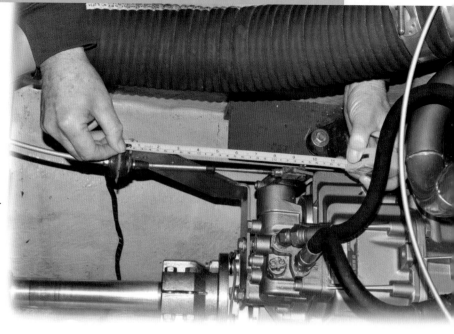

Right **To ensure that the gears engage fully, preventing premature clutch wear, the adjustment of the gear selector cable should be checked annually.**

Hydraulic clutches

The gear selector lever operates a valve which directs the gearbox lubricating oil to a piston to move the clutches and keep them engaged. With the engine stopped, there is no gearbox rotation and no hydraulic pressure, so stopping shaft rotation when sailing may cause harm. Consult the gearbox handbook to see what is recommended.

Routine maintenance

As well as weekly checks of oil level and colour, the gearbox oil must be changed at intervals specified by the engine/gearbox manufacturer. Remove the old gearbox oil using a pump, placing its suction tube into

the dipstick or filler hole. Replace with the correct quantity of the specified oil. This may be the same type of oil as the engine oil, or a different grade, or even automatic transmission fluid.

Saildrives

Saildrives have a gearbox mounted directly on a vertical leg, which protrudes through the bottom of the boat's hull. The drive turns a horizontal propeller shaft at the bottom of the leg.

   Draining the oil of a saildrive is done by removing a drain screw from the bottom of the leg – removing the filler cap will speed up the draining process. Some recent saildrive models allow the oil to be removed with the boat afloat by sucking the oil from the top – refer to the saildrive handbook for the procedure. Any whitening of the oil suggests a seal failure at the base of the leg, and this must be rectified.

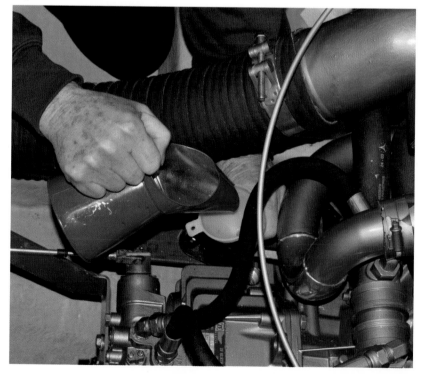

Left **Top up the gearbox oil as necessary, although unless there's a leak it should use no oil.**

Throttle & gear controls

The throttle and gear controls allow the engine speed to be controlled and the selection of forward, neutral and reverse gears. These are operated by push-pull cables running in reinforced sheaths, which often follow a circuitous route, so there may be quite a lot of friction.

Throttle and gears

The throttle lever operates the speed lever on a diesel engine or the throttle on a petrol engine. The gear selector operates the gear selector lever on the gearbox. Different types of controls are available.

Single-lever control

A single lever mounted on a special control box allows the engine to run at idle rpm with the gearbox in neutral. Initial movement of the lever moves the gearbox selector (either forward or reverse) but ensures that the engine rpm remains at idle. Further movement of the lever accelerates the engine. To enable the engine rpm to be increased in neutral, a mechanism is activated which allows throttle movement without engaging gear.

Two-lever controls

Two independent levers control the engine rpm and the gear selection. This gives a simpler, smoother control mechanism at the cost of having two levers (four on a twin-engine installation).

Two-station controls

Where there are two helming positions, a dual-station relay box is used to join and mix the inputs from the controls at each helming

Below **This control mechanism operates the engine speed control and the gearbox control with a single lever.**

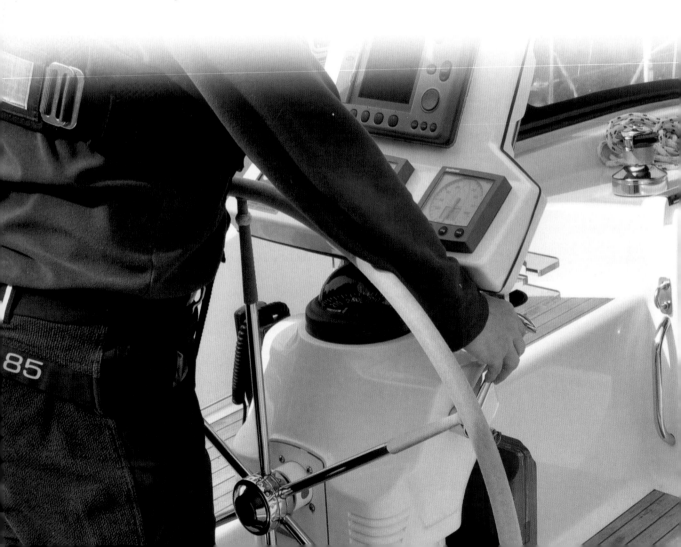

Adjusting throttle friction

Adjustment of the throttle friction requires the housing to be removed – drilling a small hole in the housing allows easy access.

The throttle and gear selectors can be adjusted once the housing is removed.

Annual greasing of the cables minimises friction in the controls. This will require the control box to be opened.

position. The controls at only one position can be used at any one time. The relay box adds yet more friction to the system, and operation can become quite 'notchy', requiring care in manoeuvring.

Routine maintenance

Electronic controls: There is no maintenance that the owner can carry out other than to check the cleanliness and security of electrical connections and fuses. A manual override is available – see the engine handbook.

Mechanical controls: Routine maintenance normally requires access to the control mechanisms. This usually involves some disassembly, but is well worth the effort once a year, to maintain as smooth a control as is possible. The procedure is:

✪ Gain access to the control levers at the helm position. If you're lucky, access will be easy from the cockpit locker or behind the instrument panel. However, you will need to access the inside of

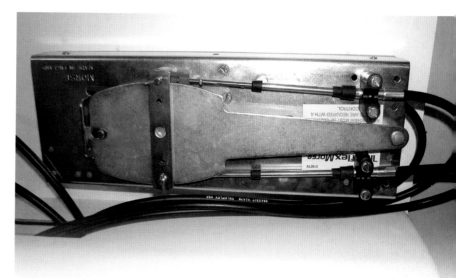

the steering pedestal if it's mounted there, or to remove the control box if it's on a bulkhead.

✪ Clean all congealed grease from the mechanism, and check the condition of all pivots, pins and nuts and bolts.

✪ Regrease with waterproof grease.

✪ Check the condition of the input levers on the engine and gearbox, and lubricate as necessary.

Above **Two helming positions require a dual-station relay box to allow control from each station. This increases friction, so regular lubrication makes control easier.**

Cleaning out the fuel tank

Marine fuel suppliers have a relatively low turnover, so boat fuel may stand idle for a long period and water may get into both their system and yours, creating an ideal breeding ground for various types of biological growth that can colonise any hydrocarbon fuel. Also rust can form on the inside of steel tanks.

Diesel bug

Fungal spores and algae can colonise diesel fuel tanks. Oxygen is required for their growth, and this is found in any water present in the tank. Water is denser than fuel, so it sits in the bottom of the tank, with any growth taking place at the interface between the fuel and the water. The biological growth can block filters. Some organisms are sulphur-producing, and the resulting sulphuric acid can damage the tank and the fuel system. If there is no water in the tank, growth cannot take place.

Below **Some fuel tanks have an access hatch, which will allow easier in-situ cleaning of the tank.**

Above **If there's water in the fuel tank, bacterial growth is likely. This growth will block filters, and damage from sulphuric acid is possible. This is what the growth can look like.**

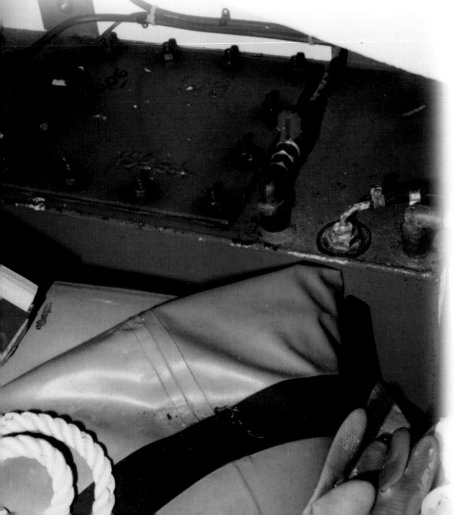

Water in the fuel tank

Water can enter the tank with poor quality fuel, from a leaking filler cap and from condensation within the tank. There are three precautions that you can take:

- Keep the tank full to reduce the chance of condensation.
- Ensure that the tank filler seal is watertight.
- Endeavour to purchase your fuel from a source which has a high turnover.

Monitoring fuel quality

The easiest way to monitor fuel quality is to regularly check the contents of the transparent bowl of the pre-filter (primary filter). Water and dirt will sit at the bottom of the bowl.

Above **If your tank has a 'sludge' trap, regular sampling from its drain will enable you to check for contamination.**

Above **A separate cock for the supply of fuel to a diesel heater will ensure there's a reserve of fuel to run the engine.**

Below **If the tank is corroded, the best solution is to replace it with a new one.**

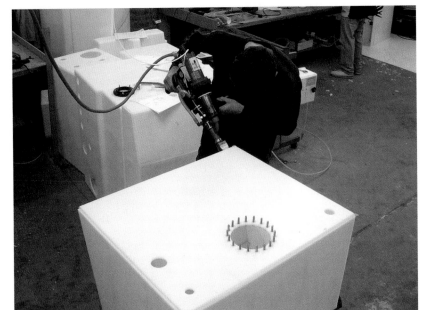

Cleaning the tank

Cleaning the tank is difficult, and therefore not often attempted on a routine basis.

⊛ **Tanks with a sludge trap:** All tanks should have a sludge trap, but rarely do. If yours has one, drain some fuel from it annually to check for water and dirt. Fitting a drain valve instead of a plug will make this easy.

⊛ **Tanks with an access panel:** If you suspect that the tank contains dirty fuel, open the access panel so that you can clean the tank – it will need to be drained first.

⊛ **Other tanks:** If you can remove the fuel filler hose from the top of the tank, you can insert a suction hose to remove the dirty fuel, water and debris. You will need to manoeuvre the hose to the lowest part of the tank.

⊛ **Fuel polishing:** This is the most effective way to clean a tank and its fuel, but it is costly. Fuel is pumped from the tank, through filters and other apparatus using specialist equipment, and then returned, clean, to the tank.

Replacing a propeller

A propeller may need to be removed, perhaps to fit a different type, or because it is damaged, or to change the anode on a saildrive. Folding propellers may need to be disassembled first. Propellers may be difficult to remove and, if refitted incorrectly, may fall off.

Propellers on shaft drives

Conventional shafts are tapered where the propeller is attached, and the hole at the centre of the propeller is tapered to fit. There are a number of different standard tapers, and the prop must match the shaft. Rotation of the propeller on the shaft is prevented by a 'key', locking the two together. The propeller is secured by a castellated nut, through which a split pin passes. To remove the propeller:

❂ Remove the split pin from the nut.
❂ Prevent rotation of the propeller – you may need to use a long piece of solid timber between one of the blades and the ground. You can't rely on the engine being in gear, and in any case the engine could start.
❂ Use a hefty spanner (wrench) to undo the nut.
❂ If the propeller won't come off the tapered shaft, use a propeller puller. If the propeller is really

Above **Folding and feathering propellers will need annual greasing.**

Below **Propellers that are reluctant to move are likely to respond to localised heating of the hub. This is not suitable for feathering props, as it may damage bearings.**

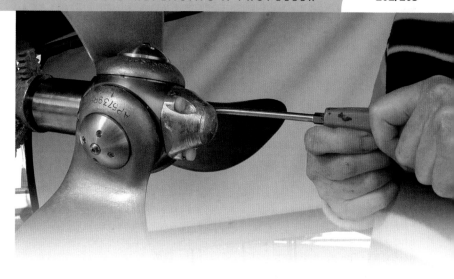

Right **Remember to replace the propeller anode once it becomes too pitted.**

stuck, heat may be needed to expand the propeller while it is being pulled off.

❂ If it's a folding/feathering propeller, the blades may have to be removed before you heat the hub – to prevent damage to seals.

Propellers on saildrives

The saildrive propeller shaft is mounted on a spline, with matching splines on the propeller hub. A nut holds the propeller in place on the shaft. The method of locking will vary according to the type of propeller fitted. There may be a simple split pin on a fixed-blade propeller, but if the propeller is folding or feathering, the locking system may be deep inside the hub and consist of locking tabs. To remove the propeller:

❂ If necessary, remove the propeller blades to gain access to the securing nut and the locking device, which may be held in place by a secondary bolt.

❂ Remove the locking device or bend the locking tabs to allow the spanner to be fitted and the nut to turn.

❂ Remove the securing nut, preventing the propeller from turning at the same time.

❂ Pull the propeller off the splined shaft.

Propellers on stern drives

These are mounted on a splined shaft in a similar fashion to a saildrive, so follow the same procedure.

Refitting propellers

❂ Grease the mating surfaces.

❂ Fully tighten the securing nut.

❂ Ensure that the locking system is assembled correctly.

❂ Use new locking tabs if they have been deformed when you removed them.

Removing a propeller

If the propeller retaining nut is deeply recessed, you will need a deep socket spanner to remove it.

Some propellers need a special puller to remove them, especially if a rope cutter is fitted.

There is a loose-mounted key to locate the propeller onto the tapered shaft.

Repacking a stern gland

A conventional shaft drive engine has a hole in the hull where the propeller shaft exits. The stern gland prevents water entering the hull at this point. Depending on the design of the gland, it may require periodic maintenance to stop it leaking or to replace worn parts.

Conventional shaft drive

The traditional stern gland consists of special packing material wound around the propeller shaft and 'packed' into a housing. An end fitting is pressed hard against the packing to compress it so that it seals tightly around the shaft. This should drip water into the boat at a rate of about two to three drips per minute with the engine running. The water will collect in the bilge and you will need to mop this up occasionally. It is likely to continue dripping with the shaft stationary. If the packing is squeezed any harder, it will be too tight and cause overheating of the shaft and seal.

This gland will need to be tightened occasionally if the drip rate increases, and eventually the packing will need to be replaced. To remove the old packing, you will need a special or improvised tool.

The traditional gland has been superseded in modern boats, which use one of several makes of 'dripless' seal. Because of the various technologies used, you will need to follow the instructions supplied with the unit.

Repacking the gland

Accessibility is the key to this operation, and unfortunately this can be a problem on some boats.

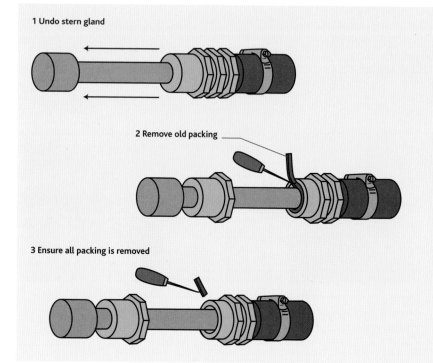

1 Undo stern gland

2 Remove old packing

3 Ensure all packing is removed

Below **A traditional stern gland relies on packing material to minimise any leakage. This will need to be replaced occasionally.**

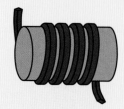

4 Wrap new packing around shaft

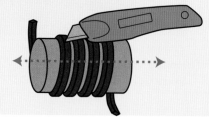

5 Cut through all coils

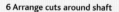

6 Arrange cuts around shaft

Above **This traditional stern gland is lubricated by grease. The white tube carries the grease from the 'greaser' to the stern gland.**

7 Push new packing into housing

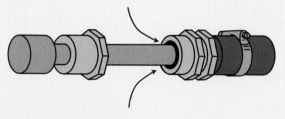

8 Tighten sealing nut against the packing

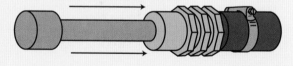

Being made of bronze and suffering from salt water corrosion, they are usually difficult to take apart. Instead of repacking the old gland, it can be less bother overall to fit a drip-less seal.

Most boats have the stern gland mounted on a piece of heavy-duty rubber hose, so that the gland can tolerate any misalignment of the shaft. This hose can perish, so its condition needs to be monitored. If this needs to be replaced, the propeller shaft will have to be moved

Repacking a stern gland 2

back to allow the hose to be removed, and you may prefer to give this job to a professional.

- ✿ Take the boat out of the water.
- ✿ Remove the bolts holding the yoke in place, or undo the very large nut at the front of the gland if this is used instead of a yoke.
- ✿ Move the yoke or large nut forward along the shaft.
- ✿ Use a packing removal tool (or an improvised one if you don't have a proper one) to dig out the old packing. This will take time, as the old packing will probably disintegrate, and it's important to get all the debris out.

- ✿ Clean the surface of the shaft.
- ✿ If the shaft is badly scored, you may need to replace it. Otherwise use wet and dry abrasive paper to smooth out any scoring, and clean up with wire wool.
- ✿ Check the size of the packing required. It should just fit round the shaft and slide into the housing.
- ✿ Wind the packing in a spiral round the shaft. About three turns should do.
- ✿ Using a sharp hobby knife, cut through all three turns at a shallow angle to the shaft. You should end up with three rings with the cuts at a slight angle rather than at right angles to the packing.

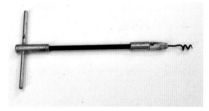

Above **This is a special tool for removing the old packing from the stern gland.**

Below **This bronze stern gland has been 'bonded' to the hull anode. The green sheathed wires connect the gland to the anode stud.**

Right **Some propellers require the blade pivots to be greased annually.**

✪ Slide each ring into the housing in turn, arranging them so that the cuts don't line up with each other. Spread them at 120–degree intervals to help prevent leakage.
✪ Slide the yoke or large nut into contact and tighten up – but not too tight.
✪ When the boat is refloated, immediately inspect the stern gland for excessive leakage and tighten some more if necessary. The aim is for two to three drips per minute.
✪ Once the boat is in use, the gland may need to be retightened as the packing beds in.

Saildrive diaphragms

A large flexible diaphragm is used to seal the hole between the hull and the leg that protrudes through it. Yanmar engines have a double diaphragm with a moisture detector between the two, which will give an alert if one fails. All others have a single diaphragm. The manufacturer's recommendations should be followed with respect to inspection and replacement.

Replacement is likely to require the engine to be moved forward about 4in (100mm), and in some cases the engine will need to be removed.

Stern drives

Because the boat is steered by swivelling the drive unit, there is a large flexible bellows to prevent water entering the hull. The bellows will need at least annual inspection, and will need to be replaced if it deteriorates. The maintenance procedures will be specified by the manufacturer.

Left **There are a number of 'dripless' seals, this being one type. The seal must be squeezed when the boat is relaunched to remove any air, as it is water lubricated.**

Servicing the generator

Normally the generator (or alternator) is a fit-and-forget item, requiring only its drive belt to be adjusted or changed on an inboard engine. With the aid of a workshop manual, more complicated repairs are possible.

Dynastart generator

Old engines used a combined starter motor/generator, known as a 'dynastart', which was belt driven and produced little current. Failure of its brushes would render the starter inoperative.

DC generators or dynamos

These units did not produce much current, and the regulator was built in. The brushes could easily be replaced, usually by removing an end cover or a band around the brush housing.

Alternators

All modern inboard engines use an alternator to generate electricity. This unit produces alternating current (AC) which can't be used to charge the battery. A built-in rectifier/regulator converts the AC to direct current (DC) to charge the battery. Carbon brushes transfer the current from the rotating assembly to the fixed part of the alternator, and these brushes occasionally need to be replaced. Additionally, if you wish to fit a more efficient regulator than the standard one, you will possibly need to get into the alternator to bypass it.

Alternators are supplied by various makers, even across a single manu-facturer's engine range, but the standard way to access the inside of them is this:

✪ Switch off the battery supply.
✪ Label all wires to the alternator, and make a sketch noting the colours and terminals. A mistake when re-connecting could damage the alternator.

Left **This engine has a second alternator fitted to increase the 12 volt electrical output. High output alternators are also available and may be a better option.**

- Disconnect the wires.
- Remove the adjustment and pivot bolts from the alternator mounting bracket and take the alternator off. Beware, it's quite heavy.
- If there's a plastic cover over the rear of the alternator, remove it to gain access to the brushes, which are easy to change.

Ideally you should have the workshop manual to hand, but the following description for a Yanmar alternator may be a guide for other types where further work is required:

- Remove the four nuts and washers from the rear of the casing.
- Remove the long clamp screws from the side of the casing.
- Pull the front of the alternator away from the centre portion carefully to remove the rotor and bearings to gain access to the regulator and brushes.
- Remove the terminal nuts on the rear of the alternator.
- Pull the rear of the alternator off, noting the position of any internal and external insulated spacers.
- To replace the brushes, the wires will need to be unsoldered, and the new ones soldered on in their place.
- Reassemble in the reverse order.

Dismantling the alternator

The case is often in three parts, secured by long bolts, which must first be removed.

Carefully prise the front end of the assembly clear of the casing.

Remove the nuts from the rear case, noting the position of the insulating washers.

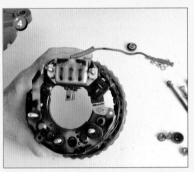
Pull the rear of the case away from the stator ring to reveal the carbon brush assembly.

Disconnect the wires from the alternator, unsoldering them if required, and replace the brushes with new ones.

Reassemble in the reverse order. Once the rear and centre sections are reassembled, insert a toothpick into the rear hole to retract the brushes so that the front section can be slid into place.

Daily and weekly checks

Most engine failures occur because of a lack of maintenance. Regular inspection can reveal faults before they cause a breakdown. A mental checklist (or a paper one) ensures that the necessary checks are carried out every time you take the boat out.

Petrol (gasoline) and diesel engines

Where routine checks are concerned, there is little difference between petrol (gasoline) and diesel engines.

Because petrol vapour is highly explosive, fuel leaks are dangerous, and an electric ventilation fan in the engine compartment is essential.

Daily checks

- Ensure the cooling water seacock is open.
- Check oil level and top up if required. Diesel engine lubrication oil rapidly turns black after an oil change, and this is normal. Petrol lubrication oil should not discolour at all.
- Check for fuel and oil leaks.
- Check the alternator drive belt tension.
- Check coolant level on engines with fresh water cooling. Top up if necessary with water/antifreeze/summer coolant. (The cooling system should not be losing water, so if frequent topping up is required, find the cause.)
- Check the raw water pump for a leak from the seal failure tell-tale.
- Check fuel/water separator bowl for contamination.
- Look for any loose items.
- Traditional stern glands often have grease lubrication that requires the grease reservoir handle to be rotated about half a turn at the start of the day. If you are under power for a long time this may need to be done every few hours.

Above **Carry out a daily check of the engine oil level – some engines have quite a high oil consumption rate.**

Below **Check the coolant level daily. This is just about right, with the level halfway between low and full.**

ENGINE STARTING

- Select ON at the engine battery isolation switch.
- Check that the ventilation fan (if fitted) runs before starting the engine. This is extremely important for petrol engines.
- After starting, check all warning lights have gone out and that cooling water is flowing from the exhaust. (On some boats this is impossible, so a cooling water alarm is a worthwhile investment, because by the time the engine's overheat warning activates, the water pump impeller will probably have failed.)

SAFETY TIP

Any time you inspect rotating machinery, it's vital that you take steps to prevent clothing, equipment, hair and so on becoming entangled in moving parts.

Weekly checks

- ✪ Check gearbox oil level and colour. Gearbox lubricant should not discolour at all, so any change indicates a problem that needs to be investigated.
- ✪ Make a more thorough check for oil, fuel and water leaks, security of components and the condition of engine mountings.
- ✪ Check the stern gland for leaks. For most, a couple of drips a minute is fine, but dripless types shouldn't leak at all. If the gland is oil lubricated, check the level in the oil reservoir.
- ✪ Check the cooling water strainer for weed. If you see lots of floating weed around the boat, then make this a daily check.

Above **At least weekly, check the cooling water strainer for weed and debris – check daily if there's a lot of floating weed in your area.**

Above **Check the raw water pump tell-tale hole for leakage. This will give an early warning of water seal wear and can save the expense of a new pump.**

Left **Regularly check the primary fuel filter bowl for water and dirt contamination.**

Essential spare parts

It is probable that, at some stage in your boating career, you will experience engine trouble, no matter how carefully you have carried out your maintenance and servicing. Having the correct spare part on board will ensure that you are on your way with little delay.

A thought about tools

If you are carrying spares because they may not be readily available in some of the places you are heading to, it's probable that any maintenance engineer will have the necessary tools, or at least be able to improvise. But if you are carrying spares in the expectation that you may want or need to fit them yourself, you must carry any tools needed to fit them as well as the spares themselves.

Essential spares

Some of these spares are used during annual servicing, but could also be required for some unscheduled event like an oil leak, fuel blockage or impeller failure. Most of these items would be part of your regular annual maintenance cost, and you are going to need them at the end of the year in any case, so it's just as well to carry them on board.

- Sufficient lubricating oil for at least one oil change
- Oil filter

- Transmission oil if different from the engine oil
- Fuel filters (primary and fine). In fact, two of each would be better in case of fuel contamination and filter blockage
- Drive belts
- Water pump impeller
- Antifreeze/summer coolant. Ideally you should use a distilled/de-ionised water mixture for the cooling system, so carry a ready-made up mixture for topping up.

Cruising spares

When cruising, it's worth carrying extra spares in case you break down far from help. The cost of these items is very modest.

- Cooling system thermostat. The thermostat controls the running temperature of the engine. If it fails in the open position, the engine will run too cool, which is merely inefficient. But if it fails closed, the engine will rapidly overheat rendering it unusable

- Cooling system hose
- Hose clips of various sizes
- Insulating tape
- Self-amalgamating tape
- General purpose electrical wire
- Cable connectors
- Cable ties
- Tube of liquid gasket
- Exhaust bandage.

Spare engine components

This list can vary greatly, depending on how far (in distance or time) you will be from help. These items will be expensive and probably never used, but could be very reassuring if you have them on board. Some suppliers may be willing to make up a full spares pack on a sale or return basis if you are off on a long cruise. Things you may wish to consider are:

- Starter motor
- Alternator
- Fuel pump
- Cooling water pump
- Throttle cable
- Gear selector cable.

Left A spare alternator drive belt should always be carried, especially if it also drives the water pump, as failure will prevent the engine being used.

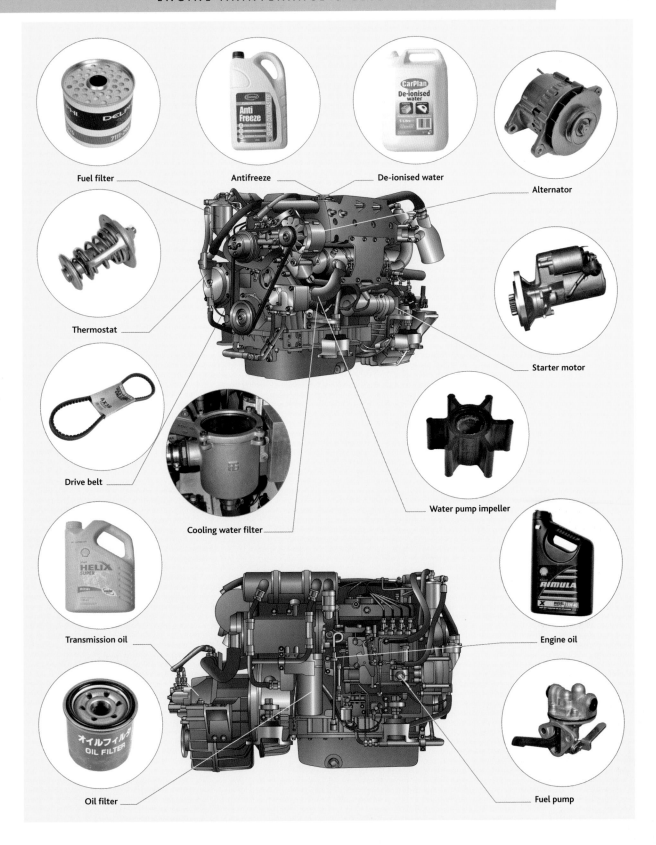

Fuel filter

Antifreeze

De-ionised water

Alternator

Thermostat

Starter motor

Drive belt

Water pump impeller

Cooling water filter

Transmission oil

Engine oil

Oil filter

Fuel pump

Troubleshooting

If you have a problem with your engine you need to follow a logical method to determine what is wrong. Have a troubleshooting chart or step-by-step guide to identify your problem, and remember that many problems have multiple symptoms.

Engine won't turn over
- Is the battery switched on?
- Is the battery flat?
- Check the voltage at the starter motor when the starter key/button is activated. If there's no voltage, check the wiring, connectors and switch.
- If there's an intermediate relay (or 'booster') is it working?

Engine turns over but won't fire
- Is the engine turning over fast enough?
- Is there fuel? (Check the tank contents and that the fuel is turned on.)
- Does the fuel system need to be bled (purged)?

Petrol engine won't start
- Do not attempt to produce a spark to check the ignition. In the enclosed engine space, with any fuel vapour present, an explosion may occur.
- Check the spark plugs, ignition leads and distributor.

Noise and vibration
Both of these problems are subjective and can increase slowly for a long time before they are noticed. As soon as you notice any unusual noise or vibration, investigate its cause. Possible causes are poorly adjusted valve gear, loose or broken engine mountings, a hole in the exhaust or something loose.

Above **A clamp ammeter can be used to check the alternator's output. Make sure it is positioned far enough from the alternator not to be affected by the alternator's magnetic field.**

Below **The colour of the exhaust is a good indication of an engine's health, but don't confuse white smoke with steam on a cold morning.**

Above **On some engines, there's a hidden fuse in the start circuit.**

Lack of power

This may be real or apparent. An apparent lack of power may be due to an under-reading log, fouled hull or propeller, or too much weight, all of which need to be considered. An important question is: 'Has this happened suddenly or has it slowly built up?' If all else is normal, probable causes are:

☸ Engine is in poor mechanical condition.
☸ Restriction in the fuel supply.
☸ Restriction in the air intake or exhaust.
☸ Incorrect set up of the throttle control/linkage. This can be checked on a diesel engine by ensuring that full rpm is available in neutral.

Above **If the starter motor doesn't function, check the voltage on the solenoid and the motor's terminals. Keep out of the way of all moving parts while someone else operates the starter.**

Exhaust smoke

The colour of the exhaust smoke is a very important part of troubleshooting. Normally there should be no exhaust smoke once the engine has reached normal running temperature.

Black smoke occurs on a diesel engine because there's insufficient air to burn the fuel that is being injected. It may be due to the engine being overloaded, and the governor is signalling that more fuel should be injected because the rpm is not responding to the throttle. Or it may be caused by a blocked air filter or exhaust, so that too little air is available.

Blue smoke may indicate burning lubrication oil, especially on a petrol engine. But in a diesel engine it is much more likely to occur because the fuel droplets that are being injected are too large. This probably

Above **A good check on a battery's health is to measure its voltage as the starter is operated.**

indicates the need for the injectors to be serviced. Some older engines have a blue haze in the exhaust all the time.

Light grey smoke is, in a diesel engine, probably an injection problem, indicating a need for the injectors to be serviced or the injection pump timing to be checked.

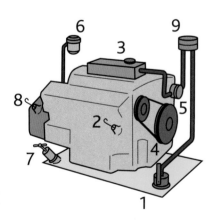

Common causes of problems:
1. Cooling water– check the seacock is open.
2. Engine oil – check the level.
3. Fresh water coolant – check the level.
4. Drive belt – check the tension.
5. Sea water pump – check for leaks.
6. Primary fuel filter – check for water or dirt.
7. Stern-gland greaser – check it is full.
8. Gear box oil – check the level.
9. Sea water strainer – check for weed.

Powerboat
maintenance

Stern drives

Stern drives combine an inboard engine with a leg similar to that of an outboard motor. They require more maintenance than either outboard motors or inboard engines with a conventional shaft drive.

Avoiding corrosion

Galvanic corrosion is the biggest problem for stern drives used in salt water. On most installations the leg cannot be lifted clear of the water, and they are often used on boats that are too large to be kept ashore. Stern drives must therefore be protected by sacrificial zinc anodes at all times. Generally these last for a full season, but they should be inspected regularly in any case, and replaced when 30 per cent of the material has wasted. Always use aluminium friendly antifouling on stern drives. These are formulated with copper thiocyanate, which is less galvanically active than conventional copper oxide antifouling.

Paint systems

The drive's paint system is of equal importance to the anodes, and it must be maintained in perfect condition if rapid corrosion is to be avoided. Barnacles are particularly damaging to paint finishes, so boats that are kept afloat should be hauled out and re-antifouled at the first sign of underwater growth. This is good practice in any case, and will frequently pay for itself in terms of reduced fuel consumption at speed.

To ensure the adhesion of antifouling, the drive must be meticulously prepared, including careful hand sanding with a medium grade paper, and the application of an appropriate primer. If corrosion is

Above **It's important to check the condition of stern drive bellows. Replace them if there is any sign of damage.**

Below **Stern drives are permanently immersed when the boat is afloat. It's therefore vital to protect against corrosion.**

Above **A stern drive ready for painting. Note that copper-based antifoulings cannot be used with aluminium drives.**

evident it must be entirely removed by sanding or careful localised grinding. An etch primer is then needed before antifouling primer can be successfully applied. Always use antifouling that is formulated specifically for stern drives – the high copper content of standard antifouling accelerates corrosion of the aluminium parts.

Other routine maintenance

Other parts of the system require servicing every 50 or 100 hours, depending on the model. Hydraulic hoses, gaiters and clamps should be checked for cracks, pinholes and growth of marine organisms. To properly check the condition of gaiters, the drive needs to be rotated in both directions, as well as lifted and lowered.

The joint that enables the leg to articulate has a number of bearings, each with grease points. These need a couple of squirts of waterproof grease using a grease gun. At the same time, attend to any steering grease points and check the fluid levels in hydraulic steering and lift/trim systems. If fluid is consistently lost, the source of the leak should be investigated.

Look for signs of gearbox oil leaking ahead of the prop, which indicates a worn shaft seal. This is a common problem with engines that operate in shallow muddy or sandy waters. Also check the condition of the gearbox oil. If it's a milky colour, this also indicates the presence of water, so the oil should be changed and the shaft seal replaced.

Jet drives

Jet drives can operate in shallow water without damage, and have no external moving parts that can injure people in the water. Until recently they have been relatively little used except on personal watercraft, but they are gaining in popularity in small boats.

Types and problems

Jet drives can be fitted to both inboard and outboard engines. In both cases the key component is a large aluminium impeller that draws huge amounts of water into the unit (up to 4,000 gallons/18,000 litres per minute) and expels it towards the back of the boat at high speed.

Gratings (or 'grates') over the water intake offer some protection against larger items of debris getting into the drive. These can still cause problems if they block the water flow, but if the motor is briefly shut down they often simply drift away.

Small stones can be picked up in shallow water. The smallest will be ejected out of the nozzle, but slightly larger ones can partially block the intake grating. Rope and other floating debris may wrap around the impeller, and will need to be removed by hand. Inboard type motors normally have an inspection hatch that gives access to the impeller, but outboards may need to be tilted out of the water for access.

TROUBLESHOOTING

Jet drives often exhibit one of two distinct symptoms when something goes wrong: too many revs or too few. An inability to achieve maximum engine speed points to motor problems – unless the main thrust bearing in the drive has failed. By contrast, if the engine revs freely the problem will be with the jet unit.

Below **Jet drives operate on different principles from other drive units, and this is reflected in their maintenance.**

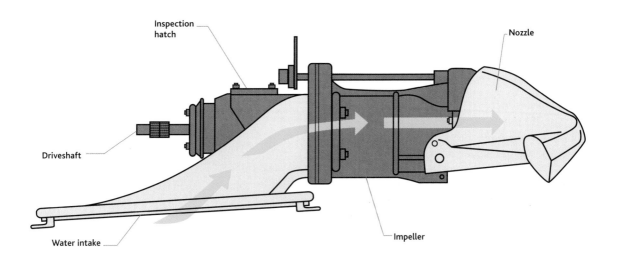

Inspection hatch

Nozzle

Driveshaft

Water intake

Impeller

Above **Opening the port to clear debris from the impeller of an outboard-mounted stern drive.**

Above **The key elements of an inboard engine jet drive system.**

Left **Check the opening is above the waterline before opening the inspection hatch of an inboard-mounted impeller.**

Gradual power loss

Debris can cause a blockage that results in a large and instantaneous loss of drive, but if power declines gradually, this points to problems with the impeller. Foreign bodies, including particles of sand and mud, progressively damage the blades. Minor damage can be repaired by removing the impeller and filing the leading edge to a uniform rounded shape. More serious damage needs to be referred to a specialist.

As the unit wears, the distance between the impeller and its casing increases, reducing the efficiency of the pump. Most systems are designed with thin metal shims above the impeller. These can be removed and placed below the impeller to restore the optimum clearance between the impeller and casing.

Keeping cool

Jet outboard cooling systems lack the dedicated water pump impeller of standard outboards, instead relying on the drive impeller to pump water around the motor. This means that, if drive is lost, the supply of cooling water is interrupted and the engine must be shut down to prevent overheating.

This arrangement also has an implication for flushing the unit with fresh water after use. To prevent the engine being flooded by water, the correct procedure is to start the motor before the water supply is turned on.

Trim tabs

Trim tabs make an important contribution to the handling characteristics of many power craft, and help to reduce fuel consumption. They require little maintenance, but all too often are entirely neglected.

How they work

These ostensibly simple devices provide a variable amount of lift at the stern of a boat to help it get onto the plane and maintain an efficient fore-and-aft trim. They also enable vessels to stay on the plane at lower throttle settings.

Most trim tabs are made of stainless steel, so corrosion is less of an issue than for stern drives, but they still must not be ignored. Boats kept afloat in salt water should have their tabs antifouled regularly, and zinc anodes fitted to the upper faces.

Trim tabs may be subjected to large loads, so each time the boat is laid up you should check that they are not bent out of shape, and that the mountings of the struts and the tabs themselves are secure.

The simplest trim tabs for small boats are self-adjusting, with the tab supported by a gas-filled strut. They assume their lowest position with the boat at rest, gradually rising when speed (and therefore the water pressure) increases.

Left **Although corrosion is less of a problem, sacrificial anodes must be replaced at regular intervals.**

Below **Trim tabs may look small compared to the overall size of a boat, but they are vital for its efficient operation.**

Above **Examine the condition of contacts on electrically-powered trim tabs. These need to be replaced.**

All trim tab struts rely on O-rings that are designed to be an exact fit on the stainless steel shaft. Any barnacles or other hard fouling (however small) that forms on the shaft will damage these seals. The easiest way to prevent marine growth on the shaft of adjustable trim tab systems is to fully raise the tab when the boat is not in use. Don't paint the struts with antifouling, as the seals rely on mating with the metal surface.

Adjustable trim tabs

The angle of adjustable tabs is altered using electric motors or hydraulic rams. The latter have the pump inside the boat, where it is protected from weather and spray. They are therefore inherently more reliable than electric types, with the majority of problems attributable to faults in the wiring between the dashboard switches and the hydraulic pump.

The hydraulic fluid should not need to be changed or topped up during the system's life. However, it is important to check the level in the reservoir periodically. If it does need to be topped up, then the system should be carefully checked for fluid leaks. Always use automatic transmission fluid – not brake fluid, which will degrade seals.

Electrically adjustable systems have a motor inside the strut, where it's prone to getting damp if water gets past the seals. If electric tabs stop working, first check the

Above **Checking the fluid level of hydraulically-actuated trim tabs.**

power supply, including fuses and connections, verifying that the full battery voltage reaches the actuators when the switch is activated.

If actuator failure is suspected, this can be confirmed by touching the wiring from each unit in turn to an independent 12 volt supply. If the actuator doesn't extend or retract, it almost certainly needs to be replaced. Most models are designed as maintenance-free sealed units.

Left **The condition of hydraulic hoses should be checked at regular intervals.**

Sailboat
maintenance

9

Aluminium mast checks

With proper maintenance, aluminium spars are capable of giving reliable service for many decades. However, they experience enormous loadings, especially in heavy weather. Regular checks are vital to monitor wear and spot problems at an early stage.

Mast foot and step

Examine the bottom of the mast extrusion for signs of corrosion or other damage where it meets the mast foot or shoe. This is particularly important for keel-stepped masts, where the base is out of sight and may be regularly submerged.

If damage here is limited to the bottom couple of inches of the spar, the most cost-effective solution is usually to slice the damaged section off the bottom of the extrusion and step the marginally shorter mast on a hardwood block to restore its original height. If a wood block is not an option, it may be possible to have the standing rigging shortened and its terminals re-swaged; otherwise, new rigging will be required.

The entire length of the spar should be checked for damage. Dents in the mast wall can significantly weaken the spar, but strength can be restored by sleeving the spar. This is done by cutting it in two at the damaged area and riveting in place a tightly fitting sleeve, made of the same thickness of aluminium as the mast wall. If damage is close to the spreader roots, an external doubling piece will add strength

Below **Unless the mast is unstepped each season, checking the rig inevitably involves going aloft at some point.**

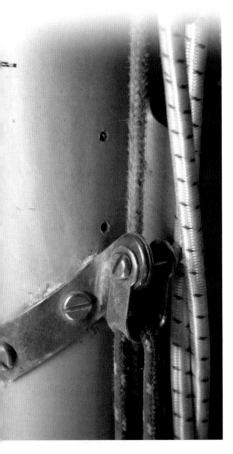

and distribute the spreader loads over a wider area.

At the same time as you examine the spar, check all electrical cables for damage, and test all mast-mounted electrics, including lights and instruments, to make sure they are functioning correctly (see pages 176 to 179).

Spreaders

These are one of the biggest causes of mast failure. They must be angled slightly upwards – generally by about six degrees – to bisect the angle the cap shroud makes at the spreader tips. If this geometry is wrong, rigging loads will tend to twist the spreader off the mast. In addition, nicks or chips on leading or trailing edges will reduce a spreader's ability to withstand compression loads.

Left **Corrosion of this aluminium mast has started next to a stainless steel fitting. The fitting should be removed and checked.**

Stainless steel fittings on an aluminium mast create the potential for galvanic corrosion. To minimise this, spar-makers use monel pop rivets and insulating barriers such as chromate paste or silicone sealant between the two metals. If there is evidence of pitting or corrosion, the fitting should be removed to ascertain the full extent of the damage, and a new application of paste used when the fitting is reattached.

Above **A sleeve inserted into an aluminium mast and rivetted in place can prolong the life of an old spar.**

Left **A dent in the sidewall of a mast will seriously weaken it. The only solution is to reinforce it with an internal sleeve.**

Inspecting wooden masts

Many of the checks for aluminium spars apply equally to wooden masts, but the nature of their construction necessitates a number of additional procedures. To avoid large areas of damage that are expensive to repair, it's even more important with a timber spar to identify any problems as early as possible.

Paint and varnish systems

The paint or varnish system is crucial in protecting the spar from water ingress, so it should be examined at least once and preferably twice a year. Any scratches, areas of chafe or bubbling paint should be dealt with immediately, dried out and recoated. Regular maintenance in this manner will maximise the lifespan of the paint/varnish system, but periodically the spar will benefit from a strip back to bare wood and a full recoating.

At the same time, check for signs of water ingress and rot. This is most likely to start near fixings, with screw or bolt holes the prime culprits, but it can quickly spread well beyond the initial point. With keel-stepped masts, pay particular attention to the mast heel in the bilge and the area where the spar passes through the deck – these places are normally out of sight, allowing problems to fester undetected. Some people advocate inserting a leather pad or canvas gasket between the fittings and the spar to prevent corrosion initiating the onset of rot.

Fittings near areas of damaged wood or coatings should be removed, and rotten or soft timber removed with a chisel. Thoroughly dry the area before undertaking remedial repairs or repainting. Small, shallow areas of rot can be repaired by removing the damaged wood and

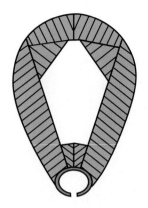

Above **Most wooden masts are hollow spars made of a number of pieces of timber glued together in various different ways.**

replacing it with new timber (see page 82). However, larger areas will need new timber scarfed in, with a minimum 8:1 taper, although 12:1 is better. Scarf joints should be staggered along the length of the spar, with each one terminating several feet from its neighbours. When replacing fittings, ensure fixings are properly sealed and don't provide an entry point for moisture.

Wooden mast construction

Aside from some gaff and lug rigs, wooden masts are generally hollow, and made from a number of planks or battens glued together, then shaped by a combination of sawing, planning and sanding. Any evidence of failure of the glue, often evidenced as the end of a plank

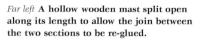

Far left **A hollow wooden mast split open along its length to allow the join between the two sections to be re-glued.**

Left **The same mast re-glued, re-varnished and good for another 30 years of use.**

starting to spring away from the spar, needs to be rectified.

Local repairs can be made by holding the joint open with a wedge, cleaning the mating surfaces and re-gluing with epoxy thickened with microfibres to create a structural adhesive – then clamping the repair while the glue cures. However, if glue has failed in one area it's likely that it is also weak in others. This means that it's often easy to split the spar into its component planks, using a chisel and wedge to spring

Above **Wooden spars are capable of a very long life and if problems develop they are generally easy to identify and rectify.**

the elements apart – although careful saw cuts along the glue line may be needed in places. The entire spar can then be checked for rot, inside and out, before being re-glued with epoxy adhesive.

Giant hose clips make ideal clamps. Conventional woodworking clamps are awkward to use on the curved surface of a spar.

Above **Gluing scarf joints. A taper of at least 8:1 is needed to ensure the structural strength of the joint.**

Standing rigging

The rig of even quite modest boats is subject to large dynamic loads, while a 40-footer can generate enough force to lift a large car. So it is vital that the rig – and that means all of its many elements – is utterly reliable.

Routine maintenance

Regular inspections are the key to early identification of problems. The lower swaged ends of standing rigging can be examined weekly – any sign of movement or cracked strands of wire is a sign of imminent failure. Also check bottlescrews (turnbuckles) are properly secured with split pins or seizing wire to prevent them unscrewing. Corrosion showing as a brown stain is not a problem, provided it only affects the surface and can be polished away.

Checking aloft

A trip aloft should be made at least once a season to check that all components appear to be in good condition, including shrouds where they pass through spreader ends. It's also important to check that the entire load-bearing length of each shroud and stay, from the top swage to the chain plate, is exactly aligned. If any element is out of line, loads are increased and a sideways component of force, which the fittings are not designed to take, is introduced.

A number of mistakes can frequently be seen in the set-up of standing rigging, the most common being clevis pins that don't match the size of the terminal they secure. Even if the mismatch is small, the metal will wear at an accelerated rate, leading to premature failure.

Crevice corrosion

Cyclic loading of stainless steel components can lead to metal fatigue and create microscopic fissures on the surface of the metal. Sea water is then trapped in these fissures, which slowly become deoxygenated – and stainless steel corrodes if oxygen is not present. Although this starts in a small way, the effects can be severe, eventually rendering an entire component useless. The most effective check for such cracks is dye testing, which reveals them as a purple hairline, although looking for pitting with a magnifying glass may be useful.

Crevice corrosion is one of the reasons insurers normally insist on the safeguard of replacing standing rigging every ten years (five years for race boats). Although risk of failure after this time remains small, it's much more common for problems to develop in older rigging.

Left **Every element of the mast and standing rigging should be carefully checked at least once a season.**

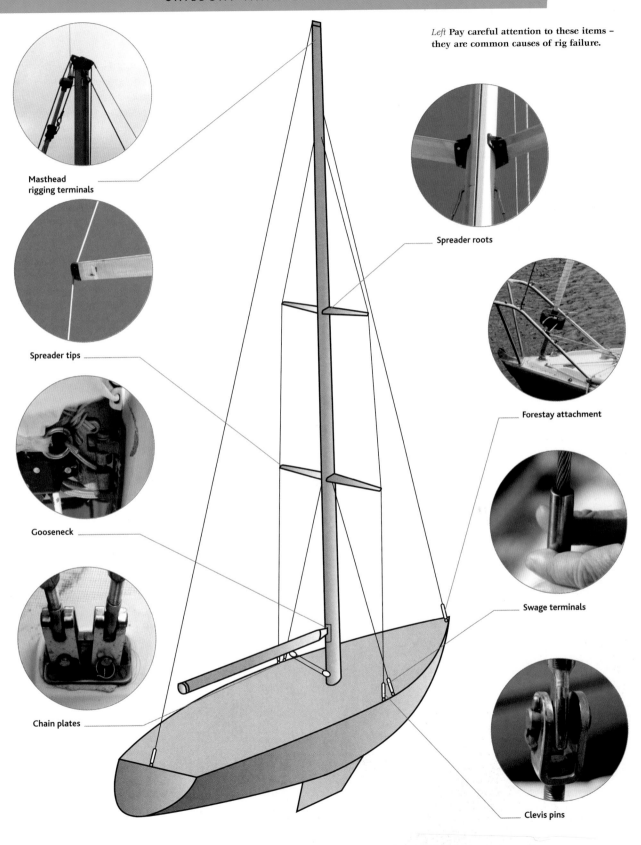

Left Pay careful attention to these items – they are common causes of rig failure.

Masthead rigging terminals

Spreader roots

Spreader tips

Forestay attachment

Gooseneck

Swage terminals

Chain plates

Clevis pins

Tuning rigging

Rigs must be properly set up to avoid structural damage and achieve their designed strength. A well-tuned rig also improves a boat's handling characteristics, whether it's a racer or a heavy cruiser, including minimising excess weather helm. Tuning a single-spreader rig is a straightforward process, but becomes more complex with additional sets of spreaders, especially if they are swept aft.

Mast rake and bend

Most boats are designed to sail with between two and five degrees of aft mast rake. Too much rake will cause excessive weather helm, while too little will give neutral or, even worse, lee helm. To measure rake, pull the main halyard to the masthead with a piece of light line (which will have little wind resistance) tied to it. Tie a heavy weight to the end of this line, suspend it in a bucket of water, and measure how far aft of the mast step the line is. As a rough guide, 8in (20cm) for every 20ft (6m) of mast height represents two degrees of rake with a straight mast. Rake is determined by forestay length, so adjusting the forestay bottlescrew will change the amount of rake.

Riggers make shrouds in pairs and are careful to ensure they are of equal lengths, so it's easy to check whether a mast is laterally vertical. If there are equal numbers of turns on the bottlescrews on both sides of the boat, the mast should be exactly upright. Initially bottlescrews should be firmly tensioned by hand, although final tensioning is done under sail. Applying light oil to the threads makes them easier to turn and helps to prevent damage.

The rig also needs to be set up with some positive pre-bend – with the mid-section of the mast curving slightly towards the bow. Use the baby stay or forward lower shrouds to pull the centre of the mast forward until the bend is equivalent to between one-quarter and one-half of the diameter of the spar. This can be judged by sighting directly up the mast.

Sailing trials

When sailing to windward in a force 3 (enough wind to get the boat fully powered up), the leeward shrouds should have minimal tension, without becoming slack. Lower shrouds should be adjusted so that the mast is perfectly straight athwartships. This can be gauged by sighting up the mainsail luff groove. The rig should subsequently be checked with reefed sails set in stronger winds, to ensure there is adequate, but not excessive, pre-bend.

Left **After inserting split pins, tape them over to cover the sharp edges and stop lines and sails snagging.**

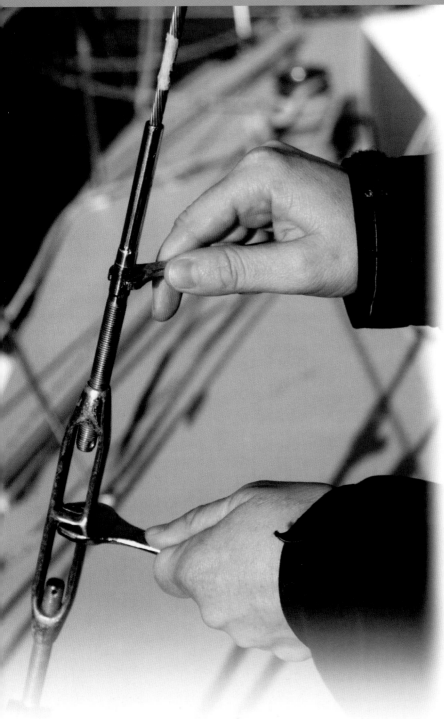

Above **Bottlescrews can be held with a temporary lashing while the rig is being tuned, before being permanently secured.**

The most common mistake when setting up a rig is to leave the shrouds too loose. When leeward shrouds are slack, they are subject to additional fatigue bending, and the entire rig is at risk of increased shock loadings. This is especially important for rigs with multiple swept-aft spreaders. Rig tension should be checked periodically. All hulls deform under their rig load, with fibreglass boats in particular changing shape over time.

The angle between this vertical line and the mast is known as the 'rake'.

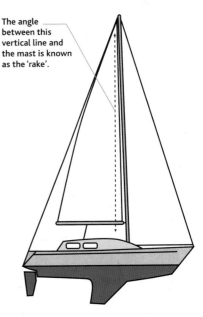

Above **Do not use a screwdriver as a lever to tighten bottlescrews as this will damage the fittings. Use well-fitting spanners.**

Right **All sailing boats are designed to have the mast raked slightly aft, generally between two and five degrees.**

Running rigging & blocks

Proper care of deck gear will extend its lifespan and minimise the number of failures. In addition, well-maintained equipment helps you to avoid undue friction, so that sail handling and deck work are easier and safer.

Routine maintenance of blocks

Check that blocks are free running and that there's no damage to the pulley, sidewalls or attachment points. They should also be rinsed regularly in fresh water to remove deposits of salt and grit. The best modern blocks use Torlon (a resilient, self-lubricating plastic) for the bearings, and need no further maintenance. However, plain bearing blocks (where the sheave revolves on the central pin that holds it in place) and those with stainless steel bearings benefit from a sparing application of silicone lubricant from a spray can. Don't be tempted to apply excess lubricant – it just traps dirt and grit.

The following steps will help to free seized or partially seized blocks:

- ✪ Rinse with hot soapy water to dissolve salt and remove grease deposits. This is sufficient to get many blocks working.
- ✪ Lubricate with WD-40, and rotate the pulley back and forth as much as possible. Repeat as necessary. Note that this product can harm some composite materials, so it should be washed away with hot soapy water once the block is running freely.
- ✪ Once the block is dry, apply silicone spray lubricant sparingly.

TIP

Boatbuilders often supply much longer lines than necessary. The extra length just gets in the way, gathering dirt and getting tangled, so don't be afraid to cut it off, leaving an excess of no more than 2ft (0.6m).

Mast and boom sheaves

Worn masthead and boom end sheaves can cause a number of problems, including lines tending to jump off the pulley and jam. The pulley may even seize entirely. If the process outlined above doesn't work, the solution is to remove the

Below **Chafe in a genoa halyard caused by wear at the masthead sheave.**

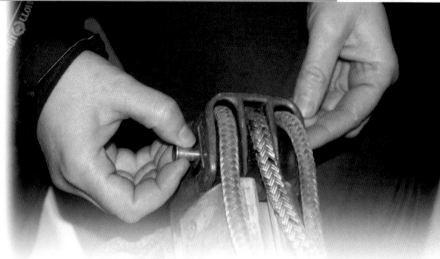

pin that holds the pulleys in the sheave box, and replace both pulleys and sheaves.

The pins of some modern sheave boxes are captive at both ends. In this case, carefully drill a hole at each end to allow the old pin out and a new over-length pin to be fitted, secured by split pins. Pins that are seized in place can be pushed out by lightly tapping a drift pin of the same diameter with a hammer.

Upgrading deck layouts and gear

Deck hardware is constantly evolving, and the advent of new materials results in equipment that's increasingly light and compact, yet more robust than its predecessors. At the same time there's a trend to simplify deck layouts. If you are upgrading the lines of an older boat to more modern, low-stretch materials, it's important to recognise the additional peak loads that a line with minimal stretch will put on deck fittings and clutches. Often the latter will also need to be upgraded to suit the new lines.

Above **Removing the pin holding the sheaves for reefing pennants in the 'box' at the end of a boom.**

Right **A modern low-friction roller-bearing block made from a lightweight structural polymer and with Torlon self-lubricating ball bearings.**

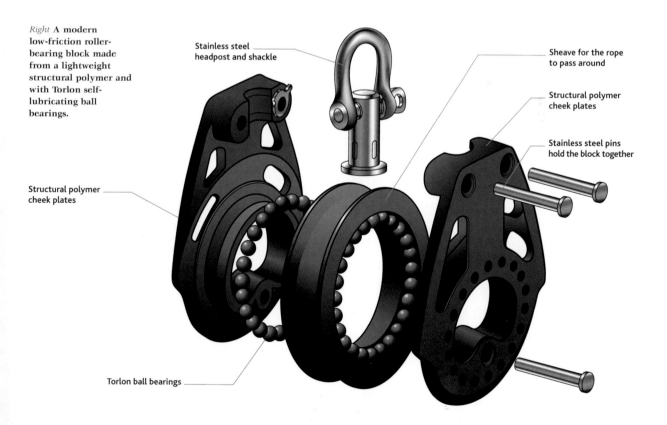

Stainless steel headpost and shackle

Sheave for the rope to pass around

Structural polymer cheek plates

Stainless steel pins hold the block together

Structural polymer cheek plates

Torlon ball bearings

Servicing a winch

Boat winches are designed to carry exceptionally heavy loads. Well maintained winches not only last longer, but minimize the risk to crew and craft from unexpected malfunction or failure.

Winches are robust pieces of equipment but still require servicing periodically. Grease can congeal over time, reducing the power of a winch, causing the ratchets (toothed wheels) to stick. The winch could then release itself without warning, – dangerous if there is a sail or heavy load on it.

Be methodical

Cruising yachts should have their winches serviced every year. Ideally racing yachts should be serviced

Below **The genoa sheet load on a 40ft (12m) cruising yacht can easily reach 1,000lb (453kg). Regular servicing is vital for performance and safety.**

several times per season. You don't need many pieces of equipment or even much skill to service a winch, but you will need to be methodical when taking the winch apart and patient when reassembling it.

Before carrying out a winch service, obtain the manufacturer's diagram of the associated parts and follow the service instructions. All good winches tend to come apart readily and require the correct grease to prevent the pawls (the hinged catches that fit into the notches of the ratchet) from jamming. Winches are normally mounted on coamings near the edge of the boat. If a bit drops off while

you are working on it, the part will roll over the side. You could place a see-through plastic bag over the winch to prevent springs and pawls jumping out and getting lost while you are working.

Taking it apart

Lay out the parts in order of removal, placing the items in the cockpit rather than on the deck and in a container to keep them all together. One essential when stripping down a winch is to scrub all gears and pawls with a paintbrush or toothbrush using paraffin liquid, or a similar solvent. It is important that you let the parts dry so that no solvent is left that would dilute the new grease. Place all the parts on a rag in a box to dry and follow the manufacturer's recommendations as you carefully grease each part, usually with a light oil such as winch grease. It is not helpful to drench everything in grease, which will make the winch sluggish.

Assemble the winch

Reassemble the winch in reverse order, making sure that the pawls can move freely. The pawls should move smoothly and automatically return to their normal position where they engage with the teeth. If they do not function correctly, clean and lubriate with a very thin film of winch grease and reassemble once more.

ONGOING CARE

- ✪ Ensure winches are firmly secured to the deck or coaming.

- ✪ Wash winches regularly to remove the salt that causes corrosion.

- ✪ Cover winches when not in use.

- ✪ Carry spare springs and ratchets.

Winch maintenance

Servicing a two-speed Lewmar winch

Remove the retaining clip and drum from the winch.

Remove the roller bearing from the winch for cleaning.

Clean the drum spindle with a cloth to remove dirt and old grease.

Clean the gearing mechanism with a brush and paraffin liquid.

Wash away dirt and old grease from the winch drum with paraffin liquid.

Remove the retaining screw from the gears to take apart.

Remove the springs and pawls from the gears. Lightly grease all parts.

Temporarily reassemble to confirm smooth operation.

Headsail roller reefing

Most headsail roller reefing systems require minimal maintenance. Any problems encountered generally stem from poor installation. However, some have stainless steel bearings that need greasing periodically, and in all cases it's vital to understand the system and how to solve the most common problems.

Halyard wrap

The genoa halyard wrapping around the top swivel is the biggest single problem you are likely to encounter. Possible reasons are:

- ❂ The forestay or halyard is too slack.
- ❂ The headsail luff is too short, resulting in the swivel being too low.
- ❂ Incorrect shackles have been used to attach the halyard to the swivel, allowing the halyard to rub on the swivel.
- ❂ The halyard leads parallel to the forestay. It should diverge from the stay at an angle of 5 to 10 degrees.

Tensioning the backstay and halyard respectively will solve the first two problems, while a strop can be added between the head of a short-luffed sail and the swivel. If the halyard leads parallel to the forestay, a fairlead fitted on the forward face of the mast will divert it to the correct angle.

Routine maintenance

This varies depending on the material used for bearings. Torlon and Delrin need only a rinse with fresh water a few times a season, but models with stainless steel bearings should be greased annually. The better models have sealed

Above **Check the top swivel rotates freely. Note also the custom-shaped shackle which ensures a correct lead for the halyard.**

Below **Removing the forestay before sliding the reefing system off. The rig is supported by halyards tied to the stemhead.**

bearings that need only an application of a little extra grease at specific grease points.

If stainless steel bearings are not sealed, an application of paraffin or WD-40 is needed first to dissolve the old grease and dirt, followed by a wash with warm soapy water. Once dry, apply waterproof grease sparingly.

Replacing the reefing line

If the sail is bent on, furl it around the foil and pull the entire reefing line out, so there are no turns left on the drum. Then untie the stopper knots in each end of the old line, unthread it and reeve the new one.

If the sail is not bent on, then the number of turns of the line around the drum must be counted as the old reefing line is unwound. After reeving the new line, turn the foil by hand (making sure you are going in the correct direction) to put the required number of turns around the drum.

With the sail fully furled, and a couple of turns of the jib sheets around the sail, there should be at least five turns left on the drum – these are needed when the sail furls tightly in strong winds. If there are insufficient turns on the drum, remove the sheets and spin the foil by hand until you have a suitable number.

The size of the luff groove in the foil needs to match the luff of the headsail, and sailmakers use a range of insert sizes to accommodate different groves. If the insert is too large, the sail will be difficult or even impossible to hoist; if it's too small, the luff may pull out of the foil.

Right **Checking the headsail luff rope size is a good match for the luff groove.**

Inset **This diverter on the forward face of the mast ensures the headsail halyard leads from the top swivel at the correct angle.**

Halyards & mainsail reefing systems

Halyards and reefing lines need to be removed from the spar from time to time, either for replacement or to be washed, though reinstalling them isn't too difficult. Reefing systems must also be tested before they are used in anger.

Removing and replacing halyards

Before removing a halyard or reefing pennant, a lightweight messenger line should be attached to make replacing it easier. This is simplest if an eye is incorporated in the whipping at the end of the halyard – the messenger line can be tied directly to that.

Alternatively, sailmaker's twine stitched through both lines will create a strong join that can be covered with tape to create a smooth profile that will pass easily over sheaves. When installing a new halyard or reefing line, keep all the others in tension so that the new one doesn't twist around them.

Installing a halyard without a messenger is more awkward. If the mast is unstepped and lying horizontally, professional riggers use stainless steel rigging wire, which can be pushed along the entire length of the spar with the new line attached to it. If the mast is stepped, a weighted messenger can be lowered from aloft, before being hooked out of the spar or sheave. Single line reefing systems have additional purchases in the boom, so pennants cannot be replaced without a messenger, unless one of the boom end fittings is removed to allow access to the blocks within the spar.

Above **A short length of rigging wire bent into a hook can be used to fish a halyard out of a mast exit.**

Below **To reeve a new halyard without a messenger, feed a length of rigging wire into the spar, then tape the new halyard securely to this.**

Modernising systems

One of the most popular upgrades of deck gear is to lead all lines aft so that sail handling can be done from the cockpit. This works best if single line reefing is installed, or additional pennants from the luff of the sail are led aft. Otherwise a crewmember will still need to go to the mast to deal with the luff cringle. Leading lines aft increases friction, so use the best blocks you can afford and plan the layout to minimise the angles through which lines are diverted.

Whatever the reefing system, it's important to check that all elements work smoothly before they need to be relied on at sea. With mainsails, this is easiest if the boat is lying head to wind. Such a check should be carried out after the sail is bent on at the start of each season.

In-mast reefing

Most problems with in-mast reefing stem from insufficient leech tension when the sail is reefed, and this can be solved by reducing topping lift tension. Routine maintenance involves washing with fresh water and lubricating bearings annually with the grease recommended by the manufacturer. If the system becomes progressively stiffer to operate after several years' use, it should be dismantled so that the bearings and gears can be cleaned in solvent and fresh grease applied.

Right **In-mast mainsail reefing systems need the boom to be maintained at an angle that allows the sail to roll neatly when reefed.**

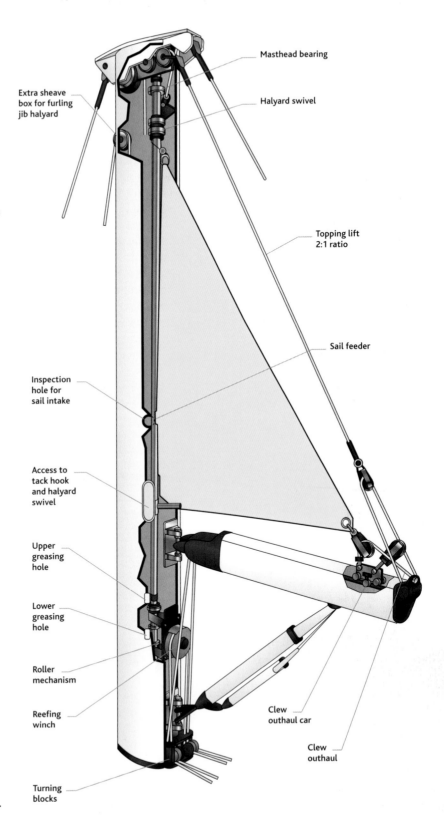

Masthead bearing

Halyard swivel

Extra sheave box for furling jib halyard

Topping lift 2:1 ratio

Sail feeder

Inspection hole for sail intake

Access to tack hook and halyard swivel

Upper greasing hole

Lower greasing hole

Roller mechanism

Reefing winch

Clew outhaul car

Clew outhaul

Turning blocks

Sail valeting & stowage

Good sail shape is a prerequisite if you want a boat to have good handling characteristics. Knowing the prime reasons for premature ageing of sailcloth is therefore vital in maintaining sails that retain their strength and shape for as long as possible.

Creasing, flogging and sun damage

Creases reduce the strength of a sail and its ability to withstand stretching, and when a sail is allowed to flog or flap the structural fibres are rapidly broken down. In addition, polyester sails are impregnated with resin to minimise stretch, but this breaks down every time the sail flaps. Motor-sailing with the mainsail flapping is particularly damaging.

Degradation caused by ultraviolet light is the other big problem. It rapidly weakens the fabric and results in the death of many little-used sails, so sacrificial UV strips on roller headsails and an effective mainsail cover are vital. Modern lazyjack 'bag' systems can encourage sailors to be too laid-back about mainsail protection. The two sides of the 'bag' must be zipped together over the top of the sail to prevent degradation of the cloth in sunlight.

Preparation for storage

Keen dinghy and small boat racers roll their sails for storage, with battens in situ but loosened, as this minimises creases. If sufficient storage space is available, this method is good for yachts up to about 36ft (11m). Flaking is the next kindest alternative, and the most viable option for larger boats. If the battens are removed, a flaked sail can be 'bricked' – rolled tightly from the clew to form a cylinder. This creates a package a fraction of the size of a rolled or flaked sail, but introduces damaging hard creases.

Modern sails use Velcro to secure the battens – a short batten prodder must be slid between the hooks and loops before the batten can be removed. Some older sails use lashings, or even stitches, to hold the battens in place. Battens in very large sails may be tensioned and held in

Above **Most modern sails use Velcro to hold battens in place. A 'batten prodder' is used to separate the two parts of the Velcro.**

Below **On smaller boats, rolling a sail is kinder to the fabric as it does not introduce folds or creases.**

place by screws, and these must be loosened before the batten can be removed. Sails should be stored away from sunlight in a dry, well-ventilated and vermin-proof area.

Sail cleaning

Sails should be washed regularly with fresh water to remove salt, and given an annual DIY wash with a hose, soft brush and mild detergent. Sailmakers use a variety of laundering methods. Some wash sails in giant tubs, but this inevitably causes some creasing. Others have warehouses in which sails are washed with a hose, which is much kinder to the cloth.

Drying sails without damage

Never allow sails to flap or flog while they're being dried. The best way to dry them is to go sailing on a fine day, or to hoist and set them while moored. On shore, they should be spread out to dry, ideally supported carefully a little above the ground.

Above **The best way by far to dry a sail is to hoist it on the mooring and sheet it in to prevent it flapping.**

Left **Sails of larger boats should be flaked for storage. It's easier to do this on the dock than on board.**

Repairing sails & boltropes

The old adage that 'a stitch in time saves nine' is perhaps most fitting in relation to sail repairs. Regular inspections of cloth, stitching and hardware will identify problems at an early stage, when only minimal remedial repairs are needed.

Distribution of loads

Before attempting to repair a sail, it's vital to understand the distribution pattern of loads through the material (see figure below). In low-stress areas, self-adhesive sail repair cloth or tape applied to both sides of the damage can last indefinitely, provided the material is first washed with fresh water and then dried and de-greased using acetone. Rounding the corners of patches reduces localised stresses, helping them stay in place much longer. Some laminate materials can be harmed by stitching, so self-adhesive patches of the correct material may be the only option for making repairs.

TIP

Make sure you use needles that are the right size for the job. Most packs of sailmaker's needles are skewed towards large sizes for stitching bolt ropes and whippings. Unless your sails are of very heavy cloth, use the smallest needles for sail repairs.

Damage in high-load areas of Dacron sails is more likely to need a stitched repair, though self-adhesive sailcloth can still be useful if it's a similar weight to the fabric of the sail. It is possible to successfully hand stitch the edge of such patches, but a machine will make the job faster and neater. Many domestic machines will sew through two or three layers of Dacron sailcloth if fitted with a heavy denim needle, although some hand finishing may be necessary if more layers of cloth are encountered.

Essential tools and materials
- Double-sided tape.
- Self-adhesive sail repair tape and cloth.
- Sailmaker's needles.
- Sailmaker's palm.
- Sharp scissors.
- Strong polyester thread.

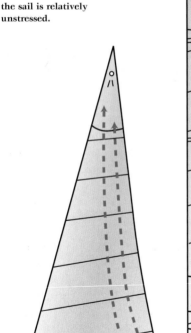

Below **How sail loads are distributed. The leech and clew carry high loads, while the lower middle part of the sail is relatively unstressed.**

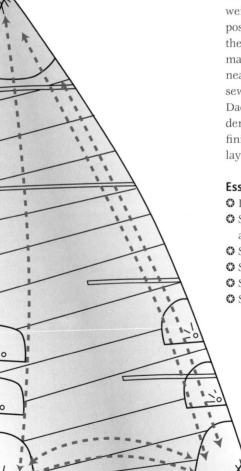

Hand-stitching a seam

Damaged stitching can easily be repaired by hand, reusing the old needle holes. Double-sided tape is invaluable in holding the two panels in position so that the seam lies flat without puckering.

Bolt ropes can be locally reattached to the luff or foot of a sail by hand sewing, with stitches going into the rope. However, if a long section of bolt rope has pulled away, this indicates that the cloth here no longer has adequate structural strength. The best solution is a patch that wraps around both sides of the sail.

If eyelets start pulling away from the cloth, they should be removed and the sail patched to restore strength to that area, before a new two-part grommet is punched into

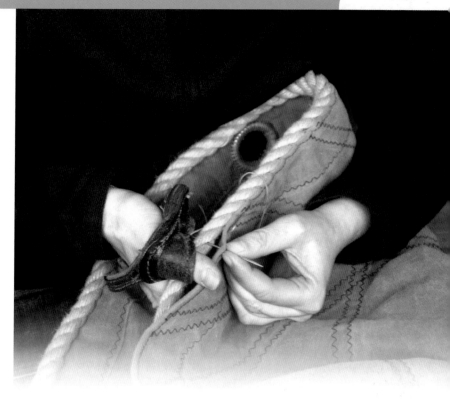

Above **Boltropes can be reattached to a sail with hand sewing. Each stitch should pass through the middle of the rope.**

place. A temporary repair can be made by stitching around the eyelet, with each stitch passing through the fitting and into a sound area of cloth around it. However, large cringles that take significant loads need to be fitted using a sailmaker's hydraulic press.

Spinnakers and cruising chutes

Small nicks and tears to nylon spinnakers and cruising chutes can be successfully repaired using self-adhesive spinnaker repair tape. However, larger rips will need a machine to stitch a new layer or panel of cloth in place.

Stitching a seam

Use double-sided tape to hold the cloth in the right place while making the repair.

Anchor the thread by making three or four stitches through a pair of existing holes.

Slowly work along the seam, using existing holes if possible.

Stitch in the opposite direction to finish the other half of the zig-zag.

Bending on sails & covers

At one time, bending on sails was a precursor to almost every sailing trip, but with roller furling headsails almost ubiquitous on today's cruising yachts, it's now generally a task that's performed once a season, at most. As well as the main working sails, it's important to know how to rig storm sails. This can vary considerably from boat to boat.

Slab reefing mainsails

First secure the foot of the sail to the boom. With the clew at the front of the boom, insert the boltrope into the groove or track on top of the boom. Pull the sail aft until the tack can be secured at the gooseneck and the clew outhaul attached. With loose-footed mainsails, insert the torpedo attached to the clew into the grove on the boom, slide it aft and then attach the tack and clew outhaul.

Most masts have a gate, a little way above the gooseneck, that allows luff slides to pass it freely. It's easiest to start by inserting those nearest the tack, allowing them to slide down, and then work towards the head. If they are not already in place, battens should be inserted next. Use a batten prodder, if necessary, to push the Velcro tab into the batten pocket (see page 242). Finally, pass the reefing pennants through the cringles on the leech of the sail, and tie them round the boom. The sail can now be flaked ready for use.

In-mast furling sails

With the boat lying head to wind, shackle the outhaul block to the clew of the sail and the head to the halyard swivel. Next, insert the bolt rope at

Above **Don't take a chance on your storm jib fitting. Hoist it on a calm day to check it will work when you need it for real.**

Below **The mainsail clew is usually lashed to the back of the boom with a lanyard. Ensure it's as taut as possible.**

Bending on a mainsail

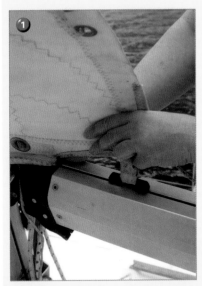

Insert the boltrope and/or torpedo at the clew of the sail into the groove, and pull the clew to the aft end of the boom.

Lash the tack of the sail to the gooseneck. In some cases a shackle is used for this in place of a lanyard.

Insert the sail slides into the gate on the mast, starting from the bottom and working up towards the head of the sail.

the head of the sail into the luff grove of the foil and hoist all but the final 2ft (0.6m) of the sail - some systems require the lower part of the luff to be fed into the bottom of the foil from above. The tack can then be attached, the halyard tensioned and the sail furled.

Roller-reefing headsails
- ✪ Shackle the tack to the roller drum.
- ✪ Tie the sheets to the clew using bowlines.
- ✪ Pass the bolt rope at the head of the sail through the prefeeder (if fitted).

- ✪ Shackle the sail and the halyard to the top swivel.
- ✪ Insert the bolt rope into the bottom of the groove in the foil.
- ✪ Hoist the sail, with one person feeding the luff and another pulling the halyard.
- ✪ Tension the halyard using a winch.
- ✪ Furl the sail, making sure that at least two turns of the sheets wrap round the sail.
- ✪ Cleat the furling line securely.

Hanked headsails
Hanked-on headsails are also attached first at the tack and clew. Hanks are then clipped to the

forestay, working upwards from the tack. The sail can now be flaked and tied to the rail until needed. Storm sails are rarely taken out of their bag, but it's vital to figure out how to set them (and how to lead the sheets efficiently) before they need to be used in gale conditions, so practise!

Canvaswork
Fitting canvas items is generally a matter of common sense. It is important, though, to ensure that every element fits properly and is secured well enough to withstand the considerable forces imposed by gale-strength winds.

Dinghy
maintenance

Regular checks

A dinghy is used in conditions that can cause corrosive and abrasive stresses on the boat from salt water, wind and waves. A little ongoing dinghy care and repair will ensure that you enjoy trouble-free sailing with your dinghy.

The sails (including the spinnaker), the hull, foil, rudder, rigging and deck fittings should all be inspected.

Sails

All sails can become damaged, especially through the stress of racing. Check the mainsail and foresail before you put the sails away for the winter. Hose down the sails with fresh water to remove salt, or immerse them in cool water with soap flakes. Repair any tears yourself or take them to the sailmaker.

Check out the spinnaker. Spinnakers are light sails and can easily get small tears where the cloth catches on the chute, so make sure any small holes are fixed before the spinnaker is put back in the sail bag. During the season as a temporary measure you can patch up the damage before a tiny hole turns into a rip. Use self-adhesive spinnaker tape to cover the hole, flattening the tape to remove air bubbles and round off the edges.

The hull, foil and rudder

There may be times when you can't avoid impact damage to the hull of a dinghy. Rotomoulded plastic can withstand quite hard knocks and sustain only minor scratches. More serious damage requires professional repair. Any damage should be dealt with straight away to avoid water seeping into the hull.

Fibreglass dinghies may sustain minor damage to the gel coat. It should be repaired without delay to avoid water seeping into the laminate, which will be hard to remove later. Check over your foil and rudder. If they have been damaged they can be built up using

Above **When removing the sails from your dinghy check them for tears before you put them away until next season.**

specialist products such as gel coat filler and marine epoxy filler (always follow the manufacturer's instructions), power sanded to shape and painted with the original colour.

Rigging

Check all the shrouds and wire halyards, including at the top and bottom of a furling jib. Wire can fray and break which can compromise the rig's strength. Tape up split pins at the foot of rigging with waterproof tape to protect the sails (and you) from getting torn on sharp edges.

Deck fittings

Cleats, rollers and jammers can suffer from salt water erosion so wash them regularly in fresh water. Spray silicone may provide added protection. If the fittings are really worn, they should be replaced.

Left **Dinghies that regularly take part in racing suffer more stress on their sails, rigging, sheets and fittings and need to be checked frequently.**

Right **These are the main parts of the dinghy that need special attention during dinghy maintenance.**

Check forestay and halyards for chafing

Renew tape to keep split pins in place

Remove foil (centreboard or daggerboard) and inspect for damage

Check jammers for corrosion

Check rudder for impact damage

Check the sails for rips and tears

Hull & deck repair

Three construction forms are generally used for dinghies: wood, fibreglass and rotational moulding. In some cases wood and fibreglass are combined in a boat with a fibreglass hull and plywood deck. The three materials have different properties and maintenance considerations.

Above **Rotomoulded boats are the product of an industrial process, rather than traditional boatbuilding methods.**

Below **The material your dinghy is made of will have a bearing on the care it needs, with wooden boats needing most attention.**

Fibreglass, plastic and wood

Fibreglass has been the primary construction form for many years, and benefits from proven longevity with a minimum of routine maintenance. Some more recent racing dinghies also incorporate epoxy resins to create a structure that maintains stiffness over a longer period. Exactly the same techniques are used to repair the hull and deck as for larger fibreglass boats (see pages 62 to 69), provided epoxy is used in preference to polyester resin where appropriate.

Since the late 1990s, rotational moulding has been widely used for large production runs. A measured quantity of powdered or granulated plastic (usually polyethylene) is placed in a hollow mould, which is heated to around 300°C to melt the

plastic. The mould is then slowly rotated around two axes to allow the plastic to flow evenly over the mould's internal surfaces.

Rotationally moulded boats have very high resistance to impact damage and scratching, but are heavier than equivalent fibreglass craft. The biggest downside is that, in the unlikely event of the boat sustaining structural damage, repairs are difficult to carry out. Specialist knowledge and tooling are required to fuse new material into the damaged area.

Wooden boats

Timber construction includes plywood, both sheet and hot- or cold-moulded varieties, as well as traditional planked clinker or carvel construction, which are discussed in more detail on pages 260 and 261.

Buoyancy tanks

The easiest way to check for leaks is to run detergent solution around any fittings and along the edges of the tank where it joins the hull or deck. The air in the tank can then be

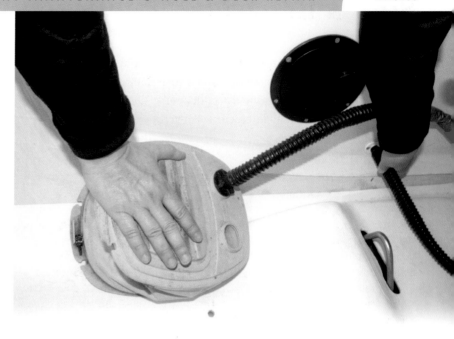

pressurised using a foot pump connected to a bung (drain) hole. Any air that escapes will cause the detergent to bubble.

Leaking fittings can easily be removed and re-bedded, but if there are leaks between the edges of a tank and the rest of the boat, the joins will need an extra layer of fibreglass laminated on top of the existing material.

Above **Buoyancy tanks are vital for a dinghy's safety and should be pressure tested for leaks at least once a year.**

Problem fastenings

Many dinghies have deck fittings secured with screws. If these pull out, some can be replaced with bolts, but with others there's no access to reach behind the fitting. Faced with this problem many owners resort to bigger screws, but this is rarely a neat or long-term solution. It's better to fill the holes with epoxy resin and microfibres (microscopic strands of fibre used to thicken epoxy resin to from a structural adhesive/filler). The screws can be reinserted to form a thread as the resin sets. If they are removed just before the epoxy hardens fully this will prevent them being permanently bonded in place.

Left **Many dinghy fittings are attached with self-tapping screws, but they should still be bedded on sealant to prevent water getting into buoyancy tanks.**

Repairing foils

A smooth flow of water over rudders, centreboards and daggerboards is vital for a dinghy to handle as designed, and for optimal racing performance. However, these items are easily damaged, especially on their fine trailing edges or along the lower edge, as a result of grounding damage.

Checking structure

Most older dinghies have foils made of marine plywood, although newer boats use fibreglass, often with epoxy reinforcements. These may also incorporate a foam or honeycomb core to create a stiff but lightweight structure.

Before undertaking repairs, it's important to assess whether the foil retains adequate structural strength. Centreboards and daggerboards are most prone to failure at the point where the foil exits the hull when in the fully lowered position. This is the first place to look for evidence of stress cracks. In a fibreglass structure these should be ground out; if they penetrate no more than 10–15 per cent of the foil's thickness, the material removed can be made good with new fibreglass. Deeper cracks almost invariably mean structural strength has been compromised and the foil needs to be replaced.

Checking the core

A second check is to make sure that water has not been able to penetrate a fibreglass skin and reach the core material, as this can dangerously compromise strength and stiffness. Visually inspect any damage and poke it with a small screwdriver. If this sinks deep into the foil, then water is certain to have reached the core. However, if the surface can't be punctured, the likelihood is that the core will be dry. The same principles apply for rudders, although the most usual point of failure for the blade is at the bottom of the stock.

Repairing edges

Start by carefully removing any loose or cracked material with a sharp chisel, then thoroughly clean and de-grease the surfaces. A filler made of epoxy resin thickened with micro-balloons can be used to repair small chips and nicks, although a 50:50 mix of micro-balloons and microfibres (which add some structural strength) is better for larger areas of damage.

Left **The dings in the edges of this Laser daggerboard will impair its performance and handling, but are easy to fix.**

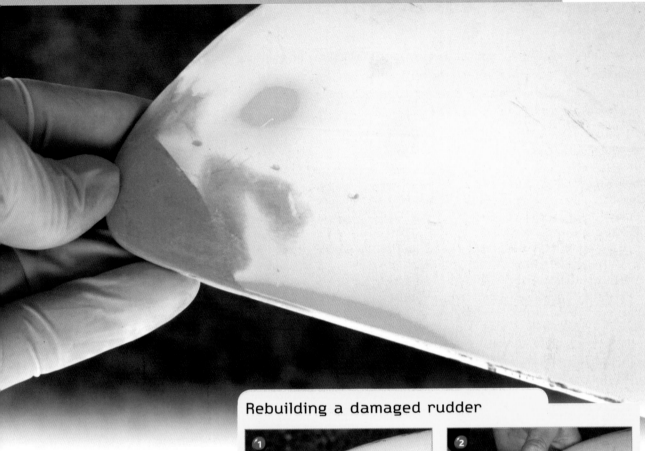

Above **The repaired rudder blade (see right) after fairing to shape. It is now ready for repainting.**

The trailing edges of foils are often very fine and fragile, so large areas of damage – over about 1in (2.5cm) in the fore-and-aft direction – will benefit from additional support. Inserting stainless steel pins into the after edge of the sound material will solve this problem.

The final and arguably most skilled part of the task is sanding the repaired foil to fair it to the original shape. This requires both patience and a fine eye, but a useful tip is to spray the area with car body paint, as this will show imperfections clearly, highlighting the areas that need further sanding or filling.

Rebuilding a damaged rudder

Start by inserting stainless steel pins to give the repair structural support.

Tape a temporary support on the underside to prevent the filler sagging.

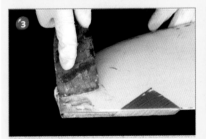

Apply the epoxy filler. Two or three applications are needed on each side.

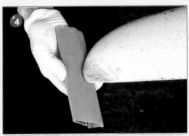

Sand the repair back to a fair finish that blends in with the rest of the rudder.

Trailers & tarpaulins

Boat trailers are all too easily neglected, yet surveys show an alarming proportion of them have safety-related defects. Similarly covers must not be overlooked — they are essential to protect the boat and your investment in it.

Bearings and braking

Wheel bearings are a common problem for trailers that are regularly submerged. Combination trailer/launching trolleys and break-back trailers, which allow a boat to be launched without the wheel hubs getting wet, are well worth the extra cost.

To replace or re-grease wheel bearings, support the trailer securely on axle stands and remove the wheel. Next prise off the domed dust cover that fits over the hub, remove the large castellated nut (and attendant split pin), and slide both outer and inner bearings off the axle.

Soak the parts in paraffin (kerosene) to clean and de-grease them, before working waterproof bearing grease into the bearings, and repacking the hub with grease. When refitting, spin the hub while tightening the castellated nut. Once resistance to spinning is felt, back it off about one-eighth of a turn and refit the split pin. The wheel should spin easily and without rumbling, otherwise the castellated nut is too tight, or the bearings have insufficient grease.

Larger trailers should have their braking systems examined annually for signs of corrosion, and grease points should be given a squirt of waterproof grease from a grease gun after each immersion in water. All trailers should be checked for corrosion twice a year. Any rust should be removed by sanding or grinding, and the area repainted with several coats of paint to prevent further damage.

Below **A break-back trailer allows the boat to be launched without immersing the wheel bearings in damaging sea water.**

Left **Regularly inspect covers for damage and repair them at the first opportunity, before the problem escalates.**

Safety cables

Small, unbraked trailers must have a wire safety coupling to keep the trailer attached to the tow vehicle if the hitch becomes uncoupled. Larger, braked trailers have a breakaway cable, which activates the braking system should the trailer become uncoupled. Cables should be replaced if corrosion or broken strands of wire are evident.

Tarpaulins

Covers are most commonly seen as providing protection against rain and frost, but they also shield ultraviolet light, which would otherwise continuously degrade the boat and its equipment. The two most common materials used are polycotton and PVC, with the latter being either laminated to a polyester base or impregnated into the polyester fabric under pressure. The second process results in a material with some breathability and greater longevity than laminated fabrics, but still at a lower cost than polycotton fabric.

Three types of cover are available for dinghies. An all-over design rigged with the mast and boom in position will protect the boat and its equipment during the season when it's in the boat park. A flat-top cover can be used over the winter if the mast is unstepped, and when towing the boat. Under covers are also used for towing, to protect against road dirt and stone chips.

Servicing wheel bearings

With the trailer supported on axle stands, remove the wheel and dust cover.

Remove the split pin from the castellated nut, then spin the nut off its thread.

Remove the outer bearing and slide the hub off the axle to show the inner bearing.

Re-pack the hub with grease. Spin it slowly while retightening the castellated nut.

Inflatable dinghies

Inflatable dinghies operate in a harsh environment, yet their very nature means they are made of lightweight and flexible materials. Despite this, good-quality dinghies have the potential to be long lasting, provided they are treated well.

Inflatable materials

Two materials are used for the overwhelming majority of inflatable dinghies: Hypalon (a rugged synthetic rubber) and PVC impregnated into a fabric cloth. Hypalon is widely regarded as the superior choice, and has potential for excellent longevity, with many 30-year-old boats still in service.

Vinyl is cheaper and more popular, but degrades faster in ultraviolet light, and repairs are awkward to make because it's difficult to get glue to stick to the shiny surface. The cheapest PVC dinghies have glued seams, but better quality models have seams bonded through a heat welding process. These can almost rival Hypalon for longevity.

Care of inflatables

Abrasion is the biggest enemy of all inflatables. Avoid dragging the boat across the ground when launching, landing and handling on-shore, as this will rapidly wear the surface of the material. Similarly, when stowing the dinghy on board take care to avoid contact with anything that could cause the material to

Above **A spoon is an ideal implement to smooth out air bubbles when applying a patch to an inflatable dinghy.**

Below **Wear and tear is often found in the join between tubes and solid transoms. This dinghy has a commendably high level of reinforcement in this area.**

Right **Examine both tubes and floor at regular intervals for signs of damage.**

chafe. In a rough sea, even a small amount of movement can create problems.

Over time UV degradation will weaken the material, especially with PVC dinghies, so if possible avoid leaving the boat outside where it will be exposed to sunlight for extended periods.

The boat should be washed with fresh water and dried thoroughly before being stowed. The practicalities of stowage on most boats mean dinghies are often packed into the smallest possible volume, but this inevitably creases and weakens the fabric. A better option is to store the boat ashore, ideally somewhere it can be left unrolled and partially inflated.

Repairing leaks

To repair small holes in the fabric, inflate the dinghy and pour a weak solution of detergent over the tubes. Bubbles will form around any leaks. The area should then be dried and the surface roughened with 100 grit sandpaper to provide a key for the adhesive, then thoroughly cleaned and de-greased. Ideally two applications of methyl ethyl ketone (MEK) should be used for cleaning, although acetone can be used for non-critical patches.

It's important to use the correct repair kit for the fabric type, and to follow instructions to the letter. Low humidity and moderate temperature (15–23°C) are also important if a long-lasting repair is to be achieved. Note that the adhesive has a short shelf life – as little as one year – and once opened readily absorbs water, so a part-used container should not be kept for use at a later date.

In the absence of a repair kit, cleaning the area and applying a blob of marine adhesive sealant such as Sikaflex 291 can provide an effective temporary repair.

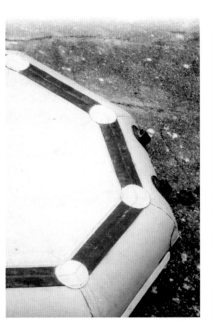

Far left **Transoms are vulnerable to chafe if the dinghy is dragged along the ground when launching or recovering.**

Left **Check the painter for chafe and to ensure the attachment is firmly bonded to the boat.**

Wooden dinghy maintenance

Wooden dinghies inevitably require more care than fibreglass or roto-moulded boats. Paint and varnish systems in particular must be maintained in good order to prevent the ingress of fresh water that leads to structural problems.

Fresh water ingress

Before the 1950s most dinghies were built of traditional planked construction, but the high cost of this means that only a handful of boats for enthusiasts are now built this way, and marine plywood construction is much more common. Fresh water is the enemy of all wooden boats, with rainwater being the prime culprit. Any chips and dings to the paint or varnish should be touched up at the earliest opportunity. A coat of quick-drying primer followed by one or two of gloss topcoat is sufficient for a temporary seal against water ingress.

Many plywood dinghies have exposed edges of ply that must be kept well protected by paint or varnish, because water penetrating here quickly gets drawn into the timber. For this reason better-quality boats have hardwood capping pieces over exposed plywood edges.

Covers

Some water will penetrate the best of covers, even if it just runs down the mast, so wooden dinghies should be stored in a way that allows water to drain. For boats kept ashore, this generally means lifting the bows so that water can run out of the transom drains. Covers should ideally be of a breathable material that won't trap moisture in the boat, and should be designed to promote ventilation.

Below **The decks and inside of wooden dinghies deteriorate rapidly if they are not protected from the ravages of rainwater and sunlight.**

Above **Store the boat with the bow raised to allow any water that finds its way inside to drain out through the transom bungs.**

Above **Paint and varnish systems must be maintained in good condition. Touch up any chips and dings as soon as possible.**

If stored outside over the winter, it's important to maximise airflow and ventilation around all wooden dinghies. The best option is usually to store them upside down on trestles, as water can't collect on the upturned hull, and there's good airflow underneath.

Traditional construction

Although plywood boats benefit from being kept as dry as possible, traditionally built clinker and carvel planked boats need to absorb a little moisture to prevent the timber shrinking and gaps developing between the planks. In salt water

environments and temperate climates, keeping the boat afloat during the summer is normally sufficient to achieve this – and unlike fresh water, salt water acts as a mild preservative.

Filling screw holes

A common mistake when replacing fittings is not to fill the old screw holes. This allows water into the structure of the boat. At the very least, use a slightly oversized drill bit to remove the timber around the threads, then fill the hole with a mix of epoxy resin and micro-balloons. A neater solution is to use a plug-cutter bit in a drill to cut a plug of the right size for the hole from a scrap piece of hardwood. Then epoxy this in place. Once the glue has set, the section of the plug that protrudes above the surrounding timber can be cut away with a sharp chisel.

Left **It's a good idea to store the boat upside down over the winter. This prevents water getting inside and maximises ventilation.**

Outboard engines

Getting a stubborn outboard started

The marine environment is particularly harsh on petrol engines, which rely on electricity to make the spark that ignites the fuel. Outboard motors are therefore inherently more prone to problems than diesel inboards, but with regular attention they can give decades of reliable use.

Outboard basics

Large modern engines with sophisticated engine management systems are reliable and easy to start, but older models, particularly two-strokes with carburettors rather than fuel injection, can be stubborn. In all cases, however, a properly maintained engine is easier to start than a neglected unit.

Starting up motors with a pull-cord is much easier when a sensible technique is employed. Unless you're a hefty bodybuilder, don't rely on arm muscles to pull the cord for anything but the smallest of engines. Grip the handle with both hands and use your body weight to give a stronger pull.

Some units with a manual choke need it to be flicked off immediately,

HOW THEY WORK

All petrol engines work by mixing air and fuel, compressing the mixture, igniting it with a spark and clearing the exhaust gases away. If the engine doesn't run at its best, then one of these processes has been compromised. Cooling is almost universally achieved by pumping water from the sea, river or lake through the engine, although a few very small units are air cooled.

Two-strokes must have lubricating oil mixed with the fuel, either in the tank or, in the case of more sophisticated models, automatically injected from a separate reservoir. Four-stroke models are more complex and tend to be a little heavier than their two-stroke counterparts, but have the advantage of better fuel efficiency and reliability. They have their lubricating oil in a separate sump (as with any modern car).

Environmental regulations have effectively imposed a blanket ban on the sale of smaller two-stroke outboards in the European Union and North America since 2007, although bigger models with sophisticated engine management systems satisfy the legislation that was introduced at this time.

Left **A high-capacity fuel filter, such as the one fitted to this RIB, is a worthwhile insurance against fuel problems.**

but others prefer a more progressive approach. The only solution is to experiment with your own engine.

Flooded carburettors

Repeatedly trying to start a reluctant engine can cause the carburettor to flood with excess fuel. If the engine doesn't start after five or six pulls, or a few short bursts of an electric starter, switch the choke to the warm running position, and open the throttle. This allows more air in, weakening the fuel/air mixture. Alternatively, wait for five to ten minutes before making another attempt to start the engine.

Although it may be worth carrying a can of ether-based aerosol spray for use in genuine emergencies, where the safety of the boat may be at risk if the engine won't start, don't make a habit of relying on these to start a problem engine. The powerful solvents in them wash oil from the sides of the cylinders, accelerating wear.

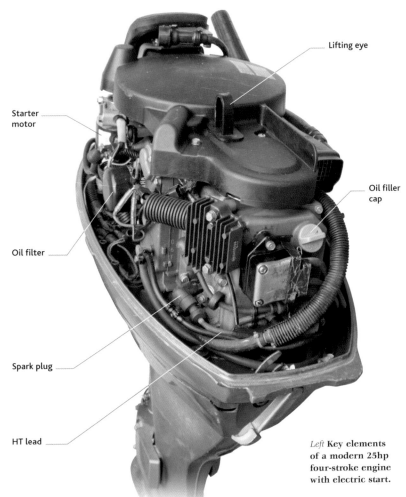

Starter motor

Oil filter

Spark plug

HT lead

Lifting eye

Oil filler cap

Left **Key elements of a modern 25hp four-stroke engine with electric start.**

Good starting technique

Good technique makes starting pull-start engines much easier. Grip the handle firmly with both hands...

...and lean backwards as you pull, using your body weight as well as your arm muscles.

If space permits, keep moving backwards to use the full length of the cord – most are surprisingly long.

Bigger engines with electric starters rely on having a well-charged battery and clean, dry electrical contacts. Some smaller electric-start motors also have a rudimentary pull-cord system under the engine cover. Many of these are not very powerful, so should not be relied on as a back-up unless you have already successfully started the engine this way.

Residue problems

Petrol (gasoline) has a relatively short shelf life, especially after mixing with two-stroke oil. This can cause problems with a carburetted engine that is used only occasionally. When the fuel left in the carburettor evaporates, it leaves a sticky residue that will progressively reduce the size of the main jet. The classic symptom of this is an engine that misfires and runs rough, with loss of power even when warm, but that improves when given choke. The solution is to dismantle the carburettor and clean the jets (see pages 270 and 271).

This is rarely a problem if the engine is used every week, or if the priming bulb of a remote tank can be given a couple of squeezes. Otherwise it's worth removing the fuel from the carburettor – most are fitted with a drain plug, although many owners simply turn the fuel off with the engine running to allow the carburettor to run dry.

Fuel filters and water separators

A clean supply of fuel to the engine is particularly important, especially for units with fuel injection systems, so fuel filters are fitted to remove dirt particles. If these become clogged, the engine will be difficult to start and unable to deliver full power. It's important, therefore, to

Above **Check the battery if an electric start engine won't start. It should show over 12.2 volts. Any less and it should be recharged.**

carry a full set of spare filters and the tools to fit them.

Small outboards have a low-capacity in-line filter under the engine cowl, while large engines may also have a bigger remote filter. Some of these are combined with a water separator, similar to those for diesel engines, that allows any water in the fuel system to be drained from the bottom of the unit.

Checking for a spark

This is a quick way to determine whether an engine that won't start has problems with the fuel system or with its electrics. Remove the spark

Left **The same general troubleshooting principles apply to outboards of all sizes.**

plug (see pages 268 and 269), reconnect the HT lead (the high-voltage wire that delivers the electricity that makes the spark) and hold it against the engine block, using pliers held in a thick glove, while turning the engine over. A healthy spark will show as a fat blue flash that will jump a gap of around 0.4in (10mm) on modern engines, or half that on elderly models without electronic ignition.

Engine block

Spare split pins and shear pins

Carburettor

Throttle cable

Fuel filter

Above To check for a spark, remove the spark plug, re-attach the HT lead and hold the plug 0.2-0.4in (5-10mm) from the engine block while turning the engine over.

Left Under the hood of a typical small two-stroke outboard. It's worth familiarising yourself with the important components.

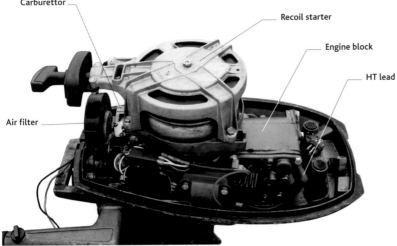

Carburettor

Recoil starter

Engine block

HT lead

Air filter

WHEN THE ENGINE FAILS

No engine is infallible, and an important principle of seamanship is to have more than one form of propulsion. Small tenders achieve this with oars to supplement the motor, while a daysailer can use its sails in the event of engine failure. It makes sense for larger outboard-powered motorboats to have a second, smaller engine that can be used to return to port if necessary. If all else fails, an anchor is an essential insurance policy while you wait for a tow.

Changing spark plugs & shear pins

Clean spark plugs are needed for optimum engine efficiency, while a broken shear pin or damaged rubber propeller hub insert will prevent any power from the engine reaching the prop.

Spark plugs

These should be cleaned or changed at the engine's regular service, but with some older two-stroke engines problems with oil fouling may still be encountered between services, especially if the motor is run for long periods at low revs. Before removing the plug, clean the surrounding area to prevent debris falling into the cylinder – an old paintbrush is ideal for this. Next remove the electrical HT lead from the top of the plug, and unscrew it using a close-fitting plug spanner.

The condition of the electrodes gives a useful indication of an engine's state of tune. Ideally they should be a lightish brown/grey colour, although electrodes in two-strokes tend to be a little darker. A white colour indicates that the engine is running too hot, either because of cooling system problems or a weak fuel/air mixture. A dark or black colour is the result of a rich fuel/air mix or oil fouling.

Electrodes can be cleaned with emery paper or a wire brush. The gap between them increases over time, so check the size with a feeler gauge, consulting the engine specifications for the recommended gap. Never over-tighten plugs when replacing them: hand tight, plus around one-eighth of a turn using a spanner is ample. Finally, push the HT lead securely in place.

Shear pins

Many smaller and older engines have these easily-replaced weak links between the propeller and gearbox. They are intended to save the unit from serious damage if the propeller strikes a solid object. If an

Below **Dirty spark plugs are a common cause of poor engine performance, especially with two-stroke engines.**

Right **Replacing a propeller split pin is a five-minute operation, but make sure you carry plenty of spares.**

engine appears to function normally but doesn't provide any thrust, the likelihood is that the shear pin has failed.

Before replacing the pin, remove the HT lead from the spark plug(s) or switch the battery off, to eliminate any danger of the engine being accidentally started while you're working on it. A split pin holds the prop in place on small engines, while the props of larger engines are secured by castellated nuts, with a split pin that prevents the nut loosening. With the propeller

off, make sure the remains of the old shear pin are removed before sliding the new one in place. When replacing the prop, the castellated nuts should be spun up finger tight, then tightened with a spanner just enough to line up the holes for the split pin.

In place of a shear pin, many newer and larger engines have a rubber hub insert in the prop that absorbs small knocks without damage. However, a heavy grounding can tear the rubber apart, uncoupling the engine from the prop. A specialist propeller repairer can insert a new hub, provided the blades are not too badly damaged, but it's worth carrying a spare propeller to minimise inconvenience in the event of hub failure.

Cleaning a spark plug

Ensure the surrounding area is clear of loose debris before removing the plug.

Use fine emery paper to clean the electrodes, then thoroughly clear the dust.

Use a feeler gauge to check the gap between the electrodes is as prescribed.

Don't over-tighten the plug. Hand tighten, plus one-eighth of a turn with a spanner.

Servicing, checks & troubleshooting

Routine maintenance and servicing are the key to ensuring the reliability of outboards, regardless of age or size. Each engine has slightly different recommendations for servicing, but most are along the following lines:

Daily routines
- Check level of fuel tank.
- Check fuel system water separator (where fitted).
- Inspect condition of battery terminals (electric-start engines only).
- Check engine oil level using dipstick (four-stroke only).
- Check flow of cooling water after starting engine.
- Check condition and operation of kill-cord.
- Check security of the mounting to transom or bracket.

Above **It's important to check the condition of the starting cord regularly.**

Left **Use a vacuum pump to drain the oil from a large four-stroke engine via the dipstick tube.**

EVERY 100 HOURS OR 12 MONTHS
- Change engine oil and filters (four-stroke only).
- Clean or replace spark plugs as per manufacturer's schedule.
- Replace fuel filter(s) and check fuel system.
- Replace water pump impeller.
- Replace cooling system anodes.
- Carry out tuning diagnostic check.
- Check gearbox oil level and top up as necessary.
- Check condition of recoil start-cord.
- Check and clean all electrical contacts.
- Check operation of power trim/tilt (where fitted) .
- Check steering system and lubricate as appropriate.
- Lubricate gear and throttle control linkages.

Cleaning carburettors

After removing the carburettor, invert it and unscrew the bowl.

Carefully lift the plastic float away from its seating and put to one side.

Next, remove the pin that holds the needle in place.

Lift the needle away to reveal the main jet. Clean with an aerosol carb cleaner.

Carburettor cleaning

Before starting work, obtain a spares kit of gaskets and other reusable parts for each carburettor. First remove the carburettor from the engine, then dismantle it, noting where each element goes (taking photos of every stage will help with reassembly). Clean the jets with an aerosol carb cleaner, though if they have a thick coating of gum or black varnish, they will benefit from a soak in liquid carb cleaner.

Main jet

Changing four-stroke oil and filters

Run the engine for at least ten minutes to fully warm it up. This reduces the viscosity of the oil, making it easier to remove. Remove the old oil by pumping it out via the dipstick, then remove the oil filter by rotating the cartridge anticlockwise.

Before fitting the new filter, smear a small amount of clean oil on each side of the rubber seal. This helps it to seal. Resist the temptation to over-tighten it. Spin the filter on until it no longer turns freely, then tighten one-eighth of a turn. Next, fill the engine with fresh oil to the level of the top mark on the dipstick (note that many smaller engines require very little oil). Check the filter for leaks after starting the engine and again after the first few hours of running.

Gearbox oil

The gearbox at the bottom of the leg has two plugs that are used for replacing gear oil. With the engine vertical, remove both plugs to drain the old oil into a container. Next, pour the manufacturer's recommended grade of oil into the lower hole, until it comes out of the top one. This procedure ensures no air locks form as the gearbox is refilled. Replace the top plug before removing the refill bottle from the lower plug. Then remove the bottle and replace the lower plug.

Left **The carburettor of a two-stroke engine showing the location of the main jet.**

Far left **The cooling water should have a continuous stream of water like this.**

Left **An intermittent stream like this indicates a cooling system problem.**

heat, penetrating oil and patience are the keys to this job.

Sacrificial zinc anodes help to protect the engine from the ravages of the hot salt water that is pumped through it. These should be changed annually, or after every 100 hours of engine use.

Flushing the cooling system

Flushing fresh water through the cooling system of engines used in a salt water environment reduces the build-up of deposits in the engine's waterways. It is important to run the engine for sufficient time to reach its normal operating temperature,

Checking the tell-tale hole

A pump at the top of the leg feeds water up to the motor. After travelling around the engine the main flow runs back inside the leg and exits underwater. A tell-tale stream from either directly under the motor or the back of the leg shows whether there's a healthy flow of cooling water. If the flow here stops or is weak, first check that the tell-tale hole isn't blocked by poking the straightened end of a paper clip into the opening. If it isn't blocked, the problem will be more serious: failure of the impeller or a partial blockage of the waterways by salt and calcium deposits.

Replacing a water pump impeller

The location of the water pump makes changing the impeller a much more involved job than with an inboard diesel engine. In most cases the gearbox must be unbolted and

slid away from the leg, which will reveal the water pump at the top of the gearbox. Corrosion between the metal used for the bolts and the aluminium engine case can make them very hard to remove, but don't be tempted to force them, as this often results in breakages. Instead,

Below **With the gearbox removed, the impeller can be inspected and slid off its shaft if it needs to be replaced.**

Right **To access the impeller, start by removing the bolts attaching the gearbox to the bottom of the leg.**

Above **The so-called 'ear muffs', attached to a regular garden hose.**

Right **The cooling systems of large engines are flushed using 'ear muffs' which direct cooling water into the inlet grills.**

otherwise the thermostat will prevent the coolant reaching the main part of the engine block.

A small engine can be run in a tank for this purpose, but larger models need a water supply from a hose. This is fed to the engine via an attachment that covers the water intake gratings on each side of the bottom of the leg. These devices are referred to as 'earmuffs' because of their appearance, and are available from outboard retailers. If possible, this should be done every time the engine is used, but for many it's only realistic to do so when winterising the unit at the end of the season.

Troubleshooting

Two key principles help enormously when diagnosing problems with an engine. Firstly, don't wait for the unit to stop operating – take action at the first sign of trouble. Secondly, a systematic and logical approach is the one mostly likely to lead you to the source of the problem.

Safety gear

Lifejackets, lifelines & flares

Never take safety gear for granted. It's vital to check the entire inventory regularly to ensure all components are in good condition, are within their expiry date and will operate effectively when needed.

Lifejackets

It's very easy to be complacent about servicing lifejackets, but research suggests that about one in three of those in service have at least one fault. It is disconcertingly common for the compressed gas inflation cylinder to work loose, so it's always worth making a quick check of the cylinder before donning a lifejacket. In addition, the following checks and servicing procedures should ensure reliable operation of the jacket when needed.

Monthly check
✪ Check that the gas cylinder is fully screwed in.

Three monthly check
✪ Check the cylinder for corrosion.
✪ Check the material in contact with the cylinder for damage.
✪ Check webbing, stitching, zips, buckles and other fastenings for damage.
✪ Check the operation of harness line clips and examine webbing for damage.

Above **Inflate lifejackets every six months to check they hold air for at least 24 hours.**

Six monthly check
✪ Inflate the lifejacket with a hand pump to check it retains air for at least 24 hours.
✪ Check all areas of fabric for damage.

The pellets that automatically inflate lifejackets should be replaced annually; they have a finite shelf life and should not be used once the expiry date is reached. The gas cylinders of lifejackets with hydrostatic inflation systems are inside the air chamber, so they are better protected than those in conventional lifejackets. Hydrostatic activation devices also have a longer service life, needing to be replaced only every three to five years. All the parts required are sold by most chandlers.

Correct storage will increase the lifespan of lifejackets. At the end of the boating season they should be inflated enough to remove creases, then hung on a plastic coat hanger.

Left **Safety is a continuous process of checking everything is in order.**

Lifelines and jackstays

Lifelines should be checked monthly, because loose shackle pins and screw-in eye terminals are common faults. The aft end of each lifeline should be secured by a lashing that can be cut to facilitate recovering a person overboard. Lashings should be checked both for chafe and the security of the knots.

Webbing jackstays need to be capable of withstanding surprisingly high loads, so most are rated with a safe working load of about two tonnes. They should be checked monthly for chafe and for the security of the fastenings at each end. Ultraviolet degradation weakens them, so in temperate climates they should be re-stitched after five years, and replaced after a decade of use. In hot climates these figures should be halved.

Flares

Distress flares have a limited lifespan (generally three years) and are stamped with their expiry date. Disposal facilities can be difficult to find, but liferaft service agents

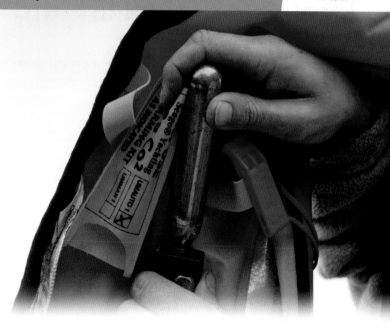

Above **Before putting on a lifejacket, check the inflation cylinder is tightly in place. This is the biggest cause of lifejacket failure.**

regularly need to dispose of out-of-date pyrotechnics and are often helpful in this respect.

Radar reflectors

Even if kept aloft, radar reflectors are not immune from problems. The security of mountings should be checked annually, and the exterior of the unit examined for cracks or other damage.

TIP

Before undertaking any maintenance of safety equipment, always check the manufacturer's specific recommendations.

Left **Check jackstays for chafe, and re-tighten shackle pins every month.**

Fire fighting, first aid & EPIRBs

We hope never to use emergency equipment – but that often means it languishes out of sight, with problems left unnoticed as they develop. A methodical regime is therefore needed to ensure maintenance is fully up to date at all times.

Fire equipment

Fire at sea can be a terrifying experience, yet most boat owners are guilty of failing to maintain their extinguishers properly. All types should be checked at a specialist service centre annually. The procedure includes checking the operation of the gauge, weighing the cylinder to confirm the correct quantity of extinguishing agent, and checking for corrosion. Even with annual servicing, dry powder and foam extinguishers have a lifespan of only five years, although gas types last twice as long.

TIP

Making a list of all the expiry dates of safety gear in the back of your logbook will help ensure that none of them are missed.

Below **Fire extinguishers are all too easily forgotten, but they need regular inspections and annual servicing.**

EMERGENCY ELECTRONICS

EPIRB (emergency position-indicating radio beacon) and SART (search and rescue transponder) devices typically contain batteries that last for five years and are not user-replaceable. The device must be sent to a service centre for battery replacement. In addition, EPIRBs need the following annual checks:

○ Carry out a visual inspection for defects.
○ Carry out the self-test procedure as per the manufacturer's instructions.
○ Check that the EPIRB identification, including the 15 Hex ID code, is clearly visible.
○ Check correct registration of the unit with the local Coastguard.
○ Check the battery expiry date.
○ Where fitted, check the hydrostatic release expiry date. These last for two years and are normally user-replaceable.
○ After testing, replace the unit in the bracket, checking that no transmission has started.
○ Confirm that there is a copy of the manufacturer's operating instructions on board.

Fire blankets should also be checked annually, because modern fibreglass models can slowly develop holes at the creases. If there's any possibility that your boat has an older asbestos fire blanket, don't risk removing it from its case, because this may disturb dangerous dust particles. Carefully bag the entire item, dispose of it at a facility licensed for asbestos waste, and replace it.

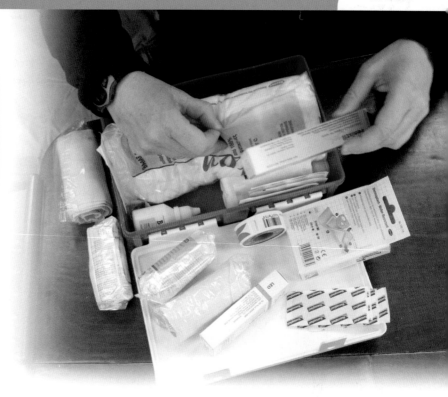

First aid

First aid kits should be checked annually to ensure there are no problems due to moisture penetration. Items with 'use by' dates should be replaced before they expire, especially in the case of drugs. First aid manuals are updated frequently with new advice, so make sure you have the latest version.

VHF care

Modern hand-held VHFs are fully waterproof, providing the antenna and battery pack are securely attached. The entire unit should be rinsed with fresh water after exposure to salt water spray, and allowed to dry completely afterwards. Note that if the waterproofing is compromised (for example, if the case is cracked or the VHF has been dropped), it must be kept dry at all times.

Above **First aid kits are vulnerable to damp, and many items have short shelf lives. Make sure yours are in-date.**

Below **Activate the self check facility on EPIRBs every month, following the manufacturer's instructions.**

Liferaft & man overboard gear

When considering liferaft maintenance, most boat owners think only of the scheduled services required. However, the raft must also be looked after carefully on board in order to keep it in tip-top condition.

Stowing liferafts

Poor stowage often results in unnecessary damage to liferafts. Valise types must not be stowed on deck, because the bag is not waterproof. In addition, their stowage must offer protection from chafe – something that is often difficult to achieve in a rough sea. Canister models are designed to be stowed on deck, but the waterproofing between the two halves of the container is easily compromised if the canister is used as a convenient step or seat.

Servicing liferafts

Traditionally liferafts have required annual servicing, and this is still the case for most commercial models, but many rafts aimed at the leisure market are vacuum packed to extend services to three-yearly intervals.

Some models are fitted with hydrostatic releases that will deploy the raft automatically if the boat sinks. Those aimed at the leisure market require no routine servicing, but the releases must be replaced every two years. The contents of any grab bags should be carefully inspected annually.

Man overboard equipment

Solid foam lifebuoys are long-lasting and require minimal maintenance other than cleaning with weak detergent solution. However, their lights are a different matter, and models with user-replaceable batteries are prone to failure. They should therefore be checked for correct operation at the start of each trip. Fully-sealed lights are inherently reliable, but should have the self-test facility activated

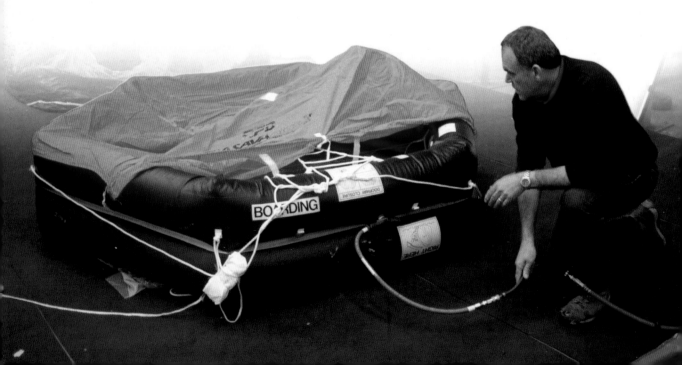

Below **Service centres inflate liferafts using compressed air. The inflation cylinder is also weighed to check it is fully charged.**

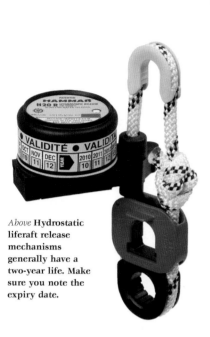

Above **Hydrostatic liferaft release mechanisms generally have a two-year life. Make sure you note the expiry date.**

monthly and the battery replaced at three- to five-year intervals.

Inflatable lifebuoys and danbuoys should be serviced annually – it makes sense to do so at the same time as the liferaft. Solid danbuoys are generally robust, but their flags can flog to pieces in a matter of weeks. A short length of plastic pipe tied to the backstay can be used to protect the flag in such a way that it deploys automatically in use.

Throwing lines are made from polypropylene, which degrades rapidly in sunlight. If any part of the line is exposed to light in its normal stowage position, its strength should be checked at least annually.

Right **Liferafts stowed in a valise (rather than a canister) are prone to damage, in this case due to chafe when operating the bilge pump (inset).**

Laying up for winter

13

Laying up a boat

Dry land is the best place for cruising yachts during cold winters. Most routine annual boat maintenance is carried out during the laying-up winter period. Arrange for a crane, winch or tractor to take your boat out of the water so you can carry out annual maintenance.

Removing a boat from the water

- **Lifting:** Mobile cranes or hoists come equipped with strong nylon webbing slings. A lifting apparatus is used to place the boat high and dry in the boatyard. Cradles and hoists will support the hull at the sides and take the weight off the keel.

- **Towing:** A boat can be towed up a ramp or slipway from the water at high tide, carried on a boat trailer. It is pulled by a tractor and parked in its spot in the boatyard.

Right **Marinas normally have cranes or hoists to lift boats out of the water, supported by slings that distribute the weight of the boat evenly on lifting.**

Below **Pulling a boat up a slipway onto dry land. The trailer will hold the boat in position while it's out of the water.**

Supporting the hull

When the boat is on its trailer or on the hard, the hull is likely to need additional support in the form of shores under the bow and stern. If the boat has a fin keel it will almost certainly require extra support.

Now is the time to check the boat is sitting properly and not under undue stress, while allowing access to all underwater areas for maintenance work. Once in position the boat is jacked up onto timber chocks, and wedges are placed under the keel.

It is important to ensure that the boat is stable and does not fall over when workers come on board. A ladder will be required to allow access to the deck.

Cleaning the hull

The first step in cleaning off the underwater areas is to remove any marine growth clinging to the hull and this is best done as soon as the boat is hauled clear of the water. While it is still wet, weed, slime and barnacles can be removed more easily than when they have

dried out. High pressure hoses combined with a scraper for more stubborn areas are the most efficient and labour-saving methods of getting rid of marine growth. Always finish the bottom cleaning with a fresh water rinse.

Above **Ladders should be properly attached and at an angle no steeper than 1:3.**

MARINE FOULING

Animal: Barnacles, coral and other marine animals seek a base to cling onto while feeding on nutrients in the water.

Weed: Numerous forms of vegetation cling to static objects as seen on rocks at low tide. If a boat is static, it will pick up marine weed of some type.

Slime: Single cell algae which produce a syrupy-type medium and grow quickly to create quite a thick layer.

Left **Remove marine growth with a jet-power washer as soon as the boat is taken out of the water. Antifouling the hull should be the last job you do before returning the boat to the water.**

Winterisation & damp prevention

When laying up a boat for winter, it's vital to ensure all systems are protected from frost damage. It's also important to minimise the ingress of damp, as this can quickly lead to significant damage from mould and mildew.

Prepare for the worst

Good laying-up practice is the key to keeping a boat in good shape over the winter, and minimising the amount of work that's needed to get afloat in the spring. Don't underestimate the extremes of climate that boats may encounter while laid up – few owners actually see their boats during the worst of the winter weather.

There are two diametrically opposed options for keeping the interior of a boat dry: sealing it up

Above **Leave cabin doors ajar to promote good ventilation through the boat.**

Left **Batteries can deteriorate rapidly over winter. They should be charged monthly while the boat is laid up.**

entirely and using a dehumidifier to extract moisture from the closed environment; or maximising ventilation (see pages 56 and 57) to prevent damp lingering. Note that many boatyards are in sheltered locations, with boats packed in tightly, so good ventilation can be harder to achieve than for boats on a summer swinging mooring.

The autumn lay-up is a good opportunity to assess whether all the items that have accumulated on board during the season really need to stay there. Anything that's removed will help reduce damp over the winter and allow the air to flow more easily around the boat, so personal kit and berth cushions should be taken home. In addition, lockers can be emptied and cleaned, and the essentials brought back to the boat in the spring.

Fresh water systems

Tanks, pumps and pipework can all be damaged when fresh water freezes. It is therefore important to empty water systems, even though it can be a time-consuming task on boats with manually-pumped water. If pressure pumps are fitted it will be easier to empty the tanks, but if they are of a large capacity it's worth running the engine (or connecting to shore power) to prevent excessive battery drain. Once the cold water system has been emptied, the hot water system, including the calorifier, can also be drained. And don't forget to check that shower sump pumps are drained of water.

It is best to service heating systems long before lay-up – at the end of summer, so that they are ready for use when the weather turns cooler. Radiator-based central heating systems rely on a combined antifreeze/rust inhibitor to prevent the contents freezing. It's important to check that this is at the manufacturer's recommended concentration.

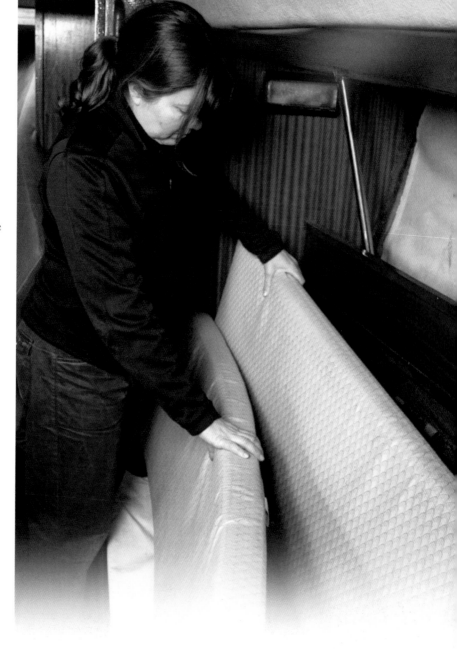

Above **Stand berth cushions on edge to allow air to circulate if it is not possible to store them safely ashore.**

Battery care

Batteries should be stored in a fully-charged state, and charged overnight every month to maintain their charge (they self-discharge at a rate of two to three per cent per month, depending on type). Alternatively, owners of boats equipped with three- or four-stage chargers that are going to be connected to a power supply can leave their batteries on board. This type of charger is suitable for permanent operation, and will not damage the batteries.

Engine winterisation

Many routine engine servicing tasks can be carried out when laying up the boat, but a number of additional tasks should be undertaken to ensure that the unit is protected over the winter, and that there are no reliability problems in the spring.

Changing and topping up liquids

As engine oil ages it gradually becomes acidic, which can slowly damage the engine. The ideal time to change the oil (see pages 188 and 189 for inboard engines; 270 and 271 for outboards) is therefore when the boat is decommissioned in autumn. Similarly, it makes sense to drain the fresh water side of indirectly cooled engines and refill with new antifreeze when laying up.

Over winter, condensation readily forms on the sides of fuel tanks, introducing water into the fuel. This water will promote the growth of bacteria in the fuel, which will eventually clog the filters. The solution is to top the tanks right up with fuel at the end of the season.

However, if the tank has not been drained and thoroughly cleaned for a few years, this task should be carried out first to prevent the risk of existing micro-organisms multiplying over winter. Once clean and dry, the tanks can be filled completely to prevent condensation.

Another exception is two-stroke outboards. Petrol (gasoline) has a limited shelf life once mixed with two-stroke oil, so it's best to drain these tanks completely when the engine is winterised.

Above **Filling diesel tanks before winter will prevent condensation in the tank.**

Below **Remove the engine's water pump impeller to prevent its vanes seizing in one position over the winter.**

Internal protection

Protect cylinders by removing the injectors (or spark plugs for petrol engines) and spraying oil into the cylinder while turning the engine by hand – using a ring spanner on the crank pulley if necessary. Then spray oil into the air filter and seal the opening. This will prevent corrosion forming in the internal parts of the engine.

A few minutes' attention will also help to prolong the life of other components. Removing the water pump impeller of an inboard engine (see pages 194 and 195) will prevent its vanes freezing in a single position, and loosening alternator and water pump drive belts will help to extend their service life.

If the boat is to remain afloat and in commission over the winter, be wary of relying on the lower freezing point of salt water to protect the engine against frost damage. Many ports and estuaries have a high fresh water content. One solution for boats kept in a marina is to run an electric heater on its 'frost' setting to prevent the inside of the boat freezing.

Outboard engines

There are a couple of additional procedures for outboard motors. If used on the sea, the cooling system should be flushed with fresh water to prevent a build-up of salt and calcium deposits and reduce corrosion. In addition, two-stroke models should have their carburettor(s) drained of fuel (see pages 270 and 271).

Above **Check fresh water cooled engines have sufficient antifreeze to prevent the cooling system freezing in cold weather.**

Left **Loosening the tension on the alternator and waterpump drive belts over the winter will extend their service life.**

Spars & rigging

Many boatyards, especially those in exposed locations, insist on a yacht's mast being unstepped as a safeguard against boats toppling over in winter gales. Lowering the rig also enables every element to be inspected easily.

Sails and boom

All sails must be removed before the mast can be lowered. If you intend taking them to a sailmaker for valeting, it's worth doing so immediately; autumn is a slack time, so generous discounts are often available.

Next, detach the boom from the rig. Start by disconnecting the kicking strap, then ease the topping lift to lower the aft end of the spar onto the deck. Remove the topping lift and tie it off at the base of the mast. Next, detach the gooseneck and lower the boom to the deck. On any boat over about 30ft (9m), this is a two- or even three-person job. Any lines that are led aft from the mast will need to be unthreaded from their respective deck gear and coiled at the base of the mast.

Above **The boom must be removed before the mast can be lowered.**

Left **Preparing a strop to lift the mast. Make sure all the standing and running rigging is secured before lifting.**

Electrical wiring

Wiring for navigation lights, instruments and VHF antennas may be passed through the deck in a number of ways. In some cases the wiring simply plugs into sockets near the mast step, which makes unstepping the rig very easy. However, often a continuous length of wire is passed through a deck gland, and the wire must be followed to its first junction below decks, detached from there and pulled out through the gland. Don't be tempted to re-use an old gland for a second season – they degrade in sunlight, so when you pull the wire through the weakened rubber, it will destroy the seal.

Standing rigging

In preparation for lowering the mast, all rigging pins can be removed and bottlescrews (turnbuckles) loosened until they are hand tight. Record the number of turns before starting work, so the old rig settings can be repeated when the mast is restepped.

Attach the strop for the crane under the spreaders, but outside the lower shrouds. Once the crane has taken up the slack, unscrew the bottlescrews from the end of each stay or shroud. As the mast is lifted off the step it will need to be guided by two or three people using ropes tied around the foot. The mast should be supported by trestles or similar supports over its entire length.

Stainless steel standing rigging and bottlescrews can be cleaned with a cloth soaked in solvent such as white spirit. While doing this, check that none of the wires are frayed or otherwise damaged. After cleaning,

Above **Masts in storage should be supported at regular intervals to prevent them bending out of shape.**

Right **The loads involved in lifting a mast are relatively small, but the crane jib must reach above the lower spreaders.**

lubricate bottlescrew threads with light oil. This is also an ideal time to treat galvanised rigging with a linseed oil/paraffin mix (see pages 230 and 231).

TIP

Standing rigging should not be left in contact with the mast over the winter, as this risks corrosion between the two metals. It therefore makes sense to coil the rigging and store it separately.

Tarpaulins

Preventative maintenance is key to keeping a boat in good order, and a quality cover can make a huge difference to the amount of work that needs to be done in the spring, especially on boats with large amounts of varnished timber on deck.

Winter weather can wreak havoc with paint finishes, and is a killer for varnish. However, if the boat is sheltered from rain, sun and frost, even varnish may only need a light sand and a couple of extra coats in the spring. A cover can also help keep water out of the interior of a boat with deck or hatch leaks until it's possible to deal with these properly.

However, occasionally tarpaulins can create new problems. Large volumes of water running off the cover may expose previously unnoticed deck leaks, so after rigging a new cover it's worth spending a few minutes with a hose to check for problems.

When choosing a cover it's vital that it complements the method of damp protection chosen for the boat over the winter (see pages 286 and 287). If a dehumidifier is used, the cover should completely seal the boat from the elements. However, if ventilation is necessary, the cover must be designed to promote a good flow of air through all parts of the boat.

Material choice

These considerations also have a bearing on the choice of material. The main options are poly-cotton, PVC and acrylic fabrics. Poly-cotton and acrylic fabrics are breathable, making them a good choice where

Above **A free-standing tent allows work to continue in all weathers and can provide workshop space next to the boat.**

Below **An all-over cover will give excellent protection, but should ideally be made of breathable material.**

Right **This cover gives good protection to the wooden deck and brightwork, without compromising ventilation below.**

ventilation is important, whereas PVC materials don't breathe, so they are ideal for use with a dehumidifier.

The area of varnished timber that needs to be protected often dictates the size of the cover. A simple over-boom cover can protect cockpit, coamings and companionway from the weather and allows for excellent air flow underneath. If the mast is lowered and stowed on deck, this can be used to support a full-length tarpaulin that will give ultimate protection to the boat.

Full shelter

If a large amount of maintenance is planned for the winter, it's worth erecting a cover that will enable you to carry on working in all weathers. A covered free-standing frame makes an excellent winter workshop that will also protect the boat. Granted, some tasks, such as varnishing, may need to wait for higher ambient temperatures, but such a shelter makes many tasks possible that would otherwise have to wait until better weather and longer days.

TIP

It's vitally important to ensure covers are securely fastened. In a gale they can represent a significant sail area that can't be reefed, with potentially disastrous results if the cover is not both well fitted and tied taut. Never be tempted to tie a cover to the shores or cradle supporting the boat – it's easily done!

Glossary

A

Alternator A device, mounted on the engine, that generates alternating current (AC) electricity, which it then converts to low voltage direct current (DC) to charge the boat's battery and supply the boat's low voltage electrical demands. It is usually belt driven from the engine crankshaft.

Anemometer A device for measuring the wind speed. When the boat is under way, the measured speed is relative to the boat and is therefore not the actual speed. True windspeed can be calculated mathematically or by instruments which interface the anemometer data with the boat's log. On a sailing boat, it is usual to mount the device on the masthead where the air is least disturbed.

Anode A sacrificial metal, usually zinc, that protects other metal items that are in contact with sea water from galvanic corrosion, allowing the zinc to erode instead. Anodes should generally be replaced when they are one-third eroded.

Anodising A chemical treatment for protecting aluminium. It is applied electrolitically in a special bath. If the anodising is damaged, corrosion can spread under the treatment, so any damage should be touched up with paint as soon as possible.

B

Babystay Part of the standing rigging that gives fore-and-aft support to the mast. The babystay runs from the centreline of the foredeck to the mast at the height of the spreaders.

Backstay Part of the standing rigging that gives fore-and-aft support to the mast. The backstay runs from the back of the boat to the top of the mast.

Ballast Weight in the keel (or occasionally bilge) of a sailing boat that provides resistance to heeling. Cast iron is the most common form of ballast, although lead is used on racing boats and some higher quality cruising sailboats.

Batten The leech of most mainsails is supported by horizontal battens that improve the sail's aerodynamic shape and increase the lifespan of the material by reducing flapping. Most sails have four battens, which are generally made of fibreglass, although some traditional boats may have wooden battens. Some racing boats use carbon fibre or other exotic composites.

Bilge The lowest parts of the boat, into which any water collects. The bilge is normally divided into a number of separate compartments which may drain into each other by means of 'limber' holes or may remain isolated.

Boltrope Rope stitched along the edge of a sail, either to give additional resistance to chafe or to enable the sail to be set in a groove in the back of the mast, the top of the boom, or the roller reefing system.

Bottlescrew turnbuckle A threaded device located between the wire rigging supporting the mast and the chain plates on the hull. Used to tension the rig.

Brushes Small carbon blocks that, in contact with a rotating shaft, are used to conduct electricity. The brushes, which are replaceable, are held in contact with the shaft by springs.

Bulkhead A transverse full or partial 'wall' running across the boat, often used to separate different areas of accommodation. Bulkheads are often important structural members, especially on older boats.

C

Calorifier A vessel's domestic hot water tank. May be heated by engine cooling water, or by mains electricity via a shore power connection. It may also be heated by a diesel or gas fuelled heater.

Cam belt A rubber belt that drives the camshaft from the engine's crankshaft. Cam belts must be replaced at specified intervals.

Carvel A method of wooden hull construction using planks of wood laid edge to edge (rather than overlapping, as with clinker construction). The joints are sealed with caulking.

Castellated nut A nut whose outer face has a series of square raised castellations. These allow a nut that can only be tightened relatively loosely to be secured with a split pin that runs through both the bolt and the castellations. Castellated nuts are commonly found on trailer wheel bearings and for securing the propellers of large outboard engines.

Caulking A method of sealing the narrow gaps ('seams') between planks of wood laid edge to edge. Cotton may be rammed into the seams and then sealed with a mastic.

Centreboard A retractable keel that may be made of wood, GRP, steel or other materials.

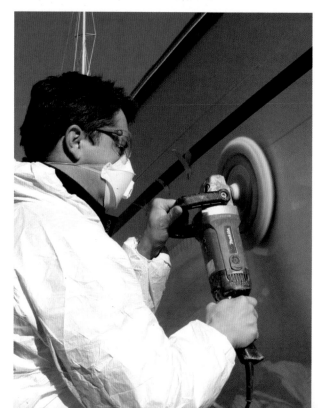

Centreboards are pivoted near their front edge, allowing them to swing upwards either directly under the hull, or within a case inside the hull.

Centre punch A hardened metal punch, the pointed end of which is used to mark the centre of a hole that is to be drilled. They may be spring loaded so that a hammer is not required to provide the necessary force.

Chain plate A fitting used to attach standing rigging to the hull or deck.

Check valve (aka 'non-return valve') A one-way valve used to prevent backflow of a fluid in a pipe.

Circuit breaker A device used to break an electric circuit in case a fault occurs. Unlike a fuse, it can be reset, rather than needing to be replaced.

Clevis pin Typically a short pin with a large diameter, most commonly used to join rigging components together. May be made of galvanised or stainless steel.

Clew Lower back corner of a sail.

Clinker A method of wooden hull construction in which the lower edge of each plank overlaps the upper edge of the plank below it. The planks (strakes) may be glued or otherwise rely on direct contact to ensure that they are watertight.

Clutch A compact rope-holding device capable of handling very high loads. Frequently used for coachroof-mounted halyards and reefing pennants.

Coachroof The cabin top, if it projects above deck level.

Coaming Raised surround to a cockpit to improve shelter from the weather and large seas.

Companionway Main entrance to a boat's accommodation.

Composite materials Advanced engineering grade reinforced plastics that are increasingly used for winch and other deck hardware components.

Compression joint A pipe joint consisting of a screwed coupling that compresses metal seals (olives) onto the pipe to achieve the seal.

Counter-bore A short hole of greater diameter than the main hole, to allow the head of a screw or bolt to be recessed. It is often filled with a dowel plug once the fitting is in place.

Cringle A reinforced eye in a sail or other canvas item.

D

Daggerboard Another type of lifting keel (see centreboard). Daggerboards lift vertically within a casing, and are made of wood, GRP, metal, or other materials. They can be ballasted or unballasted.

Danbuoy Temporary buoy with a tall pole and flag, used to help indicate the position of an object – especially a man overboard.

Deckhead Underside of the deck or coachroof.

De-zincification The loss of zinc from a copper alloy due to galvanic action.

Doghouse Raised portion at the aft end of a coachroof.

Glossary

E

EPIRB Emergency Position Indicating Radio Beacon. Electronic device for sending an automated distress signal via satellite.

F

Filler (or 'stopping') A soft paste used to fill a void or gap, which dries to form a hard surface.

Foot Bottom edge of a sail. Mainsails may be set loose footed, with only either end of the foot attached to the mast and boom, or the foot may be attached to the boom along its entire length.

Forestay Part of the standing rigging that gives fore-and-aft support to the mast. The forestay runs from the front of the boat towards the top of the mast.

Fuse The weak link in an electrical circuit that is designed to fail should the wiring become overloaded. The fuse in effect prevents the wiring itself from melting in the event of a fault such as a short circuit.

G

Galvanic corrosion The electrochemical action between two dissimilar metals that are in contact with each other or linked by a conductor such as the sea. The more 'noble' metal (e.g. bronze/stainless steel) will cause the less 'noble' metal (e.g. aluminium/mild steel) to corrode. This can be avoided by isolating the metals, using plastic gaskets or an insulating compound, or, if they are below water, linking them to a sacrificial zinc anode, which will be corroded instead.

Galvanising The process of coating mild steel with a protective layer of zinc. It is applied by dipping the steel component into a vat of molten zinc.

Garboard The planks of a traditionally constructed wooden boat immediately next to the keel.

Gimbals A double-pivot arrangement allowing an item (such as a compass) to remain level as the boat pitches and rolls. Also a single pivot-system that allows a cooker to stay level as the boat rolls.

Gland A seal on a rotating shaft. Used to prevent oil and water leaking past a rotating shaft.

Gooseneck Hinged fitting attaching the boom to the mast.

GPS The Global Positioning System, whereby a receiver can calculate its position by calculating its distance from three or more orbiting satellites.

Grommet A soft rubber or plastic ring that protects wiring or piping from the sharp edges of a hole through which the wire or pipe passes.

Grub screw A screw with no head, so that it can be tightened into a threaded hole and have no projection outside.

Gypsy A pulley with a pattern in its groove that grips the links of a chain – usually fitted to an anchor windlass. The chain and gypsy must be matched, because the wrong pattern size will cause the chain to jump off.

H

Halyard Rope used to pull sails up the rig.

Head Top corner of a sail.

Heads A generic term used for a boat's toilet compartment, or sometimes the toilet itself. Possibly derived from the fact that in old sailing vessels the toilet was in the bows, or the head of a ship.

Holding tank Storage tank for toilet waste. In some places the toilet can only be discharged overboard at an authorised pump-out station.

Hounds Point at which the shrouds are attached to the mast.

HT lead Electrical cable that delivers the high-voltage (high tension) current to the spark plug of a petrol engine. In order to create a strong spark, voltages of several thousand volts are not uncommon, especially on newer engines.

Hydrostatic release unit A means of automatically releasing and activating a liferaft or EPIRB in the event of a vessel sinking. The unit is activated by water pressure when a few feet under water.

J

Jackstay Length of wire or strong webbing onto which the line of a safety harness can be clipped. Jackstays typically run the length of the boat on each side, enabling a crewmember to reach anywhere on the boat without unclipping.

L

Laid deck One where individual planks of wood are

laid onto the frames or to an under-deck. On GRP boats the laid deck is often used for cosmetic purposes.

Lapping A process where metal surfaces are rubbed together using an abrasive compound in order to create a perfect engineering fit.

Leech Back edge of a sail.

Lift pump A small low-pressure pump used on diesel engines to deliver fuel from the tank to the high-pressure injector pump. Usually has a small handle allowing the pump to be activated by hand to bleed air out of the fuel system.

Log A mechanical device, often a paddlewheel or propeller, used to measure the distance travelled through the water by counting the number of revolutions it makes.

This can be converted (by taking account of the time taken to travel the distance) into speed through the water.

LPG Short for 'liquefied petroleum gas'. A fuel source that is stored as a liquid under pressure in a metal cylinder, but is returned to gaseous form as it passes through a regulator prior to being used in, for example, a cooker. The gas may be either butane or propane.

Luff Front edge of a sail.

Luff foil The plastic or aluminium extrusion around the forestay into which the front edge of a roller-reefing head sail is fed when hoisting the sail. Many raceboats use a foil with twin luff grooves, which allows a sail of a different size to be hoisted before the original is dropped.

M

Macerator A device that chops up raw sewage into a liquid slurry before discharge overboard or into a 'holding tank'.

Machine screw A screw that has a circular head rather than a hexagonal one. Often used for aesthetic reasons.

Mast rake Fore and aft angle at which a mast is inclined from the vertical – almost always aftwards.

Mastic A flexible sealant made from a variety of substances according to use.

Micro-balloons Lightweight microscopic bubbles used to thicken epoxy resin to create a filler that's easy to sand down.

Microfibres Microscopic fibres used to thicken epoxy resin to create a structural adhesive.

Glossary

N

Non-return valve (aka 'check valve') A one-way valve used to prevent backflow of a fluid in a pipe.

O

Olive A metal ring used to seal a compression joint.

O-ring A small tubular ring, usually made of soft rubber, that acts as a seal.

Outdrive Alternative term for stern drive.

P

Palm router A small electric hand-held router used in woodworking. Ideal for woodworking in situ, where access is limited.

Pawl A mechanical device that allows the rotation of a shaft in one direction only. These are often used in winches so that the load does not release.

Pennants Lines used to reef a mainsail, especially for pulling the aft corner of the sail down to the boom.

Priming The process of removing air from a pipe so that a fluid can be sucked through it. Also, applying a paint 'primer' to bare wood to help adhesion and reduce absorption.

Q

Quadrant Fitting on a rudder stock to which the cables, rods or hydraulics for wheel steering systems are attached.

R

Raw water The water in which the boat floats (e.g. sea water). Only used for some purpose on board, such as cooling the engine or flushing the toilet.

Regulator (on an alternator) An electronic device for controlling the way in which the battery is charged by the engine.

Regulator (on an engine) Strictly speaking, a diesel engine has no throttle. Its speed is controlled by the regulator.

Regulator (for gas) The mechanical device that controls the pressure of gas from a LPG cylinder.

Relay An electrical device that converts a low power electrical signal into a more powerful one. It uses a low current to operate an electromagnet, which then closes a pair of contacts to allow a much larger current to flow.

RIB Rigid-hulled inflatable boat – typically a glassfibre hull with inflatable tubes. RIBs are popular small motor boats with many uses, including both leisure and rescue applications.

Running rigging Ropes used to raise and control sails, or spars such as booms and spinnaker poles.

S

Saildrive A propulsion method where the propeller is driven through a leg protruding from the bottom of the hull. A large rubber diaphragm seals the big hole in the hull.

SART Search and Rescue Transponder – an electronic device used by vessels in distress to help others locate their position. In response to incoming radar beams, SARTs transmit a signal that clearly identifies the vessel in distress on the other boat's radar.

Scarf joint A long, tapered joint between two pieces of timber which allows a very large glued area to be obtained to increase strength. Scarfs should be at least eight times longer than the width of the timber being joined.

Scribe To mark a line on metal or wood by using a sharp instrument to show where it should be cut or a hole drilled.

Sealant A compound used to seal a joint. It usually retains an amount of flexibility after it has cured or set and the type is chosen according to the task it has to fulfill.

Self-tapping screw One which will create a thread when screwed into (relatively) thin metal or fibreglass and therefore doesn't require a nut. Suitable for light or moderate loads only.

Shaft drive A conventional propulsion system where the propeller shaft exits the hull towards the rear of the boat, usually at a small downwards angle.

Shear pin A weak link between the propeller of some smaller or older outboard engines and the propeller shaft. If the propeller strikes a solid object the shear pin breaks, thereby protecting the gearbox from damage. Many newer engines have a rubber hub insert instead – this is much less likely to fail than a shear pin, but if it does, it cannot be repaired on board.

Sheets Ropes used to control a sail once it is hoisted.

Shroud Part of the standing rigging that gives lateral support to the mast. Cap shrouds are the rig's longest shrouds, running to the masthead; lower shrouds run from the deck to just below the mast spreaders.

Skin fitting Through-hull fitting with a hole that passes through the hull from inside to outside. A valve must be fitted to through-hull fittings below the waterline, enabling inlet/outlet pipes to be sealed shut.

Solenoid An electromechanical device that converts an electrical signal into a mechanical motion using an electromagnet.

Spars Collective term for masts, booms, gaffs, spinnaker poles, and so on.

Spline A series of projections on a shaft which fit into grooves on a matching part to allow them to move together. Also, slats of wood inserted into the seams of a hull to seal it.

Split pin (or cotter pin) A thin metal (usually stainless steel) pin used to secure a clevis pin in place, or prevent a castellated nut unscrewing. Once inserted, the two halves of the tail of the pin are opened out to hold it in place.

Spreaders Struts projecting from the sides of the mast to spread the angle of the upper shrouds.

Standing rigging The wires that support the mast, usually made of stainless or galvanised steel.

Sterndrive A propulsion system where the drive unit on which the propeller is mounted passes through the transom at the rear of the boat. The drive unit is bolted to the engine/gearbox through the transom and can be removed for maintenance.

Stopping (or 'filler') A soft paste used to fill a void or gap, which dries to form a hard surface.

Swaged terminal Fitting attached to the end of a rigging wire in a hydraulic press, using enormous force.

T

Tack Bottom front corner of a sail.

Throttle The control that regulates the speed of an engine. On a diesel, this is correctly called a regulator or speed control lever by matching the fuel injected to the load on the engine to maintain a preset rpm (revolutions per minute).

Through-hull fitting (skin fitting) A fitting with a hole that passes through the hull from inside to outside. A valve must be fitted to through-hull fittings below the waterline, enabling inlet/outlet pipes to be sealed shut.

W

Washboard The removable door in the companionway or entrance into the cabin of a boat.

Wet or dry Waterproof abrasive paper that may be used dry or lubricated with water when rubbing down a painted surface or gel coat. It is available in various grades of roughness which are selected according to the job.

Index

Index

Acknowledgements

The publisher would like to thank the following for their kind permission to reproduce photographs in this book. (Abbreviations key: t = top, b = bottom, r = right, l = left)

Nic Compton 31 (br), 80, 90-91, 160-161, 248-249, 299

Sarah Doughty 6-7, 8, 9, 237, 250 (tr), 251, 284 (b), 285

Nick Gates 228

Rupert Holmes 2-3, 4-5, 26, 27, 28, 29, 30 (t & bl), 31, 32, 33, 34, 35, 36, 37, 38, 39, 40, 41, 68 (b), 69 (b), 92, 93, 94, 95, 97 (t), 99, 102, 103, 104, 105, 106, 107, 108, 109, 110, 111 (tl), 112, 113, 134, 218, 219, 220, 221, 222, 223, 224-225, 226, 227, 229, 230, 231, 232, 233, 234, 235, 238, 239, 240, 242, 243, 245, 246, 247, 252, 253, 254, 255, 257, 258, 259, 260, 261, 262-263, 264, 265, 266, 267, 268, 269, 270, 271, 272, 273, 274-275, 276, 277, 278, 279, 280, 281, 282-283, 286, 287, 288, 289, 290, 291, 292, 293, 296

istockphoto: 236, 250 (bl), 284 (tr)

Richard Johnstone-Bryden 10-11, 24-25, 50 (b), 52, 58, 70 (b), 72, 81, 82, 83, 84, 85, 86, 87, 88 (t), 89, 114-115, 116, 126, 132 (b), 134, 146, 148 (b), 154, 176 (b), 186-187, 216-217, 256, 295

Jake Kavanagh 55, 56, 62, 64 (l), 66, 67, 74 (b), 75, 76 (b), 96, 97 (b), 98, 100, 101, 118, 208, 294, 297,

Pat Manley 12, 13, 14, 15, 16, 17, 18, 19, 20, 21, 22, 23, 42-43, 44, 45, 46, 47, 48, 49, 50 (t), 51, 53, 54, 57, 59, 60, 61, 63, 64 (r), 65, 68 (t), 69 (t), 70 (t), 71, 73, 74 (t), 76 (t), 77, 78, 79, 88 (b), 111 (tr & b), 117, 119, 120, 121, 122, 123, 124, 125, 126, 127, 128, 129, 130, 131, 132, 133, 135, 136, 137, 138, 139, 140, 141, 142, 143, 144, 145, 147, 148 (t), 149, 150, 151, 152, 155, 156, 157, 158, 159, 163, 164, 165, 166, 167, 168, 169, 170, 171, 172, 173, 174, 175, 176 (t), 177, 178, 179, 180, 181, 182, 183, 184, 185, 188, 189, 190, 191, 192, 193, 195, 196, 197, 198, 199, 200, 201, 202, 203, 205, 206, 207, 209, 210, 211, 212, 213, 214, 215,

M Shepherd 194

Illustrations by KJA Artists. Thanks to Pat Manley & Rupert Holmes for supplying artwork references.

Thanks also to:

Aquafax Ltd (Hamble), 12-13 Mitchell Point Ensign Business Park, Hamble, SO31 4R, for help in photographing sea-cocks and toilets.

Krueger Limited, Krueger House, New Milton, Hampshire, BH25 5NN, for help in photographing marine heaters.

Marine Power Ltd, Deacons Boatyard, Bridge Road, Bursledon, Southampton, SO31 8AW, for help in photographing engine components and servicing.

The Elephant Boatyard Ltd, Lands End Road, Old Bursledon, Hampshire SO31 8DN, for help in photographing the repair of wooden boats.

Seaward Marine Ltd, Prospect Road, Cowes, Isle of Wight PO31 7AD, for supplying photographs of GRP hulls in build.

E P Barrus Ltd, Launton Road, Bicester, Oxon. OX26 4UR, for supplying engine photographs.

R G Marine Services Hythe for photographic opportunities.

Colin Bridle Marine Services of Hythe Marine for photographic opportunities.

Michael Thomas, Mike Shepard, Carlton Douglas, David Gray, Ken Manley and Gareth King, Malcolm Hammond and Roy Stoner; all boat owners who put themselves out to provide photographic opportunities.

Barry Watkin at Cowes Harbour Commission, Katie Ashcroft at Laser Performance, Graham Sunderland of Winning Tides, Seaweather's safety and survival equipment centre in Southampton, Sunsail's Milina base in Greece, Ben Willows and Gareth Ely at UKSA in Cowes, Kevin Burke at Westminster Boating Base in London, and Malena Feldt at CM Hammar in Sweden.

Alekos Steffan, Alison Molyneaux, Graham Hawkesley, Kass Schmitt, Kevin Mole Outboards, Martin Morris, and Roma Griffin.

Andrew Simpson for his pearls of wisdom.

Jane Utting for her unerring eye.